speechless

Also by Rosemary Crossley

Annie's Coming Out (With Anne McDonald)

Facilitated Communication Training

speechless

Facilitating
communication
for people
without voices

ROSEMARY CROSSLEY

A DUTTON BOOK

DUTTON
Published by the Penguin Group
Penguin Books USA Inc., 375 Hudson Street,
New York, New York 10014, U.S.A.
Penguin Books Ltd, 27 Wrights Lane,
London W8 5TZ, England
Penguin Books Australia Ltd, Ringwood,
Victoria, Australia
Penguin Books Canada Ltd, 10 Alcorn Avenue,
Toronto, Ontario, Canada M4V 3B2
Penguin Books (N.Z.) Ltd, 182–190 Wairau Road,
Auckland 10, New Zealand

Penguin Books Ltd, Registered Offices:
Harmondsworth, Middlesex, England

First published by Dutton, an imprint of Dutton Signet,
a division of Penguin Books USA Inc.
Distributed in Canada by McClelland & Stewart Inc.

First Printing, April, 1997
10 9 8 7 6 5 4 3 2 1

Permission to quote from "The Listeners" by Walter De La Mare is gratefully acknowledged to the literary estate of Walter De La Mare and the Society of Authors as its representative.

LIBRARY OF CONGRESS CATALOGING-IN-PUBLICATION DATA:
Crossley, Rosemary.
    Speechless : facilitating communication for people without voices
    / Rosemary Crossley.
        p.   cm.
    Includes bibliographical references and index.
    ISBN 0-525-94156-8
    1. Facilitated communication.   I. Title.
    RC429.C79   1997
    616.85'503—dc21
                                                            96-49707
                                                            CIP

Printed in the United States of America
Set in New Baskerville
Designed by Leonard Telesca

To Joan Dwyer,
advocate extraordinaire.

Contents

Thank You

To thank properly everyone who has contributed to *Speechless* I would need to write another book. Special thanks go to the people whose stories I tell, but every person who has ever attended DEAL Communication Centre has contributed to the book in some way, as have their teachers and caregivers. Further thanks are due to all the staff who have worked at DEAL since 1986, and to the committee members and volunteers, without whose support the center would not exist. Some of these people appear in the book, but some whose contributions were equally essential don't—Margaret Batt, Rosemary Ryall, and Nancy O'Donnell, among many others.

Sean O'Connor, Herb Schneiderman, and Doug Biklen read the manuscript and made many important corrections and suggestions. I have undoubtedly introduced more errors in the final draft—my apologies. And then there are all the friends and colleagues, here and overseas, who have lent a hand, or an ear, during the past twenty years. You know who you are—thank you. Those people helped me personally.

I also owe a tremendous debt to the pioneers of nonspeech communication, without whose groundbreaking work I would never have thought to try and help any nonspeaker to communicate. Indeed, I feel diffident about publishing this book at all—many other people in the field have more and better stories to tell. Over the last twenty years some nonspeakers have achieved amazing things due to the largely unknown work of a host of inventive teachers, therapists, and technicians. Again, there are too many to name individually, but I am especially indebted to those in the select group that created ISAAC, to those who have been associated with ACE (Oxford, UK), TRACE, the Hugh McMillan Centre, the Pennsylvania Assistive Devices Center, the Artificial Language Laboratory in East Lansing, the School of Speech Sciences at Purdue University, *Communicating Together, Communication Matters, Communicating Together, AAC,* and the firms that develop and manufacture the technology that give voices to the mute.

There are also the individuals and organizations in many countries who have supported and researched the use of facilitation to extend nonspeech communication to individuals otherwise unable to access current communication technology successfully. First among these was the Facilitated Communication Institute at Syracuse University, whose publications, training programs, and conferences have made it the major international information clearing house on facilitated communication. They are deserving of thanks from everyone who uses facilitated communication or who is associated with its use.

All this said, no book gets published without an agent—thank you, Jane Dystel—an editor—thank you, Deborah Brody—and a team of people who turn a manuscript that looks like the cat slept on it—no thanks to you, Beggar—into an elegant volume like the one in front of you. Thank you all.

Last but not least, I must thank Chris Borthwick and Anne McDonald, two people without whom, quite literally, this book would not have been written.

1

And the Walls Came Tumbling Down

On the floor in front of me was the most extraordinary child. About the length of a four-year-old but skeletally thin, her body was in unceasing motion. The muscles and tendons on her arms and legs stood out like cords. As she lay on her side her legs were bent backward, her arms were pushed out behind her, her head was pushed back between her shoulders, and her tongue moved in and out continuously. Unthinkingly, I asked the nurse who was showing me around the hospital, "What's wrong with her?"

"That's Anne McDonald. The spasm is getting worse, and she's getting harder and harder to feed. In six months her head will touch her heels and she'll die."

"Hello, Anne," I said. She gave a skull-like grin, but her tongue didn't stop moving. It was 1974. I was twenty-eight, I had an arts degree, and had trained as a computer programmer in the days when the largest data-processing system in Australia had 90K of RAM and occupied an entire room. Having discovered that computer programming was deathly dull and that I was very bad at it, I had opted out and gone to teach at a center for children with cerebral palsy.

After two years teaching I was now starting work at St. Nicholas Hospital in Melbourne, a Mental Health Authority institution for children assessed as severely and profoundly retarded. Anne was thirteen and had lived there for more than nine years.

> I went to St. Nicholas Hospital when I was three. The hospital was the state garbage bin. Very young children were taken into permanent care, regardless of their intelligence. If they were disfigured, distorted or disturbed then the world should not have to see or acknowledge them. You knew that you had failed to measure up to the standard expected of babies. You were expected to die.

When Anne McDonald entered St. Nicholas she could not talk intelligibly, walk, or feed herself. When she fought her way out of the hospital fourteen years later she still could do none of these things. Only one thing had changed. She had found a means of communication.

> Never seeing normal children, we were not sure what they were like. Where did we fall short? In your ugly body it was totally impossible that there could be a mind. Vital signs showed that your title was "human" but that did not entitle you to live like normal children. You were totally outside the boundary which delineated the human race. (Anne McDonald in *Annie's Coming Out,* p. viii)

My job at St. Nicholas was to set up play groups for 160 residents living in four wards of forty cribs.

To picture the hospital, think of a Romanian orphanage with everything painted white. The children lacked food, clothes, medicine, therapy, toys, and love, and this neglect was effectively concealed by the trappings of the clinic—high white walls, polished white floors, gleaming stainless steel, crisp white sheets. If the children were pale, the nurses said, that was because they were sick, not because they hadn't been outside the wards for months. If they were thin, that was because they were sick, not because they were starving. The children, almost all quadriplegics without speech, could do nothing, and so the staff developed goals of their own that were unrelated to the children. Cleanliness, internal and external, was god. Internal cleanliness could be gauged by the bowel book, which served as the ward bible; external cleanliness was measured by the number of bottles of rubbing alcohol emptied each week in polishing every stainless-steel surface to a mirror.

> Nurses were discouraged from cuddling children. A crying child needed to be punished for its own good, so it would learn to accept the absence of affection and be happy. Punishment consisted of locking the crying child in a small dark storeroom. The hospital defined a happy child as a quiet child. Silence was not only golden but sullen; the nurses never saw the looks we gave them when a child was put away. . . . Time was when the strongest emotion I felt was hate, and hate makes you strong. Tender emotions were dangerously softening. Implacable hatred of the whole world which hunted handicapped children into middens like St. Nicholas twisted my relationships with people for years. (*Annie's Coming Out*, pp. 16–19)

There was in St. Nicholas almost no therapy—the single, dedicated physical therapist struggled with an overwhelming caseload. Anne's file showed she had received physical therapy for only one three-month period in the sixties, and the muscle spasms resulting from her cerebral palsy had never been addressed. Anne spent her waking hours lying on the floor because there was no chair suitable for her to sit in, lying on her side because by 1974 her body had arched backward into a half circle, with the diameter of the circle being drawn by the line of her arms extending rigidly behind her. She couldn't bring her head or arms forward without help, and she rarely saw her hands or feet.

Like the other children, Anne also rarely left the ward. There were no organized play activities, no educational programs, and most children left the hospital only once a year for the annual picnic at the beach. The physical therapist and I tried to relieve the terrible monotony of hospital life. I put up posters and mobiles and set up activity programs. In this Siberia of children waiting to die, life was an intrusion. We tried to introduce fingerpainting. The nurses complained because the children got their hands dirty, the cleaners complained because the children got the floors dirty, and when we took it all outside the gardener complained (and I am not making this up) because the children got the grass dirty. After some arguments with the hospital bureaucracy I was able to arrange for volunteers to take some children, including Anne, across the road in a motley assortment of prams and pushers for occasional walks in the park.

> In the ward the floor and walls were covered with white vinyl. The cots were covered with white sheets. You either lay on the floor or in a cot. The only floor I knew was vinyl, and as far as I knew all surfaces were like vinyl or like sheets. I had no memory of ever having felt any other, and so I processed all the pictures I saw as being representations of vinyl at foot level and sheeting higher up, with differences of color. When Rosie took me outside I was amazed at the feel of grass—in pictures it just looked like a green vinyl floor.

Another activity program brought together Anne and nine other socially responsive children with severe cerebral palsy for a session of preschool activities, one afternoon a week. As all the children in the group had been labeled severely or profoundly retarded,[1] and none had ever attended school, a

---

[1] "Mentally retarded" is the term commonly used in the United States to refer to people who have scored significantly below the normal range on an intelligence test. In Australia we now talk about "intellectual impairment" or "intellectual disability" or "intellectual disadvantage." In Britain the equivalent group of people is described as "learning disabled." "Severely" and "profoundly" retarded imply IQ scores below 35 and 20, respectively. In fact, none of the children in St. Nicholas had ever been given an intelligence test, largely because the severity of their impairments seemed too obvious to need confirming.

preschool program seemed about right. Anne appeared to enjoy all the activities and always tried to participate as much as her body allowed. The only way she and the others could communicate was to point to or look at their choice of drink or snack.

This was before the development of speech synthesizers and laptop computers, and the most complex communication aid in use at the cerebral palsy center had been a wooden board carved with the letters of the alphabet, which hung on the back of an adult's wheelchair. There some students who could use their hands or who had sufficient control of their head movements to point accurately with a head stick had been taught to type. For those who couldn't type and who had no intelligible speech the only option had been to signal yes and no while their families and teachers played twenty questions to find out what they wanted. Students who couldn't control their head movements to nod and shake had signaled with whatever movements they could control.

At the day center Janet, a teenager with tongue-thrust—repeated involuntary tongue protrusions caused by brain damage—had used this to communicate, clamping her tongue between her teeth to signal yes and holding it back for no. Anne reminded me of Janet, and so early in 1974, I told her about Janet's signals and suggested she use them. "Do you understand what I've been saying?" I asked. Anne held her tongue out with a tremendous grin. This should have alerted me to Anne's potential, but she had already fulfilled my highest expectations. At St. Nicholas, answering yes or no put you in the genius class. I gave her no opportunity to extend her communication any further until three more years had passed, and I was studying for a graduate teaching qualification. One of my assignments in literacy was to try and develop a communication system for a hospital resident. Obviously, I thought, nobody at St. Nicholas is going to learn to read or type, so I decided to try and teach a child to use Bliss symbols. (Blissymbolics was the name given to an ideographic written language devised by an Australian, Charles Bliss, with the aim of fostering international cooperation. At a Canadian center for children with cerebral palsy, teacher Shirley McNaughton and others had successfully adapted the system for use by nonspeaking children. Anne selected herself as the project child.

When the nurse had originally said to me that Anne was soon going to die of starvation, this wasn't because there wasn't enough food, but because staff shortages and the feeding position they were using to cope with Anne's muscle spasm combined to ensure that she got very little of what food there was. Because Anne could not sit in any of the chairs available at St. Nicholas, there was a tendency for her to be fed in the most extraordinary position. Her head was wedged between a nurse's knees, facing away from the nurse, and her body left hanging, arching back under the nurse's chair. This meant that all her weight was being taken by her neck, which both made it extremely difficult for her to swallow and exacerbated her tongue-thrust. This made it almost impossible for her to avoid accidentally pushing out a mouthful of food. At this time the nurses had ten severely disabled children to feed in an hour. In the circumstances, the first mouthful of food a child "rejected" was the last mouthful that the child was given. In Anne's case her tongue-thrust caused many meals to come to a premature conclusion.

In April 1977, I took Anne home for a weekend because I was afraid she was dying. Chris, my partner, agreed somewhat reluctantly, on the basis that we would host a visit every month or so until Anne either started gaining weight or died.

> Chris is tall and dark and hairy. He talks very fast with a stutter that sounds like a machine gun. He can't light the fire without reading the paper he is using first. (*Annie's Coming Out*, p. 44)

It was then three years since the nurse had told me she would be dead in six months. Anne had made it to the age of sixteen, but she was losing weight. She had lost two pounds in the last twelve months—an insignificant amount to you, and a minor blessing to me—but Anne now weighed only twenty-eight pounds. Unless something happened to stop the decline she would just fade away. About 160 children had died in St. Nicholas since Anne first came there, and one more would hardly be noticed.

> Death lived in the wards at St. Nicholas. He was often more
> friendly than the nurses. Death walked around my cot, but
> he never thought that my ribs were well enough covered to
> stand the worms a feed. (*Annie's Coming Out*, p. 28)

That weekend Chris and I took Anne to an art gallery, not
because I thought she would get anything much out of it, but
because it was the last day of an exhibition we wanted to see, and
we couldn't leave her by herself. At the gallery Anne showed
unexpected interest and concentration. At one point I wheeled
her up to a Toulouse-Lautrec print—a fat man in full evening
dress, arms akimbo, probably drunk, up on one toe, dancing by
himself—and she burst out laughing. Recognizing the incon-
gruities which make that scene funny required a degree of sophistication which was not expected in the wards at St. Nicholas.
Anne's laugh could have been a coincidence, of course, but it
seemed worth taking a chance on—she could be my guinea pig.

Two days after our visit to the gallery, I carried Anne into the
deserted ward dayroom at five o'clock, after all the other children had been put to bed. I said, "Annie, I think I can teach
you to talk. Not with your mouth, because nobody can do that,
but with your hands, by pointing to pictures of things. But
before I can do that I have to see if you can point."

After placing Anne on her side on the floor so that her arms
were in front of her, and her head was pushed forward so she
could see what her hands were doing, I knelt behind her to
maintain her in position. Then I picked up objects at random,
placed several in front of Anne, and asked her to point to one
of them. I started with two items and built up to six, which I
switched around after each selection. No more could fit into
the semicircle that was within Anne's reach. She pointed correctly to everything I named using her right hand, though
slowly and with enormous effort.

Anne had shown she could recognize and point to named
objects. The goal of the next session was to find out whether
she could also indicate named pictures. This time I sat her up
in a baby buggy major, an enlarged umbrella stroller, at a low
table—after all, a communication strategy she could only use

when she was lying on the floor wasn't going to be much use to her. However, when Anne was sitting in the baby buggy her head retracted and it was impossible for her to move her right arm. If I brought Anne's head forward but left her arm unsupported, she was unable to lift her arm above the table because it still retracted. If I put her arm down to the table, the force with which it pressed down created so much friction that Anne couldn't move it across the table. In order to enable her to point I had to bring her head forward and raise her right arm. Only when Anne's upper arm was supported above the table did she have enough control over her forearm and hand to point clearly to widely spaced items. My role was to act as a responsive item of furniture, facilitating Anne's movement by moving when she moved, giving input to the extensor muscles of her arm when flexor spasm made her arm contract across her body, and constantly repositioning her hips and trunk to try and maintain her body and head in a straight line. Supporting Anne was neither easy nor comfortable, partly because she was so short that I had to stoop over, and partly because her muscle spasm was so strong that it took all my strength to inhibit it (and I'm no ninety-pound weakling).

What Anne and I were doing in 1977 later came to be called "facilitated communication." At the time, though, I was simply trying to adapt an ordinary nonspeech communication method to a very particular set of disabilities. I didn't know whether this would work on Anne, and I certainly wasn't looking at it as something that could ever be applied to anyone else. It was (and is) simply a way to help improve someone's ability to point.

With her arm supported Anne correctly selected playing-card-size pictures and Bliss symbols on request. At this point I discovered limitations—not in her understanding, but in her reach. Unless we could find a way for her to access more items than could fit within her range of movement, her vocabulary was clearly going to be very small.

Initially I devised a hierarchical system of choices. The choices were laid out on sheets of paper in sets, like the Venn diagrams used in the mathematics of set theory.

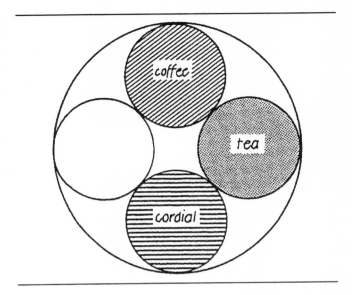

(*Annie's Coming Out,* p. 49)

Menu, submenu—it's a system familiar to any of today's computer users. On your computer you click on the category you want—"Format," say—and a subset of options come up. Click on one of those—"Document," say—and a sub-subset of options appears, from which you choose those you want. Anne wasn't using a computer, but the principle was the same. Choose a category—"drink," say—from a set of possible needs and you got another sheet of paper with the subset of options available—"coffee," "tea," "cordial," or "something else," the empty circle. "Something else" was the catchall option, "other," which allowed you to access options not included in the first subset. If Anne chose it, I had to play twenty questions to find out what she wanted. Obviously she would have to be taught the system. I envisaged her identifying the circles by color and position—green circle on the right of the drink set, for example, meant tea—with pictures added when necessary. I would have to remind Anne of the options each session, of course, and so to make it easier for me to remember which circles were which I wrote each choice on its circle.

Anne coped with the circle system surprisingly easily—if she watched a set of options being drawn up and used it once she was able to remember it, and could point to nominated options on request days later, without reminders. The aim of the system, though, was to allow Anne to communicate, and most of my time was taken up with neither teaching nor testing but with following through on what she communicated. She chose a drink—I made the drink. She wanted to go for a walk—I took her for a walk. And that is where her communication could well have stopped. She had fulfilled my expectations, as she had when I showed her how to signal yes and no in 1974. I probably would have gone on as I had then, using her new skill but not extending it, if it hadn't been for my friend Sean.

Sean O'Connor's primary interests were mathematics and model airplanes. He hadn't worked with people with severe disabilities and was unconstrained by any preconceptions. I asked him if he had any ideas that would extend the circle system. Sean asked me, did I know how Anne was remembering the choices?

"Could she be recognizing the words?"

"No, of course not. She's severely retarded."

"So you've checked whether Anne can recognize the words, and she can't?"

"No, Sean, of course I haven't checked it. There'd be no point. I keep telling you, she's *severely retarded.*"

"Then that's just an assumption. Unless you check it out for yourself, you don't *know.*"

All right, then, I'd check. The next time Anne chose a drink using the circles I wrote out the words "coffee, "tea," and "cordial" on white cards in black letters and mounted the cards on blocks so I could move them around easily. As always I talked to Anne as if she could understand and explained what I was doing—"I want to see if you can recognize words, whether you can learn to read." I told Anne what was on each card, moved the blocks around, and asked her to point to what she'd had to drink. There were no color or position cues. She pointed correctly to "coffee." I checked that she could identify the other two words and added more of those she'd seen before on the other circles. No problem. She could learn to recognize words. What else could she do? Could she string words together?

As all the words I'd used on Anne's circles were nouns, the next step was to add some verbs and see if she could point to sequences of blocks to create sentences. The task gave her no problems, and she learned new words as quickly as they were presented. On May 2 she made her first sentence: "Annie likes coffee." Then "Annie likes tea" and "Annie likes walks." A week later she made six sentences, all quite different, with five different verbs, ranging from "I want a book please" to "Annie not Rosie house yesterday," a not very subtle reminder that I hadn't taken her out on the weekend. We only stopped when we ran out of time. It seemed obvious that Anne wasn't learning language as she went—she had language which was waiting on a means of expression. If she had to depend on a vocabulary chosen for her by someone else, her communication was always going to be restricted, no matter how many sets and subsets it contained. The only limited set of items which could give her unlimited communication was the twenty-six letters of the alphabet. Given that in a week she had acquired almost as many words as would fit on the table in front of her, it was now clear even to me that I had to try to teach her to spell.[2]

For Anne to learn to spell she had to transcend more than her physical handicaps. The environment she was living in was very different from that of most first-world children and one of its many differences was its almost complete lack of written language exposure. The hospital wards contained no books, newspapers, magazines, or junk mail (or real mail, come to that). For two years Anne's ward had had a television, but most of the time she was not placed where she could see it. Her total lifetime exposure to print was a few programs of *Sesame Street*, some game shows, and the accompanying commercials. If she was going to learn to read, this had to change. From now on while I worked with other children, I would sit Anne at a table with a book propped up in front of her—the kind of book which has

---

[2] This rapid learning is not particularly extraordinary; children without disabilities learning language acquire new words at a similar rate.

one or two sentences and a picture on each page. Every time I walked past I would turn the page and read the sentences on the new page. For good or for bad Anne had nothing to do but study the page until I walked past next.

Because St. Nicholas had been intended for infants, Anne and the other residents all slept in cribs. Staff routines meant that the children were in their cribs from 4:30 in the afternoon till 7:30 in the morning. It was now possible to use this down-time—I photocopied book pages and stuck them to the bars of Anne's crib after discussing them with her. Few students can ever have been more motivated to do their homework.

The *Sesame Street* alphabet song and a set of magnetic letters served to teach Anne the alphabet. Again her visual memory stood her in good stead and by May 17 she was able to identify all letters correctly. Before this I had given her small groups of letters and asked her to touch the letters in the correct order to spell some of the words on her blocks. Now she was to try selecting letters from the whole alphabet, set out on a magnetic board. First her favorite—"coffee"—easy. Then I dictated a nonsense sentence—"I hate fat cats"—to check whether she'd got the idea of adding "e" to "at" words to make "ate." Anne pointed to "i h f c." At first I thought it was rubbish, but then I realized she'd given the initial letter of each word. No, I said, I want the whole thing, which meant at least ten minutes of hard work. With a sour look Anne started to point to "I h a t e f a t"; then she started laughing and finished, "r o s i e." Her spelling was coming along, but her tact could use a little work.

At this point I suggested that Anne try and spell whatever she wanted to say, blithely promising that I would work out what it was and show her the standard spelling. She challenged me the next day when she spelled "n s d l l y g o s k o o l m e." Wolcott Gibbs wrote of *Time* magazine's style that "Backward ran sentences until reeled the mind." Anne's sentence might have run forward, but interpretation had to run backward. Yes, "me," that's a word. So are "skool" and "go." Who or what could be going to school? A combination of questioning and guessing led to Sally, the young daughter of our next-door neighbor, met on Anne's weekends with us. That left "n"—an accident?

"n, n-n Sally go skool me . . . *When!* When Sally go skool me?" Anne confirmed that she wanted to have lessons with Sally, who had just started school. The "en" sound matches the letter *n*, but the "wh" sound is harder, both to distinguish and to represent.

I gave Anne a list of the common "wh" words, and from then on she used "wh" correctly. She continued to produce some phonetic or invented spellings, but surprisingly few compared with a typical child learning to spell. Anne had a good visual memory, she had no activity other than reading to distract her, and she was also helped by being able to use ready-made letters rather than having to make her own—children learning to spell usually learn to write at the same time, and the concentration needed for the motor task of getting letters onto the page may distract attention from spelling.

Anne was every teacher's dream; a highly motivated tabula rasa, a first-grade student with the concentration of a sixteen-year-old, she had absolutely no distractions. Give her anything to study and she studied it. Put a fact in and it stayed there. Her hearing was acute, her memory excellent. At this stage an undiscriminating learner, she devoured whatever I offered. So what should I offer?

What do you give a child who has nothing? Anne had never had an intelligence test. She didn't get one now. It was ludicrous to suppose that such a test could usefully compare someone in Anne's situation with nondisabled sixteen-year-olds who were in their tenth year of schooling. Her ability to learn was indicated by her ability to learn—by the concepts she grasped, by her ability to generalize, by her memory of what she was given. These helped make her a fast learner. Fast learning isn't always better learning, but Anne had a lot to catch up on. If the process had been any slower I might have given up, daunted by the task of compensating for ten years of missed education. The only help the hospital gave Anne to fill the gap was unintended—it gave her time. If she had been anywhere other than St. Nicholas, much of her day would have been (and should have been) taken up with therapy aimed at improving her physical status and developing functional skills, such as the ability to drive a motorized wheelchair. None of that therapy was available in the hospital, and neither were any social or recreational activities. Hypothetically, all of Anne's waking hours not taken up by meals were available for education. Even so, a major selection exercise was going to be necessary.

The elementary-school syllabus is enormous. Which bits did Anne have to do? Which bits couldn't she do? Which bits weren't essential? What knowledge that was essential wasn't in the syllabus, because it was presumed children would acquire it outside school? Anne had to learn to read and spell. She couldn't learn to write or play sports. She didn't need to learn things for which she had to rely on others, like road safety or dental hygiene. Luckily, much schooling is repetitive—in elementary school you're given some basic information about the history of your country, and every year after that you learn more detail, most of which you forget immediately after the exams. If Anne got a quick overview of basic history and geography at middle school level, and remembered it, that would leave her with as much information as the average adult.

Cumulative subjects like languages and mathematics, where each stage builds on previous knowledge, were harder to compress. Fortunately Anne was interested in numbers, knew the numbers 1 to 12 from the clockface, and had picked up basic counting from *Sesame Street* and my preschool program. Again, it was important to select the useful bits, the knowledge that she would either use (in managing a bank account, say) or that she needed to have to understand what ordinary educated adults said and wrote. You might not know exactly what the speed of light is, but you do need to know what order of magnitude it is to know what is meant by a light-year and to understand the news about *Voyager*. Anne couldn't use a calculator or a pen, so it was more important for her to learn the tricks of mental arithmetic—how to multiply 63 by 25 or 24 or 26—than it was to spend time on complicated long-division sums. Anne's interest in mathematics in fact led her to try and go further, but there were only a few advanced topics which could be studied without a broad mathematical background, and her success was limited.

Of course, what children are taught in school is only a fraction of what they know as adults. The syllabus presumes that children share many experiences outside the schoolroom, that they are immersed in a common culture. Anne had to catch up with the experiences she'd missed. Going to a cinema and an airport were treats, certainly, but so were visits to a service station or a Laundromat, places that were as unfamiliar to Anne as the far side of the moon. She'd never been in a supermarket. That was a particular hit; she was utterly amazed by the sight of all that food in one place. Her reaction surprised me. Television commercials showed supermarkets—surely Anne had got the idea? No, she said, she'd thought they'd been made up for the ads, like dancing cows and singing toasters. After all, if all that food really was on the open shelves, people would be grabbing it and eating it, wouldn't they? That's what she'd have done if she could have reached it! She'd never seen a hamburger, or tasted pizza, and the only potato she knew was white mush. On her visits home with us, which took place every week or two, Anne was easy to entertain. Not many guests find making toast, washing up, and defrosting the refrigerator thrilling new experiences, but she did.

One of the joys of rearing or teaching children is that their wonder and excitement at all the new things that confront them each day allows you to relive your own childhood. The limits of their language and their understanding, however, mean that explanations have to be simplified, detail being added gradually as they grow up. Once Anne started reading and spelling it became clear that she could handle sixteen-year-old level language and concepts. By that first Christmas Santa Claus was out and discussions of the historical significance of the winter solstice were in. She enjoyed everything, and her enjoyment was infectious. When we went to the amusement park her excitement even attracted groupies, people who followed her from ride to ride—not nastily, but just to see what this appallingly handicapped child was going to do next. When she came down the high slide grinning from ear to ear everyone applauded.

In addition to the pleasure of seeing Anne discover the world, there was the thrill of discovering her personality.

Almost every conversation brought out something new. Even something as ordinary as her food preferences—avocados, say, or taramasalata (Greek fish-roe salad)—were interesting, given the bland mush served at the hospital. It was fascinating to find out what she did and didn't know. Her only sources of information had been the ward radio and an occasional television program, and while her knowledge of current affairs was extensive, she didn't know what a dollar bill looked like.

Most people who knew Anne found her developing communication and academic skills enormously exciting, but there was a certain lack of enthusiasm among the doctors who ran St. Nicholas and who had labelled Anne profoundly retarded. In a reaction which was to become all too familiar, they first declared that Anne could not be spelling, and then refused to come and see what she was doing on the grounds that there was nothing to see. Professionals from outside the hospital who did come observed that Anne looked toward letters before she moved her hand toward them. They could see that she was selecting the letters (with great difficulty) by controlling the movement of her hand and arm below the elbow—something that support of her upper arm couldn't influence. They pointed out that her facial expression matched the content of what she was spelling, and that she spelled comments about verifiable incidents that had taken place when her supporter wasn't around. Other professionals who didn't come to watch suggested that intentionally or otherwise I, and the other people who supported Anne's arm while she spelled, were making Anne hit letters by moving her rigid arm like a pointer. Obviously they had never met anyone with severe athetosis—Anne's arm was anything but rigid!

By August 1977, three months after Anne had made her first sentences with word blocks, the Mental Health Authority was receiving conflicting reports of what was going on. The MHA asked two psychologists to test Anne and see if they could find out whether or not she really could read and spell. Dr. Leo Murphy, dean of special education at Burwood State College (now Deakin University), and Jean Vant, former senior psychologist for the MHA, thought of a simple test. They came to

St. Nicholas with a short passage they had written themselves, just to make sure that there could be no possibility of Anne or myself having previous familiarity with the text used. While I was out of the room they gave the typed text to Anne to read.

The text in front of me was a passage about a relative of Jean Vant's whose name was also Annie and who was a lush. For some reason another relative had to give her a bottle of gin once a year. After I'd read it Mrs. Vant gave me three comprehension questions to answer—"What was my aunt given?", "What was her name?" and "Where did the present come from?" Then Rosie was called in.

I started spelling the answer to the first question, and I'd got as far as "G I" when Mrs. Vant said "Oh, I know what you're going to say." At that stage I hated being second-guessed. It was foolish, but not being sleek and fat I had only my pride to live for. I was determined to pass the test, but to do so on my own terms. I changed the answer from "GIN" to "GIFT." To get the "gin" in I spelled "JEAN'S AUNT IS CALLED GINNIE" and to show off my vocabulary I spelled "SHE GOT THE GIN FROM ANNUITY."

Puns or no puns, correct or not, Anne's answers matched the questions and showed that she was able both to extract meaning from written material and to spell answers without cues from me. Jean Vant wrote that in my absence Anne "was given a passage to read whose contents were known only to Dr. Murphy and myself, then three typed questions relating to it" to answer with my support and that she herself had supported Anne's arm while she spelled answers to other questions. She concluded, "I have observed her [Anne] working with the magnetic letter board both as the person supporting her and the person who was asking the questions. I am satisfied in both instances that she did indeed answer the questions and in each case had read the material and the questions." Her final report, endorsed by Dr. Murphy, was provided to the MHA in

September 1977, and the director of the Mental Retardation Division called me over to his office to tell me how stunned and excited his superiors were. Once the implications sank in, their excitement subsided rather rapidly. The next week it was suggested that I should resign.

To balance the Vant/Murphy report, the hospital superintendent had the hospital pediatrician conduct another assessment of Anne. The pediatrician used the Denver Developmental Scale. The Denver is a screening tool designed to check whether preschoolers without obvious physical or sensory impairments are developing normally, and if you use it for an older child that means that you have decided in advance that the child you are assessing has no skills beyond those expected of a four-year-old. Anne was seventeen. The pediatrician reported that he had dangled a plastic ring on a string in front of her when she was lying in her crib and that she had looked at it but made no effort to reach for it. How was Anne expected to reach for it, given her physical problems? How many seventeen-year-olds had he met who would reach for plastic rings? The pediatrician's finding was that Anne had at best the potential of a twelve-month-old.

The hospital had always assumed that the children would die or move to another institution before becoming eligible for a disability pension at age sixteen, and hadn't made any arrangements to take it away from them. Anne bought several useful items of equipment out of her accumulated pension money. An electric page-turner enabled her to turn book pages by pressing a large button, and this meant that she could read much more than previously—almost continuously when there wasn't anything else happening or she wasn't in her crib, where it was back to photocopies stuck on the bars. The first full-length book I chose for her was *Mary Poppins*, which she didn't like. After that she chose her own books, on the basis of what she'd heard people talking about, either in person or on radio. Her favorite programs, apart from news and current affairs, were *The Science Show* and *Music for Pleasure*, a classical music program. By the end of 1977 she had read *The Double Helix*, James Watson's story of the discovery of the structure of DNA, half on the page-turner and half on her crib bars. Purchase of her own TV set gave her and other like-minded residents the chance to watch the school programs rather than soap operas. Most important, purchase of a therapeutic posture chair meant that gradually and painfully Anne's extensor spasm could be counteracted so she could bend at the hips.

By the end of 1977 Anne's spelling and use of language seemed about average for her age, but it was impossible to be sure. Because of the time and effort needed for her to spell any-thing, she was not writing essays or engaging in deep discus-sions of the universe. In December, Melbourne State College made a videotape of Anne spelling. I had asked her to think up a snappy message for the student teachers who would see the tape and she spelled, "too many tests—not enough teachers." The six words took her more than half an hour. This was slower than usual, as I was being particularly rigorous for the video. I didn't accept letters until they had been selected several times, and I didn't complete words as one would in ordinary conversa-tion (after "eno" I would normally have said, "Enough?")—but it wasn't that much slower. Anne's ordinary communication was no more than four times as fast, perhaps fifty words an hour. Her early sentences consequently tended to read like telegrams, with all inessential words omitted. When she got the chance, though, her sentences were complex enough. On one occasion during the debate about Anne's abilities the director of nursing ordered me to come to his office as soon as Anne had finished the sentence she'd just started. I whispered to her to make it as long as possible. She spelled, "Till the doctors come and see me and let me tell them with the board what I want them to do they have no right to presume to dictate to me and you should ignore them." Thirty-six words. It certainly showed mastery of embedded clauses, even if it didn't save me from the wrath of the director of nursing.

Despite intensive lobbying, the next year produced no improvements in the life of Anne and the other hospital resi-dents—they all still had their last meal of the day at 3:30 and were put to bed immediately afterward. While Anne's educa-tional program continued, I was now teaching eleven other children with cerebral palsy to read and to spell, so she couldn't have as much individual attention as previously. Except when she came home with Chris and me weekends, her opportunities for communication were significantly reduced, often to a few yes/no answers and a couple of sentences a day.

Anne turned eighteen, the age of majority in Australia, in January 1979. In February she complained that a staff member had tried to hurt her. Whether her complaint had any foundation will never be known—it may only have been the result of a vivid nightmare—but the effects on Anne of making the complaint were dramatic. Her liberty was severely curtailed. She was not allowed to leave the hospital at all—no walks, no weekends at our place—and her visitors were both restricted and only allowed to see her in the presence of nursing staff. We contacted a lawyer, but after one visit he was banned too. A senator who'd taken an interest in Anne and visited her previously was also forbidden entry. Anne was in closer confinement than if she'd been in jail, where she'd have been legally entitled to visits from both lawyers and senators. By April she'd had enough and decided she wanted to leave the hospital in which she had now lived for more than fourteen years.

Anne was legally an adult, but the Health Commission, the body governing the MHA, was not prepared to accept that she was able or entitled to make decisions about her life. While tribunals and appeal mechanisms existed to protect adults against inappropriate incarceration in psychiatric hospitals, no such safeguards existed for those who had been placed in care by their parents. Most of those who left St. Nicholas did so in shrouds. Some had been transferred to other institutions when they grew out of their cribs. No one had ever moved back into the community. The possibility had never been contemplated; the children admitted to St. Nicholas were so terribly disabled it was not expected that they would live to adulthood. In the unlikely event that they did survive, they would never have the capacity to fend for themselves. The only way that Anne could get out was to file an application for a writ of habeas corpus in the Supreme Court of Victoria.

The writ of habeas corpus was originally a restraint on the

power of princes. It asks anyone restraining a person's liberty either to produce a legal justification for the imprisonment or to let the person go—strictly speaking, to give up the body. The medieval lawyers who developed the writ had certainly never envisaged a shrimp of a girl who could neither walk nor talk using it to seek freedom from her doctors, but part of the strength of habeas corpus is in what it does not say. Being non-specific, it allows all kinds of citizens to object to restraint of liberty by the state in all its forms. And the medical profession may be our modern barons—wealthy, autocratic, and, in general, obeyed.

Anne's application for habeas corpus was heard in the Supreme Court of Victoria in May 1979. The central issues were two: Could Anne communicate? And, if she could communicate, had she in fact communicated a wish to leave the hospital? The official position was that there was no evidence that Anne could communicate by spelling and no evidence that she had the understanding to appreciate what leaving the hospital meant. The report by Mrs. Vant and Dr. Murphy seemed to have disappeared from Anne's files. Instead the Health Commission cited the pediatrician's Denver assessment, and her size. They pointed out that Anne was eighteen years old and the size of a five-year-old—was that normal? She must be severely retarded.

> I couldn't feed myself when I was sixteen, and thus it was clear I must have no more IQ than a child who couldn't feed itself. This was validated by weighing me. As I was the weight of a one-year-old[3] this must be my mental age. This would all be very humorous if the measurers had not believed their results and used them as evidence for why I should be locked up.

Fortunately, another pediatrician, Philip Graves, was prepared to put his career on the line and tell the court that the intellectual assessment of people like Anne depends on "their capability

---

[3] Slight exaggeration, this. Twenty-three-month-old, maybe.

of communicating and expressing their ability." He went on to say, "We know that [Anne] has got a severe handicap, but I don't think we can extrapolate from that to say anything very definitely adverse about her intellectual abilities." He also told the court that Anne's stunted growth was due to malnutrition rather than retardation.

The judge seemed prepared to accept that size wasn't important, even if the Health Commission wasn't, and so we were back to test results. A number of positive reports were available to the court, but they had all been generated as a result of efforts by Anne's lawyers. The report which would be most convincing was the Vant/Murphy report. It was limited in its scope and its conclusions, and it didn't say as much about Anne's abilities as the later reports, but it had been obtained by the Health Commission from psychologists of its own choosing long before there was any question of legal proceedings.

Somewhat surprisingly the Health Commission affidavits, which were said to include all the comments on Anne's intellectual functioning contained in her file, made no mention of the Vant/Murphy report. Under cross-examination the superintendent of St. Nicholas said that there was no such report. Fortunately for Anne, Dr. Murphy had sent me copies of his correspondence with the Health Commission, including the report. After Anne's attorney read the report's findings to the court the superintendent said he had never heard of or seen such a report before. Confronted with a letter from his director which said that he had been sent a copy of the report, he admitted receiving a copy and placing it on Anne's file. So why hadn't he included the report in his affidavit? "Because I don't believe Mrs. Vant. . . . I don't believe her any more than I would Miss Crossley!" And that really said it all.

Have you ever played hide-and-seek with a one-year-old? My nephew Felix plays it most charmingly. When he is to hide he runs around for a bit, then he squats down in full view with his hands over his eyes. If he cannot see you, after all, how can you possibly see him? Professional groups that are challenged often behave in a surprisingly similar fashion. They seem to think that if they refuse to acknowledge the existence of inconvenient evidence no one else will either. While the Health Commission could certainly arrange to suffer collective amnesia, what on earth gave them the idea that Mrs. Vant, Dr. Murphy, and I would all be similarly stricken?

Anne won her case. On May 17, 1979, she left the hospital to live with Chris and me.

After leaving St. Nicholas Anne fought for the right of people without speech to communicate and to have control over their lives. First there was herself—she had to go through another court case to be allowed to sign a contract to write a book. To win she had to undertake more tests, tests that she did reluctantly. At the time she spelt out "I don't like any suggestion that my communications aren't mine." Later she wrote "I've only got one life and I don't want to spend it all proving I exist." Second there were her old friends, locked away when a government inquiry published a report saying they could not communicate early in 1980.[4] Immediately after the report's release I was removed from St. Nicholas and Anne was banned from visiting everyone she had lived with for fourteen years. *Annie's Coming Out*, the book that Anne and I co-authored, was published at the end of 1980. It added to public disquiet about conditions in the hospital and in 1981 the government announced that it would be closed and the residents would be rehoused in the community.

To catch up on her missed education Anne attended evening classes at a local high school, sat and passed a public exam, and began a college degree. Her lack of formal schooling didn't seem to be much of a problem, despite the fact that when she left the extraordinarily barren hospital environment her unusual memory skills declined and soon became much the same as anyone else's.[5] Her main worry was the sheer amount of time she needed to generate essays.

---

[4] Dwyer (1996) quotes evidence obtained under Freedom of Information that shows that the inquiry did find evidence of sophisticated communication but did not publish it.

[5] This may have been the delayed effect of malnutrition—the swapping of a child's eidetic memory for the linear memory of later life, as discussed by Stephen Rose in *The Making of Memory*.

Anne wasn't learning-disabled, but that didn't mean she wasn't severely handicapped. Anne has athetoid cerebral palsy. She'd been a breech delivery, and came out backside first. This can impose abnormal pressures on the structures at the base of the brain; Anne didn't breathe spontaneously after delivery, and she had a subdural hemorrhage in the brain-stem region. All messages from the brain to the muscles must pass through this area. She had suffered massive but localized brain damage.

Cerebral palsy (CP) is the generic name for the variable movement problems which are caused by damage to the developing brain before or during birth or in early infancy. Most are caused by damage to the motor cortex and involve spasticity. Athetosis (or choreoathetosis) is another, less common, form of CP, and it is caused by damage not to the cortex but to the basal ganglia. The basal ganglia are structures at the top of the brain stem which coordinate and dispatch instructions originating in other parts of the brain to the rest of the neuromuscular system. If you have athetosis your whole body may move even when you want to sit still, either with spasmodic, unpredictable jerks (often stimulated by sudden noises or surrounding movement) or with a slow writhing, with each limb moving in turn. Your head may also move and your face may grimace and your tongue move in and out; you may be able to control this most of the time, but you'll still probably lose control when excited or stressed. The writhing movements are often most evident in the hands and fingers and may attain a smoothness and grace that voluntary movement only occasionally achieves.[6]

In athetosis, as in quadriplegia caused by spinal cord injury, the problem is the connection between the brain and the body. In spinal quadriplegia there is a break in transmission of signals between the brain and parts of the body, but spinal quadriplegics can talk, and no one suggests that there is anything

[6] I remember the opening of an art exhibition. Anne is at the end of a light, bright loft gallery. Everyone else is at the bar. With nobody impinging on her, with nothing requiring active response, she is sitting at rest, looking at the pictures and listening to Vivaldi. Her arms move from the elbow, slowly, gracefully, and her fingers float like seaweed in a tide pool.

wrong with the controlling brain. In athetosis, too, the problem is in signal transmission, but in athetosis the damage is a little higher, affecting control of the muscles of the head and neck. Essentially Anne was labeled as intellectually impaired because she could not talk.

The brain is damaged in athetosis—there is no question of that—but what does brain damage mean? The view held by most people, who don't have neurological training, is that brain damage means all-over cognitive dysfunction, what Donald Duck calls a "blinkus in the thinkus." If any part of the brain is damaged, we expect the whole mind to be affected because most of us have very little idea of how our brains are thought to work.

Part of the reason for this is that there are remarkably few important statements about the way our brains work that can be made with any certainty. The rest of the body is relatively straightforward—we know what the bits are for. Try cutting up a sheep's brain. You will see that there are two fairly symmetrical halves (hemispheres) of varying shades of pink, white, and gray, covered with a thin transparent skin. The upper surface has creases and ripples, rather like the sheep's fleece, and the lower back of both hemispheres is joined by a bulbous white structure which narrows into a sort of stem. It is impossible to say what bit does what, or what connects to what bit (except that if you had the rest of the sheep you would be able to say that the brain stem joined onto the spinal cord).[7]

So which bit does what? Instead of proceeding from structure to function, as the anatomists did, early neurologists were forced to proceed from function to structure—in fact, from dysfunction to structure. A person had a stroke and lost the ability to speak, for example, and at a later postmortem it was possible to see that an area above and in front of the left ear

[7] The inclusion of the brain stem in the structure we call the brain is (like much else in this area) somewhat arbitrary. The stem could just as well have been seen as a complex relay station attached to the spinal cord—the "caudal/cerebral interface," say—in which case Anne would not have been labeled as brain-damaged (though the reality of her disabilities would of course remain).

was damaged. After conducting many postmortems of people with similar histories, the French surgeon Paul Broca was able in the 1860s to map a specific area of the brain which appeared to be essential for speech. He determined that in almost all cases the damage that stopped speech was sited on the left or the right depending on the right- or left-handedness of the person, and found that in almost all right-handed people speech was predominantly localized in the left side of the brain (which controls the right side of the body). In the nature of things it was impossible for Broca and his colleagues to see a brain working, and more information on what was happening where in an undamaged brain had to wait until the development of computerized scanning techniques.

In the last twenty or so years the use of new technologies like CAT, PET, MRI, and SQUID[8] has exponentially increased knowledge of brain geography. The new information about *where* has not provided many answers about *how* and *why*—it has, rather, generated new questions—but at least we know that the brain doesn't work as a single unit and isn't damaged as a single unit. For our brains and bodies to function properly thousands (or millions) of individual operations have to be carried out and thousands (or millions) of control units have to work, and any one (or any thousand, or any million) of those units can be knocked out without necessarily affecting the others. Anne had lost the ability to communicate her thoughts, not the ability to think.

Once Anne was out of the hospital we could really throw ourselves into improving her communication. She wanted her spelling to be fast, independent, and easy. Naturally, we first turned to technology. It has been said, with a combination of naïveté and optimism, that any person who has sufficient intelligence to communicate and who can control one muscle can now be linked to a computer and enabled to generate messages. It isn't that easy. While a lot of technical know-how has gone into developing the current generation of communica-

---

[8] Computed Axial Tomography, Positron-Emission Tomography, Magnetic Resonance Imaging, and Super-conducting Quantum Interference Device.

tion aids, which enable many people with severe physical impairments to communicate, they still all require at least one controlled movement, which has to be reproducible many times with reasonably consistent timing and strength.

Most disabilities subtract. If you have a hearing impairment you have less hearing than the average person, if you have paraplegia you have less movement, and so on. If you have athetosis, though, you have more movement, not less. Anne's arms and legs move when she doesn't want them to. That's a practical nuisance and a social embarrassment, but involuntary movements are no more than a symptom. Unfortunately, the problems only start there. Newborn babies have a lot of involuntary and reflex movement. Their arms and legs move in patterns similar to athetosis and they have similar startle responses— throwing their arms out in response to a sudden sound, for example. As the baby interacts with its world it replaces most involuntary movements with controlled movements (we all retain some involuntary, reflex movements, mainly for protective purposes) in a complex process of movement modification and inhibition.

Inhibition, in the motor not the emotional sense, is a vital part of this process. Inhibition is the neurological mechanism which overrides your spontaneous or reflex movement impulses and so allows your conscious control to take over. It is one of the most important of the brain's control functions. Anne has difficulty getting her body to respond to her will largely because further down the chain of command unwanted messages are being generated and cluttering up the wires, and she can't shut them off.

The functional problems in athetosis are caused by this difficulty of overriding involuntary and reflex movements and replacing them with smooth voluntary movements. The amount of difficulty varies with the extent of the brain-stem damage. Some people with athetosis are able to walk, albeit unsteadily, and may have only minor articulation problems. Anne is reflex-dominated, doomed to have her arms fling out at every sudden noise, and has almost no controlled voluntary movement.

Many people who need to use non-speech communication strategies also have problems using their hands, and over the years a variety of other ways of pointing and operating communication aids have been devised. In the seventies there were three hands-free selection strategies: eye gaze, simple electric scanners, and head sticks.

A person using eye gaze selects from widely spaced items by looking at the one desired. For selections to be clear the user must have a stable head position and good eye coordination and fixation. Anne's head position was anything but stable and she had a fluctuating strabismus, which meant that her eyes looked in different directions. While both eyes had fortunately retained vision, it was not clear which eye she was using at any given moment, so her gaze wasn't usable.

In the seventies the simplest electric scanner looked like a clockface with only one hand, which went around and around until the user hit a separate switch with a fist, foot, finger—whatever body part he or she had best control over. Items—pictures, symbols, words, or letters—were selected by hitting the switch when the pointer touched them. Anne's postural problems and spasm made positioning a scanner and a switch difficult, but it wasn't impossible. She had enough physical control to hit a large switch. Once we got a scanner, though, it became clear that one essential requirement was missing—timing.

Anne could make a deliberate movement and hit a target, but the speed of the movement varied, and she couldn't predict in advance how long it would take. She started to move toward the switch when the pointer was on the item before the one she wanted, but if her movement happened quickly the pointer stopped one item too soon, and if it happened slowly the pointer would pass the item wanted and stop one or two items too late. Slowing the speed of the pointer helped, but Anne's accuracy was only above fifty percent if the pointer stayed on each item for the same time as her slowest response, about thirty seconds. At that speed a clockface scanner would take thirteen minutes for one traverse of the alphabet. It could, of course, be sped up by using different scanning strategies and setting up the letters in frequency order, but nothing could change the fact that consistency in response time is essential for functional single-switch use.

A head stick is a pointer mounted on a headband, used to indicate items or to depress typewriter keys. It, too, requires a stable sitting position and good head control. In St. Nicholas, Anne didn't have a wheelchair, much less a stable sitting position. Her extensor spasm was so severe that it could not be accommodated in anything approaching an ordinary chair. Use of the posture chair had changed this, and after she left St. Nicholas, Anne bought a wheelchair and started to use a head pointer. She still couldn't bring her head forward though, and to inhibit her involuntary movements, she turned as far to the left as she could go, wedging her head against the back of her chair.

The first commercially available electronic aid specially developed for people without speech was a mini-typewriter about the size of a Walkman called the Canon Communicator. Released in 1977, it was the first internationally marketed, easily portable piece of equipment specifically designed to replace speech. Its small size made it especially useful for people with a limited range of movement. It had paper tape output.

Once Anne got herself into the correct position she was able to type on a Communicator positioned above shoulder height about a foot from the left side of her chair. She used the head stick for several years with an early speech synthesizer, which spoke her messages and a nine-button switch set which gave her access to a word processor, as well as the Communicator. Anne never liked the appearance of the headband, or the stares that it drew, but the real issue was speed.

When Anne's posture improved, so did her hand use. She still could not point quickly or accurately without stabilization, but her facilitated spelling was much faster than it had been, and much faster than typing with the head pointer. This became increasingly important when she had to write essays. She would compose wonderful paragraphs in her head, but after slaving for hours to produce a few hundred words she would be exhausted and have to stop with only a fraction of what she had composed down on paper. She often ended up in tears of frustration.

A time trial confirmed our subjective impressions—with a head pointer Anne could generate a maximum of one hundred words an hour, with her hand four hundred (a speaker can easily generate nine thousand and a mediocre typist two thousand). A two-thousand-word essay was difficult enough with arm support, impossible without. Head pointers were out except when Anne wanted to show that she could spell without having her arm held, and once she'd done that on national television she rather lost interest.

There are now scores of high-tech communication options for people who can't talk, but the basic input strategies remain essentially the same. Instead of looking at a set of pictures, one can use eye gaze to control a computer which will speak a selection. Instead of a head stick, a light pointer which activates sensors on a computer interface can be used, or a head-mounted mouse which controls a cursor to select items on a computer screen. Switches now come in all shapes and sizes and can be operated by any detectable movement, and there is a wide range of sophisticated scanning techniques incorporating a variety of predictive techniques to reduce the time and effort required to generate a message. However, the control issues haven't changed. One still needs to be able to produce a controlled movement frequently, consistently, and on time to use a single switch to operate a communication aid.

To date only the use of myelo-electric switches, which detect the impulse to move a muscle even though the impulse isn't strong enough to actually cause the muscle to move, can avoid the need for movement. These can be functional for people with conditions such as motor neurone disease, otherwise known as amyotrophic lateral sclerosis or Lou Gehrig's disease, which result in weak messages being sent, but they don't resolve the problem of missing or variable speed messages, or interference from other systems. Every attempt to tap some of the small movements that Anne could control—movements of her eyes and face in particular—failed due to the overriding interference from larger movements that she couldn't control.

If Anne couldn't control her movements she could take control of her education. Her initial response to the Toulouse-Lautrec lithograph was not an isolated incident, and neither was her interest in Watson and Luria. She was and is fascinated by the visual—painting and films in particular—and did a major in fine arts from the University of Melbourne, along with a double major in philosophy of science from Deakin University. Because Anne's production of written work was so slow, she only did a few units a year. She also took breaks while *Annie's Coming Out* was being made into a film, and when she moved to the United States for six months in 1992 with Chris and myself (she loved CNN, the Metropolitan Museum of Art, and Ben and Jerry's ice cream, not necessarily in that order). She finally completed her degree in 1993.

Still, what Anne did and did not do after leaving St. Nicholas isn't particularly surprising; the interesting question is why everyone had originally assumed that Anne couldn't learn. The answer was partly simple ignorance. Recent textbooks firmly state that there isn't any necessary link between athetosis and intellectual disability. The trouble was that the old textbooks, the ones that had been around when the doctors at St. Nicholas were trained and when Anne was born and diagnosed, *had* said that most people with cerebral palsy were mentally retarded and that the degree of retardation correlated with the severity of the physical impairment. When the textbooks changed, no effort was made to reevaluate the people who'd been labeled under the old rules. Medical knowledge may be updated, but a label is forever.

The biology we are born with influences the biology we believe in. We find any theory which confers superiority on us acceptable and any theory which questions our superiority dubious. People who have been diagnosed as having intellectual impairments have committed no crime. They have been judged unable to look after themselves and are unwanted by their families and so have been locked up. We all need to feel superior to somebody, and if we can no longer be superior because of skin color we need to find a new underclass. One way to impose order is to subject everybody and everything to the same set of measurements. Measurement imposes its own values. To be below average is to be subhuman, even though the nature of the average is that half the population will be below it.

Even the apparently objective measurement of head circumference varies depending on the bias of the measurer. My own head circumference varied both downwards and upwards depending on who was doing the measuring, and I fluctuated between being microcephalic and hydrocephalic without ever being just right. Today we have moved from measuring the outside of heads to measuring the inside. We are more sophisticated in our knowledge of brain function but no more sophisticated in correlating what goes on inside with external performance. We judge people by the physical manifestations of brain function. Regardless of their ability to perform the items on our test scales we feel able to use the test scores to give them a ranking, with those at the bottom being discarded.

2

Not Being Able to Talk
Doesn't Mean You've Got
Nothing to Say

To be speechless is to risk being placed totally outside the boundaries which delineate the human race.

Few of us will ever do anything more complex than learn to speak the language which surrounds us in infancy. Virtually every baby has grasped the basics of its surrounding language by the age of one. The child has a very small vocabulary, but has established the groundwork to achieve full mastery of language within the next few years. Nobody teaches a baby to speak. Nobody teaches a baby to understand. The baby learns to associate the peculiar sounds made by big humans with the surrounding objects, people, and happenings.

Felix, aged fourteen months, was visiting his grandmother for Christmas. When his father carried him through the kitchen Felix pointed at a pot holder and said, "Wahla," and every relative within earshot congratulated him as if he'd won the Nobel Prize. If he'd said "wahla" during playtime it would probably not have been recognized as a word attempt, much less understood, but when Felix said it he was looking at, leaning toward, and pointing at a round pot holder with a design of three koalas (pronounced "ko-wahlas") on it. Supported by context and body language, his meaning was unmistakable, and there was much excitement and reinforcement of the "Yes, koalas" or "Three wahlas" variety. Felix knew he'd made a hit.

How many variables would have to be changed for us to stop recognizing that Felix was using our language and that what he was saying meant something? The connection between "wahla" and "koala" would probably have been missed if Felix hadn't been able to coordinate his pointing, eye gaze, and vocalization, or if he'd said "wahla" without indicating its referent, or if his attempt at "koala" hadn't been as close—"ah-ah," say.

Felix has numbers of interested people hanging on his every word, people who expect him to produce words of wisdom any moment now, and who are prepared to search for meaning in every vocalization. People extract meaning from Felix's sounds because they expect them to contain meaning, and that expectation motivates them to spend the necessary effort.

The development of speech is a complex process, and there are many points at which it can break down. A baby who can't hear won't get to first base without special intervention. Rarely a child who can hear will have something wrong with his decoding system, and will be unable to attach meaning to the sounds he hears—he, too, may be left without language. A baby who has difficulty storing information will be slow in acquiring vocabulary and syntax, and this will impair comprehension. A baby who has difficulty retrieving information will have difficulty in using the vocabulary she has. Production of intelligible speech will be impaired if there is any kind of glitch in the several motor systems involved. If Felix had been born with an obvious disability, his family might have been told not to expect him to speak. They mightn't have looked on his early vocalizations as meaningful.

If you don't have any of these problems, by the age of two or so you've got it all together; you know that the "world is open only to subjects who make use of their competence to speak and act," as the German philosopher Jurgen Habermas put it. You then do a lot of work refining your pronunciation and extending your vocabulary and your command of syntax. You learn a lot of social stuff about greetings and farewells and please and thank you and what words get you into trouble and when to whisper, and by the time you start elementary school you're really amazingly good at it all. Five-year-olds may have speaking vocabularies of five thousand words and understand many more than they say. Estimates of adult vocabularies vary widely from speaker to speaker and researcher to researcher, ranging from ten thousand words to fifty thousand plus: a pretty fair guesstimate would be "lots."

About one person in a hundred can't say those words.

Presumably there have always been people who waved their arms around, who made funny noises (but didn't speak), and who didn't do what people asked them to. Historically these people were at best social outcasts, at worst legal outcasts also, barred from inheritance and with their rights restricted because of their muteness. They were often paupers, and groups of them tended to gather in the haunts of the poor and devalued. Sometimes they were locked up in asylums for the insane. Apparently without language, certainly without education, they were generally judged to be severely intellectually impaired. Most of them were deaf. They had been deaf from birth or early childhood, and had thus grown up without speech and without the vocabulary or grammar of the surrounding language. They were what would now be called prelingually deaf.

Visual language, the language of mime and gesture, developed wherever there were communities of deaf people, but it was limited and idiosyncratic, used for everyday needs, and not as a medium of academic instruction. Some people had seen and had developed the capacities of individual deaf children, especially in wealthy families, but there had been no general appreciation of the fact that a deaf child might be as able to learn as well as a hearing child, providing the instruction was provided in an accessible medium. The first systematic attempts to educate deaf people occurred in France in the second half of the eighteenth century, largely through the efforts of one man, the abbé de l'Epée. The abbé learned the local sign language, and used that as the vehicle of instruction to teach deaf-mutes to read and write.[1]

---

[1] For a detailed and absorbing history of deaf culture, see *When the Mind Hears* by Harlan Lane.

The success of the abbé's work had important implications. First, it demonstrated that deaf people were not intrinsically mentally impaired, as had been thought. They lacked a means of acquiring information; they did not lack the ability to process and use it.

Second, and equally important, it showed that the acquisition of written language could be divorced from the acquisition of speech. Because children typically spoke before they read, and because common methods of teaching reading involved reading aloud, it was thought that speech was a necessary condition for literacy. The abbé's students showed that this was not so.

From eighteenth-century France deaf education spread throughout the world. Given language and understanding, people who were deaf moved out of the asylum into the school and the workplace.

In the eighteenth century only one severe impairment not associated with deafness was recognized. It was the aphasia found in adults who have suffered strokes. The first recorded case of such aphasia may be that in Luke Chapter 1, verses 20–22 and 62–64.

And when Zacharias came out of the temple, he could not speak unto them; for he beckoned unto them, and remained speechless . . . and he asked for a writing tablet, and wrote; and they marvelled all.

Zacharias was struck dumb but could still write. People who had speech but then lost it have usually been seen as less alien than people who have never had speech at all.

The earliest detailed accounts of attempts to educate a mute but hearing child were written by a French doctor, Jean-Marc-Gaspard Itard, in the early nineteenth century. Itard described his efforts at educating Victor, a child who had been found in the forests of Aveyron in 1799, aged about eleven (Itard, 1801–11). We don't know what Victor's diagnosis was or where he'd come from. Victor could hear, and appeared quite adept physically. Over several years, however, Itard never managed to teach him to speak more than a few words.

My hopes were totally disappointed. All I could obtain from this lengthy training was a few blurred monosyllables, some blurred, some shrill, some deep. . . . Finally, seeing that my efforts were leading nowhere, I gave up my efforts to teach Victor to speak. . . .

And it was speech that Itard wanted. Victor did, in fact, learn to spell, but Itard did not regard this as real communication. To Itard, real communication was speech, and he gave up his work with Victor and went on to try and extract speech from the deaf.

Over the next 150 years few people made any attempt to provide hearing, nonspeaking children with a means of expression, possibly because most died young. In the nineteenth century improved sanitation, pasteurization, and antisepsis started to reduce infant mortality.

The twentieth century brought immunization, improved perinatal care, and eventually antibiotics. Consequently more babies with cerebral palsy survived infancy. It was still some time before anyone attempted to educate any who had more than the mildest physical impairments, but gradually educators became aware that a severe speech impairment did not necessarily indicate a similarly severe learning impairment (although acquisition of such motor skills as writing might be difficult).

Even when this had been widely accepted, however, the most severely disabled children—those with little or no controlled movement and with no comprehensible speech—were seldom given the benefit of the doubt. Doctors who knew that children with cerebral palsy weren't necessarily mentally retarded still thought that children who were *severely* physically handicapped *must* be severely retarded. Indeed, many people today (including many doctors) still assume just this, despite the acknowledged achievements of a number of nonspeaking quadriplegics using idiosyncratic communication strategies.[2]

Only since the late 1960s have there been attempts to develop widely applicable communication strategies for children

[2] See Christy Brown's *My Left Foot*, 1954; Christopher Nolan's *Damburst of Dreams*, 1981; and Ruth Sienkiewicz-Mercer's *I Raise My Eyes to Say Yes*, 1990.

with severely impaired speech and hand function. Before then "the odd lucky child received a wheelchair tray, with magazine pictures related to basic needs" (McNaughton, 1990). Initial efforts were directed to the design of communication displays—typically, flat boards on which words and phrases were displayed (often along with pictures or other symbols) from which the user chose what he or she wanted to say. During the next decade the new field acquired a title—augmentative and alternative communication, or AAC—and its own terminology.[3]

Fortuitously, developments in technology took place at the same time as theoretical developments in nonspeech communication. Initially devices such as the Possum scanning typewriter designed in England for people who could not use their hands to type because of polio or other paralytic conditions were utilized as communication aids. The Canon Communicator, the mini-typewriter which Anne used with a headpointer (see chapter 1) was the first widely available portable device specifically made for people who couldn't talk. It came on the market in 1977, just as the first personal computers, which went on sale in 1975, were making it possible for people with severe disabilities to use microchip-based technology to compensate for their output problems. Now they could produce text without touching a keyboard—text that could be spoken in a robotic voice.

At this time augmentative communication was still generally seen as relevant only to people with severe physical impairments who had intact intelligence, and the aids and strategies which were developed reflected this. People who were not able to point with their hands were accommodated by using eye pointing, mouth sticks, or scanning systems. Large communication boards or eye-pointing charts were mounted on wheelchairs, to be followed by computers and speech synthesizers.

Somewhat surprisingly, the introduction of nonspeech communication strategies for people who were not deaf generated

---

[3] *Augmentative* communication strategies supplement speech that is limited in vocabulary or intelligibility. If speech is either absent or totally unintelligible then nonspeech communication is used as an *alternative*. Similar equipment and strategies are used in both cases.

considerable controversy. In an echo of the speech/sign debate in deaf education, many people, including many speech therapists, resisted augmentative communication because they thought that all intervention should be directed toward developing speech, no matter how limited or unintelligible. Nonspeech communication was initially backed by teachers and therapists working outside academia. The benefits soon became obvious, however, and the field became professionalized. In the 1980s a number of texts on augmentative communication were produced for university use. The ultimate evidence of academic respectability and acceptance is a refereed journal, and *AAC* commenced publication in 1985.

The early communication technology did not attempt to meet the needs of nonspeaking people who walked. In fact, for using communication aids the ability to walk was a disadvantage because walkers did not have wheelchairs on which to carry large communication boards or heavy speech synthesizers.

Efforts were made to address the communication needs of some walking nonspeakers by using deaf sign with a restricted vocabulary and simplified signs. But the program had only limited success, partly because many of the users had difficulty reproducing the signs, and partly because they did not live in signing communities.

Some fortunate walking nonspeakers with developmental disabilities were given a selection of pictorial symbols displayed on a small board, or bound in a book, and could compose a message by selecting the appropriate symbols—simple one-symbol requests like "ice cream," or more complex utterances encoded by strings of symbols. They weren't offered alphabetic systems, because it was assumed that they all had significant cognitive impairments. People with significant cognitive impairments, it was thought, could not learn to spell.

The first breakthroughs in enabling people who were deaf or who had cerebral palsy to communicate by spelling were made by individuals working in isolation. The same thing happened with autism and retardation. In Chicago in the 1960s Rosalind

Oppenheim taught a group of nonspeaking students with autism who were labeled severely retarded. She described her experience of teaching them to communicate through handwriting:

> Many autistic youngsters have major problems in controlling pencils, chalk or crayons. This disability appears to be more pronounced in nonverbal children. . . . [W]e usually teach writing by manipulating the child's hand, and thus feeding in the motor patterns. We believe that the autistic child's difficulties stem from a definite apraxia. . . . There seems to be a basic deficiency in certain areas of his motor expressive behaviour. So, in teaching writing, we find that it is usually necessary to continue to guide the child's hand for a considerable period of time. Gradually, however, we are able to fade this to a mere touch of a finger on the child's writing hand. We're uncertain about precisely what purpose this finger-touching serves. What we do know is that the quality of the writing deteriorates appreciably without it, despite the fact that the finger is in no way guiding the child's writing hand. "I can't remember how to write the letters without your finger touching my skin" one nonverbal child responded. (Oppenheim, 1974, p. 54)

The clarity and freshness of Oppenheim's observations are reminiscent of Itard's writing more than 150 years previously, but her book conflicted with received wisdom and sank without trace, though occasional reports of individuals diagnosed as autistic communicating through spelling continued to emerge. In 1985 Arthur Schawlow, an American physicist and Nobel Prize winner, and his wife, Aurelia, chronicled their son's use of a Canon Communicator to type requests and comments. In Canada David Eastham learned to type with facilitation and published collections of poems, and in England Helen Fox filled shelves of books with facilitated handwriting (Biklen, 1992).

These remained isolated instances, however, until recently. While nonspeech communication was generally accepted as suitable for people with hearing impairments and severe physical impairments, its use is still controversial for people diagnosed as autistic or intellectually impaired, with most debate centering on the claimed production of complex spelled communication by people with these diagnoses.

3

Cabbages and Kings

There isn't anything new about the concept of augmentative communication for people with severe physical handicap. In *The Count of Monte Cristo*, written in 1845, Alexander Dumas gave an account of the use of nonvocal communication quite detailed enough to be copied by anybody who needed to use it.

In Dumas's classic book, Monsieur Noirtier, "one of the finest Jacobins of the French Revolution," has ruptured a blood vessel in his brain and is paralyzed. He is wheelchair-bound and has no speech. He can, however, use his eyes.

> It had been arranged that the old man would express assent by closing his eyes, refusal by blinking them several times, and a desire for something by looking at the ceiling. If he wanted to see his granddaughter Valentine, he would close his right eye only; if he wanted his servant, he would close his left eye.

Using the yes and no signals, much can be communicated.

> Valentine entered a few moments later. Her first glance showed how much her grandfather was suffering and how much he had to tell her.

"Oh grandfather!" she cried. "What's happened? You're angry about something, aren't you?"

"Yes," he said by closing his eyes.

"With whom are you angry? Is it my father? No. My stepmother? No. Are you angry with me?"

Noirtier closed his eyes.

"You're angry with me?" cried Valentine, astonished. "I haven't seen you all day. Did somebody tell you something about me?"

"Yes."

As Dumas would have recognized as much as anyone, for free communication you require access to the full resources of language. The system that Valentine and Noirtier have devised is sophisticated and powerful. Adapted to computers, it is still used today.

"What do you want, grandfather?" asked Valentine. She began to recite the letters of the alphabet, stopping to watch his eyes at each letter. At N he signaled, "Yes."

"Ah, it begins with an N," said Valentine. "All right, is it Na? Ne? Ni? No?"

"Yes."

"It begins with No?" said Valentine. "Good." She went over and took out a dictionary, opened it before Noirtier and began to run her finger up and down the columns. At the word "notary" he signaled her to stop.

"Is it a notary you want, grandfather?"

"Yes."

"Do you want me to send for one right away?"

"Yes."

"Is that all you want?"

"Yes."

And so a lawyer is summoned. Noirtier's son Villefort, who was on bad terms with his father, tries to discourage the lawyer from staying.

"You have been sent for by Monsieur Noirtier here," said Villefort after the first exchange of greetings with the notary. "His paralysis has deprived him of the use of his limbs and his voice. It's hard even for us to grasp a few scraps of his thoughts."

Noirtier appealed to Valentine with his eyes, an appeal so serious and imperative that she immediately said to the notary, "I understand everything my grandfather wishes to say."

She explains the code, and tells the lawyer,

"And however difficult it may seem for you to discover his thoughts, I'll demonstrate it to you in such a way that you'll have no doubts on the subject."

"Very well," said the notary, "let's try it. Do you accept this young lady to be your interpreter, Monsieur Noirtier?"

"Yes," signaled the old man.

"Good. Now, why did you send for me?"

Valentine named all the letters of the alphabet until she came to W, where Noirtier's eloquent eyes stopped her. Then she began to ask him "Wa-We-Wi-" He stopped her at the third syllable. She opened the dictionary under the notary's attentive eyes. "Will," said her finger, stopped by Noirtier's eyes.

"Will!" exclaimed the notary. "Monsieur Noirtier wants to make his will! It's quite clear."

"Yes," signaled Noirtier several times.

"This is marvelous!" exclaimed the notary to the amazed Villefort.

"Yes, but I think the will would be even more marvelous," said Villefort. "The words won't put themselves on paper without my daughter's inspiration, and I'm afraid she's too interested a party to be a suitable interpreter of Monsieur Noirtier's obscure wishes."

"Monsieur de Villefort," said the notary, who was looking forward to relating this picturesque episode to his friends, "nothing now seems easier to me than what I regarded as impossible only a few minutes ago. This will be a valid will if, according to the law, it is read in the presence of seven witnesses approved by the testator and sealed by a notary in their presence. . . ."

And so Monsieur Noirtier goes ahead and makes his will.

Dumas was using the weight of plausible detail to give a veneer of probability to an implausible plot in which, for example, Noirtier is disinheriting Valentine to protect her against the poison of her stepmother, Valentine is about to marry the son of a man Noirtier killed some years ago, and Villefort is being hounded by the Count because he (Villefort) had imprisoned him (the Count, in the days when he was Edmond Dantes) to protect Noirtier (in the days when Noirtier was a prominent Jacobin). Because of these flagrant absurdities it was important that the detail was plausible, and Dumas has given a textbook account of successful communication with a nonspeaking person. The technique he describes is very similar to that used today in enlightened intensive care units for people in the same situation as Monsieur Noirtier.

Unfortunately, however, not all doctors have read their Dumas, and this has left a gap in services. After *Annie's Coming Out* was published, people whose children had been in accidents and who had survived unable to speak would occasionally ask me if I could suggest anything. One of the first people I saw with accidental brain damage was Wanda.

Sixteen-year-old Wanda had been standing at a bus stop when a friend on a motorbike pulled up and offered her a lift. She'd accepted, which of course meant she didn't have a helmet on when the accident occurred. She'd suffered massive brain damage, had reportedly been in a coma for six months, and was left a spastic[1] quadriplegic without speech. After she returned home a family friend had asked me to visit her, to see if I could make any suggestions about improving her communication.

---

[1] Wanda's disability occurred after infancy, and so is not called cerebral palsy, but her brain damage had produced changes in her muscle tone similar to that condition. Wanda had excess muscle tone—her muscles were tight—and this affected all four limbs, hence the term "spastic quadriplegia."

The family had a small farm in the ranges on the outskirts of Melbourne, with a wonderful view across paddocks and hills. When we arrived Wanda was dressed in a denim skirt and was lying back in a reclining lounge chair, looking out at the horses she could no longer ride. She could smile, and her right arm had enough vertical movement for her to have started feeding herself. Her speech had been reduced to undifferentiated vocalization, but she could respond to questions with facial expressions, or eye movements. Monica, her mother, was confident Wanda could still read—she'd written jokes on a blackboard, and Wanda had laughed—but she hadn't been able to find a means of expression for her. Monica had read *Annie's Coming Out* and had tried making a large alphabet board, but it hadn't worked. If a pen was placed in Wanda's right hand, Monica said, she could write, but this wasn't any good because the letters all came out scrawled on top of one another.

I held up a piece of cardboard and asked Wanda to point to the compass points and the corners. The explanation for her scrawls was immediately obvious. She had good vertical movement in her arm but almost no lateral movement. She couldn't move her hand across the alphabet board or the pen across the page, so the letters came out one on top of the other until they were unreadable. If her parents wanted Wanda to write clearly all they had to do was move the paper after each letter. If you want to hide a tree, hide it in a forest. Wanda was different in so many ways that the reason for her specific communication problem had been hidden in the overall presentation of abnormality. Similarly, someone who sustains brain damage in his mid-forties is likely to have any reading difficulties attributed to brain damage rather than to the deterioration in eyesight which is almost universal at that age.

Anyway, it was clear that a large alphabet board like the one Anne used wasn't going to work because Wanda wasn't able to move her hand across it far enough to reach all the letters. Up to that time I'd always used boards with the letters widely spaced because most of the people that I had worked with had problems extending a finger and had to point with a fist, and because when people had extremely limited physical control over large movements it seemed absurd to ask for the fine pointing needed to use a small board. Wanda was the exception which tested the rule. She had, as it happens, a deformity of her right hand which helped compensate for her lack of lateral movement. After the accident her right hand had contracted into a fist, as is common in spastic quadriplegia, but her little finger had been damaged in a different way and was permanently extended. It would make a useful ready-made pointer. I drew up an alphabet board about two inches square, about the size of the stick-on alphabets sometimes included with video cassettes, held it in front of her right hand, and asked her to spell her name. She pointed to W A N D A quickly and clearly. Her language had found an effective outlet. From then on she was on her own. When I saw her next, ten years later, she was using a Canon Communicator, typing her sentences slowly with one finger on the three-inch-square keyboard.

Moving from a large alphabet to a small alphabet doesn't seem a great technological advance, but eventually it made it possible for other people, people who had even more severe injuries, to communicate. One such was Derek.

Derek was nineteen when he and his girlfriend were driving back from the country in his mother's car one night and he lost control and hit a tree. The girlfriend was fine; Derek suffered massive brain-stem damage which left him a quadriplegic without speech. Tall and handsome, he had always been very active, participating in skiing, yachting, and other sports. An only child, he'd had more opportunities than most young men his age. After the accident his mother, Hilda, said, "Everyone always said I spoiled Derek. Maybe in some ways I did. But now I'm so glad I gave him the boat and the skiing holiday in Switzerland. After all, I can't give them to him now, and at least he's got them to remember."

Coincidentally, Hilda had been my literacy lecturer when I was doing my diploma of education in 1977 with Anne as my practical work. Hilda had built a swimming pool in the backyard for Derek's hydrotherapy when he came out of the hospital, and she asked if Anne would like to use it too. On our visits there we always saw Derek, and I was always nonplussed by the extent of his disability. Derek was almost as severely disabled as it was possible to be and survive off life support systems. Indeed, his nasogastric tube had only been removed at his mother's insistence, and it was entirely due to her persistence he was able to eat solid food. He had no speech and no smile, he gave little evidence of being aware of his surroundings, and his usual posture could be characterized as decorticate rigidity—that is, both his arms were bent and held tightly across his chest with the fists under his chin, and his legs were stiffly extended.[2] The only action which to a stranger seemed to be anything like a response was that he did swallow food if it was pushed to the back of his mouth, though even that had been described as a reflex movement.

If I'd known then what I know now, I would have recognized Derek as a classic case of PVS—persistent vegetative state. The name persistent vegetative state was originally proposed in 1972 to describe patients with brain damage who survived in a state that was no longer coma but was not recovery—patients who showed "wakefulness without awareness." The prototypal PVS patient was Karen Anne Quinlan, the young woman described as comatose about whom the euthanasia debate raged in the seventies. PVS or no PVS, however, Hilda believed Derek had retained his intelligence, and she said she could ask him to blink for yes and not blink for no. I found this response difficult to interpret; a lot seemed to depend on how long you were prepared to wait for the blink. I would chat to Derek, and occasionally I'd ask him to perform some movement—an eye movement, a head movement, anything that could be the basis for

---

[2] The terms *decorticate* and *decerebrate* rigidity are used to describe different patterns of excess muscle tone caused by lesions to different levels of the corticospinal tract. While *decorticate* suggests massive cortical or intellectual damage, all it in fact means is that the pathway by which the cortex controls the activity of the lower brain structures, the midbrain and the pons, has been interrupted. It does not say anything about the "higher" cognitive functions at all.

an alternative communication system—but without any result. Every now and then I'd be encouraged by something that would look like a possible response, but then it would fade and Derek would seem to lapse back into unresponsiveness.

Hilda made Derek an alphabet board, to be used by scanning—her idea was that he would blink when she was pointing to the right row, and then again when she was pointing to the right letter in that row. I thought that was too optimistic. We didn't know whether his hearing, his vision, or his comprehension were up to it, much less his memory and literacy skills. Hilda didn't seem to use the board much, and I thought she kept it around mainly because it showed other people that she believed Derek was intellectually intact. I tried it once or twice and got ambiguous results. It was possible Derek was trying to spell something, but if so he never got a whole word out before he shut his eyes. As far as I was concerned the verdict was "not proven."

After I finished my course I drifted out of touch with Hilda. Over the next few years she asked me back again once or twice to see Derek, as she felt he'd improved. I tried him on a head turn yes/no system ("Turn your head to your right when the answer's yes, Derek, and to your left when the answer is no"), without much success. I tried supporting his arm so he could point to an alphabet board; he may have pointed to the first two or three letters of his name, but it was impossible to be sure.

By 1983 Anne was using a Canon Communicator with a head pointer. When Hilda heard about this she asked me to try the head pointer with Derek. I agreed, despite a sneaking feeling that it wasn't really appropriate. After all, Derek still hadn't given me any unambiguous indication that he even understood speech. I talked to him as if I thought he was intelligent and could understand me, and because of that Hilda thought I shared her optimism, but I didn't—I just thought it couldn't do any harm. I wasn't looking forward to the session, and gloomily expected yet another failure.

To defuse the situation for all of us it was set up as a social visit, Anne and Chris and myself dropping over to Hilda's for dinner. To start, I helped Derek extend a finger and supported his arm so he could touch a small communication board I'd been trying out since seeing Wanda. I asked him to spell his name. After just possibly pointing to DER his arm went into spasm and that was that. Anne's head pointer was lying on a chair. I still didn't think Derek had the controlled head movement necessary to use it, but because this was going to be absolutely the *last* session, I wanted Hilda to be sure that I'd tried everything. I picked it up and fitted it on Derek.

"Finish spelling your name, Derek."

Slowly, almost imperceptibly, but clearly, the pointer tip moved to E and K.

Hilda was quite calm—after all, she'd expected this all along. Derek twisted the left side of his mouth into a sort of a grin, the first change in facial expression I'd ever seen from him. I was trying not to cry. It was difficult, because I couldn't let Derek (or Hilda) see that I'd ever doubted him (or her). I asked Derek if there was anything he wanted to spell. He spelled I WANT T and paused for quite a while. Then he added EA—"I want tea." It was a slow process—about twenty minutes in all— and by the time he'd finished I was under control again. We had a rather subdued dinner. Hilda commented that she thought Derek had been going to spell something else and had changed his mind. I'd been wondering about that myself.

One reason why I'd been so unwilling to accept Derek's abilities was that I hadn't wanted him to be intelligent, hadn't wanted him to be aware of his circumstances. An intelligent Derek, able to perceive and feel the hopelessness of his situation, was more disturbing than an unaware Derek, and demanded involvement at a different level. He had to be helped to express his wishes, and we had a responsibility to try and carry them out. Derek challenged my concept of personhood. He couldn't laugh or cry, his body was an irrelevant obstruction. His humanity could show in his language alone.

Just pointing to those few letters showed that Derek had some usable vision, his hearing was functional, his visual and auditory processing was functional, his comprehension was

functional (and possibly unimpaired), his short-term or
working memory had to be virtually unimpaired (the fact
that he had retained his message for the length of time it
took to spell it demonstrated that), and his long-term
memory might be unimpaired—he had at least retained literacy skills. It was hypothetically possible that his cognitive
abilities might be unimpaired, but given the nature of
Derek's disabilities, comprehensive cognitive assessment was
probably impossible and certainly irrelevant. Derek's living
options and employment prospects were going to be determined by his overwhelming physical impairments, not by his
intelligence or education. What was important was to give
him as much control over his life as possible and enable him
to interact with other people.

A few days later we visited again. I set up a communicator,
put the head pointer on Derek and he typed out, "Kill Me."
Hilda seemed surprisingly unmoved. It was a delicate moment,
and I said tactfully, "Well, Hilda, I'll go and see if Anne wants
anything and you can talk to Derek." "Oh?" said Hilda. "What
about? What did he say? I haven't got my glasses on." And so I
had to tell her, and she burst into tears, and I'm sure Derek
would have burst into tears if he could have, and there I was
patting both of them on the back. Hilda said, "Oh no" and "I
love you" and "We can't" and all the appropriate things a
mother can say in these circumstances with a comparative
stranger like me present. When Hilda retired to get herself
together again I spoke to Derek and said that since he'd only
experienced life as a severely disabled *noncommunicating* person
since the accident, it was probably worth giving life as a severely
disabled person who *could* communicate at least a six-month
trial to see if it was any better. Anne had once wanted to be
killed, I said, but now led a reasonably happy and fulfilling life.
While everybody wouldn't find Anne's life to their liking, and
what made a life worth living was a matter of individual
opinion, I thought he shouldn't make any irrevocable decisions
yet. He'd probably been lying there for six years thinking, "If
only I could talk I'd ask them to kill me," and he hadn't had

any reason to give much thought to the changes that the very act of talking could make in his quality of life. Then I left Hilda alone with Derek and went and discussed it all with Anne.

> When Derek said he wanted to be killed I wasn't surprised. I have often wanted someone to kill me, but one cannot ask someone else to do such a thing. I would have been happy to help Derek if I could have. There would have been real justice in helping someone out of the world I had fought to enter. Well, we're all different, and what we live for differs too. What is quality of life for one person is death for another.

After this I visited Derek a couple of times a week till he got his own head pointer and Communicator and Hilda became confident in using them. Derek started to go out more often, to the theater, movies, and restaurants—partly because of his new communication, and partly because taxis had been introduced to Melbourne that could take wheelchairs. He continued to get into the pool every day with Hilda and his attendant and he listened to books on audiotape. He flew to Queensland, Australia's Florida, for a tropical holiday. He and Anne became friends and shared activities and attendants.

Derek's communication never did become much more fluent. For Christmas 1984 Anne gave him a pocket computer which I programmed with whole sentences such as "What about a drink?" but it was limited, and moving the pointer to select items remained difficult. When the state's first non-speech communication center opened a few years later Derek tried all the communication equipment on the shelves. Nothing available at the time offered him any advantages over the head pointer and Communicator. He typed to his attendants if they had the time and the patience to wait for a message. If not, they used yes/no and multiple choice questions to find out what he wanted. His communication slipped back when he was unwell, which he was quite often. He had frequent infections and a series of painful physical problems. I didn't raise the subject of death again, but about a year later Derek did. He asked me to kill him if Hilda died. I took that to mean "and not until," which was something of a relief.[3]

Despite daily therapy and every effort on his and his mother's part, Derek made only small gains in physical ability during the ten years he lived after his accident, remaining totally dependent on the assistance of others in every aspect of daily living. Nonetheless, with communication he could show the kind of person he was inside, and take control over at least some aspects of his life. Derek died in his sleep in July 1986, a day before his twenty-eighth birthday. His funeral was attended by scores of people whose lives he had touched since he became disabled.

In the medical system PVS serves as the postcoma catchall. Conventional wisdom has been that despite apparently being awake, patients in a persistent vegetative state have no communication, no consciousness, no hope of recovery, and no understanding, which does make their care very much simpler. As one therapist stated the accepted view, "Vegetative patients are not 'locked in' [like Monsieur Noirtier]; we know they have suffered very extensive brain damage. The pathophysiology of such damage precludes the sparing of cognitive abilities against a background of severe physical impairment." (Snow 1991, p. 25)

The therapist had overlooked Carolyn.

When I first met Carolyn in mid-1984 she was an attractive seventeen-year-old with red-gold hair and blue eyes, lying in a hospital bed in what was said to be a persistent vegetative state. At first sight Carolyn appeared to have an even worse prognosis

---

[3] People with severe disabilities who say they want to die raise considerable anxiety in professionals, let alone their families. In the case of people whose communication is restricted it is tempting to choose either not to "hear" the message (if you're the person receiving the communication) or to presume that the receiver got it wrong if you hear it secondhand. One reason given for being skeptical about the communication claimed for people paralyzed and mute as the result of severe brain damage is that "a surprising number of the messages are said to express the patient's desire to die." In many situations professionals have to insulate themselves to some extent from the reality of life and death for their patients, so they can continue to provide care. Nonetheless, being surprised that people who have lost almost everything that makes life worth living should want to die indicates an excessive degree of insulation.

than Derek. She had been knocked off her bike by a car almost a year previously and had suffered a major head injury, fracturing the base of her skull and sustaining massive frontal lobe damage, especially on the left side. There were gaps in her skull, and in her brain. After the intensive care people had finished with her she was a tube-fed quadriplegic without speech living in a ward in a rehabilitation hospital.

Carolyn had been seen by the therapy team and assessed as not suitable for treatment—specifically, the medical director had said that "the patient's condition has not improved since admission. . . . [A]t no stage has she given a consistent cognitive response to stimuli, confirming the impression of a chronic vegetative state with a very poor prognosis. It was not considered that rehabilitation had anything to offer this unfortunate patient."

Joanne, Carolyn's mother, asked me to see her daughter, although she also said, "There isn't much to work with." The only positive thing Joanne could offer was that she'd occasionally held magazines up so that Carolyn could look at them and she thought she'd seen Carolyn's eyes moving across the page. Carolyn had been told I was coming. When her mother introduced me she gave, to my surprise, something that if it had come from anyone not said to be in a PVS would have been taken as a smile.

Carolyn wasn't going to be able to use a communication board with her hands because her arms had contracted across her chest. She did have a definite eye blink, and I thought she was using it to signal agreement with what I was saying, but she wasn't able to reproduce it consistently on command. A few years earlier that might have stopped me from trying anything further, but after Derek I pressed on regardless.[4]

We sat Carolyn up in her bed, stabilized her with pillows, and put on the head pointer, trying to avoid touching the places where her skull had been replaced with metal plates. I asked

---

[4] In fact, many people with disabilities can spontaneously produce quite complex movements, sometimes including speech, that they cannot reproduce on request. At the time I didn't know this.

her to spell her name, and she did, very slowly. She almost nodded off to sleep several times, and Joanne squeezed her hand at intervals to keep her awake.

"Ask her to spell it again," Joanne said.

"Come on," I said, "she hasn't been able to say anything for months. We shouldn't waste her time. Carolyn, do you have anything you want to say?"

I held a Communicator out in front of her, repositioning it after every few letters so it was always centered on the pointer, to ensure that all letters were accessible. GET ME A TYPEWRITER. Her movements were still very slow. Joanne was impatient and kept interjecting, to try and speed her up. Every time this happened Carolyn lost her concentration, went into spasm, and became slower still. Anything else? I HATE HOSPITAL. Carolyn slid the pointer across the plastic keyguard on the Communicator till she got to the letter she wanted and then dropped it into the hole. Even the tiny forward movement needed to press the key was a great effort for her. The trouble was that Joanne seemed more impressed by how slow Carolyn's typing had been than that it had happened at all. "How patient you must be," she said. "I could never be that patient." I wasn't sure that this was what Carolyn wanted to hear. Did she want to go home? Joanne asked. LOVE TO. Joanne wanted to take her daughter home, but the Motor Accident Board, which was responsible for Carolyn's costs, was making objections.

I visited Carolyn as often as I could. Her spelling became more fluent and Joanne became much more relaxed about the whole thing, but it still took a couple of months before Carolyn was spelling freely to her mother. To me she spelled out her opposition to the hospital's plan to move her to a geriatric nursing home. The problem was that nobody anywhere in the system was prepared to accept Carolyn's ability to communicate. In a repetition of Anne's experience at St. Nicholas, all of the professionals who had previously assessed Carolyn agreed that it was impossible for her to be spelling, and in consequence none would come and see what she was doing. A month after she had started to use the Communicator she was moved to a geriatric nursing home. It was an extraordinarily depressing environment for anyone, let alone a seventeen-year-old. I spent a lot of time in the months that followed helping Carolyn's mother in her battle to obtain the resources that Carolyn needed to move home. There were endless problems—problems that had very little to do with communication and a lot to do with interlocking, inflexible, and insensitive bureaucracies.

Anne visited Carolyn in the nursing home, to show her that it was possible for someone as disabled as she was to be out and about.

> Close to death, Carolyn was still beautiful. She was different from many people who became disabled in that she didn't have any prejudices about people with disabilities. I've met a number who didn't want anything to do with me because I'm disabled. Even though they're still more disabled, they retain the prejudices they had before their accidents. Carolyn obviously hadn't been prejudiced before, and she adjusted better to her disabilities as a result. She'd been brought up right. I get tired of people who give more sympathy to those who become disabled than those who are born disabled. While it might be horrible to lose speech, it is no better never to have had it. Carolyn seemed to realize this, and didn't act as if she was the only one suffering.

Later Carolyn visited Anne at home and tried out all the communication equipment that she had available. She was able to move her head more easily than Derek, so the technology had more to offer her. She was especially interested in a computer system which Anne had, and used it to write a letter. Because the computer keyboard was too big for either Anne or Carolyn to access directly, they had to punch out a two-digit code on a small number pad to generate each letter. Carolyn watched Anne use it and had no difficulty catching on to the idea, which boded well for future learning.

Fortunately, before Christmas 1984 her mother at last succeeded in taking Carolyn home.

It wasn't (and isn't) unusual for there to be doubts about the communication abilities of people with severe brain damage. What was very unusual about Carolyn's case was that the matter was actually settled conclusively. In February 1985, about twenty months after the accident and nine months after I had started working with Carolyn, I had a phone call from her. Her speech had come back the previous day. Her voice sounded a bit rusty and lacked intonation, but it was quite clear.

It was a week before I could go to see her. Her face had regained nearly full expression and she was obviously and understandably happy. Single word utterances—"Hello," "Yes," "No," "Boring"—were all used spontaneously and appropriately. Any doubts about her literacy skills could now be resolved, because she could read aloud or give spoken answers to written questions.

Carolyn was still able to type more words with the head pointer than she could say. However, now that she could speak she was reluctant to spell. I couldn't resist the temptation to test her. I asked her who the prime minister was; she said, "Fraser," which was the name of the man who'd been prime minister at the time of her accident. I gave her a clue—"Bob"— and she said, "Hawke," which was correct. I asked her some general knowledge questions, many of which she had answered in typing previously. She wasn't very happy with the testing, and she often said "I don't know." There were a number of possible explanations for her performance, including boredom, but in retrospect it seems possible that the problem was with her speech rather than her knowledge. Since that time I have seen numerous people with limited speech, and they all tend to say "I don't know" when asked questions for which they cannot immediately retrieve a spoken answer. It might be more accurate for them to say, "I know the answer, but I can't get it out," or "Hang on a minute, it's on the tip of my tongue," but the Catch-22 is that these responses require more fluent speech than most of these people have.

We went on.

"Five and five make . . . ?"

"Twenty-five."

"No, five *plus* five . . ."

"Oh, ten."

I held up a stuffed Garfield cat toy. "What do you call this, Carolyn?"

"Puss. Boring!"

"Yes, it's a cat. Is there anything else you can tell me? What does your mother call it?"

"I don't know."

"G—"

"Garfield. Boring!" By this time she was saying "Boring!" rather a lot.

"Anyway, Carolyn, have you got any questions to ask me?"

"How—long—before—I—talk—more?" she said, with a perceptible pause between each word.

My honest answer was that I had no idea.

Four months later Joanne arranged for Carolyn to be given an intellectual assessment by a clinical psychologist. His report said: "In view of the severity of the injuries reported in regard to the brain, this young person was able to produce quite staggering results. In regard to the digit span sub-test she was able to recall six digits recited forwards and up to three recited backwards."

A typical person without overt disabilities can recall six to eight digits recited forward, with most recalling seven. Carolyn was shown a card with pictures of nine common objects and was able to name eight immediately, but ten minutes later could give the names of only two, and two hours later still the same two. She was able to do simple additions and subtractions and successfully counted to forty in threes, starting with one. She defined a sentence as a group of words going together to make sense. Asked why we pay taxes, she said, "For the government, for people who do not work." She was able to tell the examiner the name of the prime minister and the last prime minister. "She recalled three or four facts from a short passage of some seventeen or eighteen facts read to her."

On the tests she was given Carolyn's overall performance was below average. What does that actually mean, for someone in Carolyn's situation? Most of the tests required information or skills she had learned before the accident. Some of that wasn't available to her, either because it had gone for good, or she hadn't recovered it yet, or she couldn't express it in words. The most important area of difficulty was in recall of new material—the nine items on the card were themselves trivial, but learning new material depends on the ability to lay down long-term memories, and it appeared that in Carolyn this skill might be impaired.

But what is missing is never the whole story: as with Tennyson's "Ulysses,"

> Tho' much is taken, much abides; and tho'
> We are not now that strength which in the old days
> Moved earth and heaven; that which we are, we are.

The questions Carolyn could answer she answered as a young adult, not as an infant. Her answers were the ordinary answers of an ordinary person, and so was her behavior. "She smiled appropriately and manifested some frustration at times when she could not give the examiner answers." She was very aware of her disability, and blamed herself for the accident which caused it.

Somewhat unusually, the psychologist sensibly refrained from calculating an IQ score or mental age. He concentrated on the "very positive, encouraging signs in relation to the assumption of significant intellectual strength." His report portrayed Carolyn as a complex individual, a young woman with obvious deficits who had some of the skills and knowledge of an eighteen-year-old. Any assessment which had reduced Carolyn's performance to scores and ratings would have produced a false picture. Say, for argument's sake, that Carolyn's overall test scores could be attained by an average ten-year-old. Would that make Carolyn a ten-year-old? No, because while she was missing some answers at or below a ten-year-old level she was also understanding some concepts way above a ten-year-old level. In concatenating the complexities of people like Carolyn into one or two figures we miss their personhood, the experiences they've had that a ten-year-old hasn't had, all of which have shaped the person who is with us now.

Astoundingly, the staff at the rehabilitation hospital still didn't accept Carolyn's communication. Hospital staff gave a public presentation on persistent vegetative state, during which they said no recovery could be expected. A member of the audience mentioned Carolyn—a patient diagnosed as being in a persistent vegetative state in whom there had been some recovery. The medical director responded, pooh-poohing reports of her awareness and describing her speech (which he had never heard) as "grunts."

Carolyn could have spoken to the doctors herself, but after what they'd said about her around her bed she wasn't about to. We had to bring in an independent witness. Joan Dwyer, then chair of the Victorian Equal Opportunity Board, accompanied me on a visit to Carolyn in August. Since my last visit, in April, Carolyn had suffered a number of severe epileptic seizures. Epilepsy is common in people who have sustained brain damage, and sometimes has more severe effects than it does in people who are otherwise not disabled. In Carolyn's case, the effects were almost like small strokes; she would lose some of her hard-won skills, then she would regain them, and then she'd have another epileptic episode and lose them again. Her speech was less clear than it had been in April, but her hand skills had improved and she had regained some handwriting and typing skills.

When Joanne and Carolyn showed me the psychologist's report I was pleased, but I was also mildly surprised that Carolyn hadn't done better in math. Before her speech came back she had been doing complex sums with the head pointer. Of course, it was possible that I had overestimated Carolyn's skills previously, or that the seizures had since affected her ability. To check whether she could handle processes other than addition or subtraction, I asked her to answer some sums—24 divided by 8, a quarter of 36, 5 squared, the square root of 9, and so on. In nearly every case her first response was "I don't know." The psychologist would probably have accepted that response at its face value.

Whenever Carolyn said she didn't know an answer I told her that I thought she did. I asked her to point to the answer on a number board (by this time she was able to point quite clearly with her hand to letters and numbers, using a pen as a pointer). Her answers on the number board were correct, to her delight. After a few successes she stopped saying "I don't know" and started to say "I know" before pointing to the answer of the next question. It was almost as if Carolyn did not know in one modality what she knew in another.[5]

Carolyn often had difficulty retrieving directly the spoken form of the word she wanted, but she could use visual language to cue her speech. There had been a lot of publicity about the unbecoming behavior of a high court judge, I said. Could Carolyn remember his name? "No," she said, but then pointed to MU and said, "Murphy," the correct answer. Asked for a synonym for eucalyptus, she pointed to GU and then said, "Gum tree." If she couldn't retrieve a name she wanted—the name of one of her dogs, for instance—she'd sometimes ask her mother to say the first letter, and this cue would enable her to get out the word. If we couldn't understand something Carolyn said she would spell it aloud clearly and accurately.

Joan Dwyer wrote to the medical director of the rehabilitation hospital describing her visit. Her letter and the psychologist's report together forced a revision of attitudes toward Carolyn. Nonetheless, the system's attitude toward other people left in similar situations showed no sign of changing. The therapist I cited earlier as saying that the "pathophysiology" of PVS "precludes the sparing of cognitive abilities" was a member of the team which had assessed Carolyn, and she made that comment several years after Carolyn had recovered speech.

A few years ago Anne and I ran into Carolyn at the beach, where she was checking out the available male talent. Her walking had not come back, and she was using a wheelchair. She looked marvelous. When she smiled, she was really beautiful.

---

[5] Ten years later, this situation was to be duplicated almost exactly with Fiona, whose disability was quite different (see chapter 9).

Her burnished gold hair had grown, completely covering the scars on her forehead, and her blue eyes sparkled like sapphires.

While I was still working at St. Nicholas, a group of concerned people got together to give me some support and help the children I was teaching. We hoped to provide them with a new deal, so we called the group DEAL and decided it stood for Dignity, Education, Advocacy, and Language, all things the children needed. After I was dismissed from the hospital in 1980, DEAL continued to agitate on the children's behalf. Gradually over several years it expanded its operations and started to lobby on behalf of all people with severe communication impairments. It was clear to us even then that there were substantial numbers of people in the community who had the potential to communicate but had never been given the opportunity because of general ignorance of nonspeech communication techniques and technology.

In 1985 DEAL applied to the Australian government for funding to establish the country's first center solely devoted to developing communication for people without speech. To our considerable surprise we received a grant to rent premises, hire a small therapy team, and purchase a reasonable range of communication equipment. With the assistance of some additional funding from the Victorian state government, DEAL Communication Centre was able to open at the start of 1986.

When DEAL opened we were swamped with enquiries from the families of people whose communication needs had not been addressed, or who had been labeled "unsuitable for rehabilitation."

One such was Michael. He was just eighteen. He'd been an apprentice butcher until one night he'd been savagely bashed by a gang of young suburban hoods in an argument over a taxi. He'd got home, his mother said, gone to bed, and lapsed into a coma.

Unless you deal frequently with people who are said to be in a coma you're unlikely to realize what a loose term "coma" is, and what a multitude of states it covers. The standard rating scale for people with acquired brain damage is the Glasgow Coma Scale, more remarkable for what it omits than what it says. The Glasgow Scale scores three functions—eye opening, verbal (oral) responsiveness, and motor responsiveness—all of which depend on motor skill. To respond at the highest level of the scale you need to be conscious, able to understand speech, and able to control the motor functions that are necessary to open your eyes spontaneously, to speak, and to make controlled movements. A person at the bottom of the scale does not open his or her eyes, makes no audible responses, and has no movement. The obvious problem is that a person may lack all of these motoric abilities and still be conscious and able to understand speech.

Hilary Pole, for example, was an Englishwoman who had myasthenia gravis, a neuromuscular disease, and gradually lost virtually all ability to move while retaining unimpaired her intelligence and memory. Ms. Pole could receive all stimuli; she just could not respond to them. Tracheotomized in order to use a respirator, she could hear but not talk. She could see perfectly well, but only if someone raised her eyelids for her. Her body was completely flaccid, with one exception—for part of her medication cycle she retained control over one-sixteenth of an inch of movement in the big toe of her right foot.[6] The movement of this toe was sufficient for Ms. Pole to communicate, at first using roughly the same system as M. Noirtier and later a microswitch and a Possum scanning typewriter. She set up a national organization for people with disabilities, edited its newsletter, was decorated by the queen, and wrote comic verse.

> Bottoms large, bottoms small,
> We poor nurses get 'em all,
> To rub and polish, keep 'em clean,
> It's surprising what we've seen. . . .

If her disabilities hadn't come on gradually there is no way that the abilities she had preserved would have been recognized,

---

[6] Strictly speaking, this would mean she would not in fact get the *very* worst score on the coma scale—if, that is, the examining doctor happened to arrive at the right time and find the correct toe and register the movement.

and if she hadn't had a devoted and supportive family she wouldn't have been able to use those abilities.

Hilary Pole had a disease, certainly, not a sudden accident. Whatever the differences in causation, though, the existence of a conscious, aware individual who fulfilled all the conditions for deepest coma must surely raise questions about the usefulness of a motoric scale for assessing awareness. It isn't even as though motoric dysfunction like Pole's is the only explanation for failure to respond. The higher levels of response in each category involve responses to noise or to speech. A person who has suffered hearing damage as the result of the same insult which caused the coma or has a receptive problem will not perform as the scale expects, regardless of the level of consciousness.[7]

Michael's mother called DEAL three months after the assault. Michael was in an intensive care unit at a major teaching hospital, semiconscious and tube fed. The hospital speech pathologist said he opened his eyes occasionally but wasn't tracking. His mother said that he responded to jokes, could make eye contact, and moved his head if you said his name. She'd asked him to move his hand, she said, and he had.

When DEAL's speech pathologist first met Mike she began at the beginning. He could eye track, he could roll one hand outward, he could move his eyes and blink on command if you didn't ask him to do it too fast or too often. His head sagged forward, which meant that he couldn't use a head pointer. He was able to use lateral eye movements to answer yes/no questions—look to the window for Yes, look to the door for No. As an additional complication he had gaze palsy, and if he moved his eyes to the right the right eye turned fully but the left came around only to the midline, and if he moved his eyes left the right eye only half followed. He was able to stay awake for up to ninety minutes at a time, though if he was trying to follow instructions he tired after about ten minutes. He was still

---

[7] An important, recent study describing 40 patients diagnosed as PVS, 30 of whom showed awareness and communicative ability, stated that "Since all [aware] patients followed verbal commands it is assumed that none were deaf. . . ." This P.T.O. is obviously a reasonable assumption for those who did respond, but leaves unaddressed the hearing of those who didn't. (Andrews et al, 1996, p.14)

described as comatose, and a team from Carolyn's rehabilitation hospital had assessed him as unsuitable for rehabilitation.

Michael could follow simple instructions (they had to be simple—he was physically unable to perform any complex actions). We took in an eye-pointing board, on which any letter of the alphabet can be selected by using two eye movements. This would allow Michael to communicate by spelling if his eye movement control and literacy were adequate for him to use it.

AN E-TRAN EYE POINTING DISPLAY

A	H	V		D	C	N
			R			
3	W	1		F	2	G
P	8				X	M
	E		Cut away		T	
9	U		area		6	Q
J	Z	Y			K	L
			T			
S	5	7		B	4	O

The eye-pointing board is made of transparent plastic, and requires a partner who is positioned on the opposite side of the board from the user so she can read the user's eye movements. To select a letter the user looks first at the segment of the board containing the letter and then to the corner of the board which corresponds in orientation to the position of the letter in its segment. The most frequently used letters are each in the center of a segment, and are selected by looking at the appropriate segment and then straight back through the central hole at the partner.

Michael was able to spell—simple words at first, and then complex messages. He was able to tell staff that he had double vision, ask questions about what was going to happen to him, and tell jokes. He was regarded as having been left significantly intellectually disabled by his injuries. The DEAL speech pathologist administered a battery of tests designed for use with people with limited speech, and Michael's results showed that he retained good reasoning, memory and comprehensive skills. By the time a rehabilitation hospital had been found that was willing to accept him he had recovered some speech, but it was dyspraxic, dysarthric, and difficult to understand.[8] His communication was a good deal clearer and more fluent on the eye-pointing board; his spelling wasn't wonderful, but it hadn't been wonderful before the bashing. After some months of rehabilitation during which Michael learned to drive a motorized wheelchair and started to use a computer, he too was transferred to a geriatric nursing home.

Unfortunately the nursing home staff thought that using the eye-pointing board lessened Mike's motivation to improve his speech. They took the board away and put it in a high cupboard where nobody could get at it. Even though Mike was an adult, it was automatically assumed that his wishes should be subordinate to everyone else's view of his best interests. Mike's loss of autonomy wasn't a necessary result of his disability. While he was physically unable to enforce his will, and he didn't have the vocal power to order people around, he was recognized as having opinions and, given the right circumstances, was able to communicate them. What hadn't been recognized was his right to have his opinions about his own body accepted and acted on. Mike thought that he could communicate more easily and fluently using his eye-pointing board. He was right, but that's

---

[8] "Dyspraxia" is a motor-planning problem which causes difficulty in producing coordinated movements at will. "Dysarthria" is an impairment in the control of the muscles involved in speech which results in articulation problems. The combination meant that Michael sometimes couldn't get words out at all and when he did they were slurred.

irrelevant—if he wanted it, it should have been made available to him, regardless of whether it was going to help him or not. Vegetative state may not always persist, but the infantilizing of people with severe disabilities and limited speech certainly does. In what was surely the ultimate Catch-22, Mike couldn't even have speech therapy unless he requested it in speech.

When I last saw Michael he came burning along the nursing home passage in his motorized chair, a spunk with crew-cut bleached hair. We had a brief chat. His speech was soft and hard to understand, but he still had a great sense of humor. For people with disability it's a survival trait.

The persistent vegetative state is an ethical battleground, with most of the hostilities centering on the proper disposal of the body. Maintenance of life support, termination of life support, termination of alimentation (starvation), active euthanasia, use as organ donor, use as incubator—each of these positions has been espoused by disputants. This is not the place to canvass the ethical issues, but the debate about persistent vegetative state is instructive in the way that doctors and ethicists have reacted to the existence of a population with profound disabilities, a population who challenge our notions of life and death.

4

Just a Gnat Bite

When Anne started to grow we eventually had to give up carrying her up the narrow stairs in our nineteenth-century terrace, and we moved to a big turn-of-the-century brick-and-stucco house. It had thick walls, twelve-foot ceilings, and a row of cypresses planted close together along the front, and was as soundproof as you could expect any place to be not built for the purpose. It might have been designed for Penny.

Penny's mother, Mary, had met Derek's mother, and in 1985 she asked me if I would see her daughter. Penny was twenty-nine. She had been admitted to the hospital on New Year's Day 1975 with viral encephalitis. Encephalitis is an inflammation of the brain and spinal cord, which is caused by a number of viruses transmitted in a number of ways. Penny had probably picked up her virus from an insect bite. Initially stricken with a severe headache and high fever, she soon lapsed into a coma in which she remained for seven months. She continued on a respirator for another eleven months, during which time she was diagnosed as being in a persistent vegetative state.

Nearly eleven years after the gnat bite Penny couldn't talk and she couldn't walk or feed herself and had no self-help skills. These were her lesser problems. Her major problem was that she screamed ear-piercingly much of the time. At the infectious diseases hospital they eventually put her in a building by herself—not just a separate room, a whole separate building (the ward was due to be closed down, but they kept it open just for her). A nurse later wrote about her first night in the nurses' home. "I had an anxious night as I was kept awake by a woman screaming. The next day I was told, 'Oh, that's only Penny. She screams all the time.' And scream she did, every day and night, until I left three years later."

Eventually Penny was moved to a brain trauma unit in a psychiatric hospital. A public road went through the grounds of the hospital and at night the switchboard operator got calls from car drivers who used to say, "What are they doing to that woman?"

Because of her screaming Penny hadn't been able to visit a public place since her illness. Despite seeing no signs of recognition or response, her parents had remained in close contact, visiting every week. Years afterward Mary said it was like living with a constant feeling of grief. "We felt it would have been better had Penny died. Death is final but to have Penny like that, the grieving was always there."

In September 1985 Mary and her husband, Len, brought Penny to our house for the first time. Len carried Penny into the house (the hospital had a wheelchair shortage) and sat her in a special armchair brought from the hospital. She had difficulty maintaining a sitting position, slipping down frequently and having to be repositioned. She seemed to have balance problems and gripped the arms of the chair tightly, which made it hard for her to use her hands to point. She didn't smile at all, and her expression was sullen. Her body was heavy and immobile, a total dead weight. She was screaming when she arrived, screamed almost nonstop for the next two hours, and was still screaming at her departure. The only immediate evidence of comprehension was a definite eye blink on request.

I showed Penny a speech synthesizer and asked her to press the buttons for yes and no. At first glance there seemed to be little wrong with Penny's hands. Looked at more closely, though, her low muscle tone made large movements difficult (or impossible); her fine motor skills were poor (she didn't appear able to move her fingers independently, for example, and so couldn't isolate one finger to press a button); and she was hanging on to the chair as if it were a life raft. I gave up on her hands for the moment, fitted her with a head pointer, and held up a small alphabet board covered with a plastic guard with holes in it to stop the pointer slipping, of the type which Anne and Derek sometimes now used.

I asked Penny if she could read the letters on the board. She pointed to "Yes." Then I asked her to point to the first letter of her name. Nothing. I tried everything—nothing but a lot of noise. I was sure she couldn't do it, and with her parents sitting there and watching me torture their daughter I felt dreadful. My usual approach was (and is) to try and talk to people with communication impairments as if they could understand everything I was saying and to expect them to behave like other people of the same age insofar as their physical impairments allowed. After all, what harm could it do? At worst I would inflict some avoidable stress on someone whose daily life was a series of unavoidable stresses while making a complete idiot of myself. In Penny's case I was feeling like an idiot already and was going to feel even worse if, as seemed morally certain, she wasn't able to do what I'd been asking. Nonetheless, I reacted as though she understood what I wanted and had the capacity to do it if she chose.

After a quarter of an hour of asking Penny repeatedly to spell her name I pretended to lose my temper (with the screaming, not a difficult acting job) and told Penny to tell me why she was screaming if she wouldn't do anything else. There was a long pause. I was ready to give up when Penny spelled out, clearly and accurately, HELP ME TO TALK. LOVE YOU MUM AND DAD. This didn't answer the question, but was the first sign for over ten years that she had retained language.

Penny seemed to have relatively little difficulty controlling the pointer and indicated each letter with a definite push into that letter's hole in the guard. After she hit each letter I said it aloud, after each word I said the sentence so far, and at the end of the sentence, I recapped the message. She didn't stop screaming. The only time she didn't scream was when her eyes were shut and she appeared to have turned off; any effort, any functional level of arousal, and she screamed.

A corollary of acting as if you are certain that someone has skills is that you can scarcely act surprised when they show you the skills you said you were sure they had. I told Penny about the various communication aids that were available and asked her again about the screaming. She spelled, slowly but without hesitation, LEARN TO LIVE WITH IT. I HAVE TO. I'VE TRIED EVERYTHING. We talked about yes/no problems. BLINKS DON'T ALWAYS WORK. Questioning of her and her parents established that while she could generally control single blinks, she couldn't produce the sequence of controlled blinks needed to converse in the manner of Monsieur Noirtier, and sometimes she couldn't blink at will at all. Did she have anything she wanted to say? Did she want something to eat or drink. I'M NOT HUNGRY. I'VE GOT TOO MUCH TO SAY. WHAT HAPPENED TO THE NEIGH[bors]? All her sentences were grammatical, though compact, and all were correctly spelled. Before her illness Penny had been working as a secretary. Right at the end of the session I asked her a couple of sums, 45 divided by 9 and 105 minus 9, to check if she retained some math concepts. She answered them correctly by pointing to the numbers on a small board containing ten digits, and that was the visit.

Even I found it hard to believe that this screaming but otherwise inert individual was spelling, but on her third visit an incident occurred which showed that it really was Penny communicating and that she had at least some memory of her life before the illness, her life of eleven years ago. Her sister Helen's birthday was coming up, and her parents asked Penny if she'd like to give her anything. YES. What would you like to get her? ROSES CHOCOLATES. Len and Mary seemed overcome but I couldn't imagine why. In Australia Roses Chocolates isn't two presents, it's the name of a popular chocolate assortment, and it seemed a reasonable present. Mary explained that the girls had always given one another Roses Chocolates because the birthday girl would pass them round and the giver would get some.

After Penny had visited a few more times I realized that she'd been particularly noisy on her first two visits, and while she still screamed for most of the time, she didn't always scream quite as much or quite as loudly. Unfortunately, this relaxation in tension also affected her muscle tone for the worse. When she was tense—when she screamed more—this partially overcame her intrinsically low muscle tone. When she was more relaxed and screamed more softly, her head would flop forward onto her chest, and she couldn't lift it without help. In some ways I had seen her at her best on that first day. On her sixth visit, in answer to a question from me about what function her screaming served, Penny typed, NOISE IS ENERGY, a gnomic answer which caused much discussion at the time and was only elucidated years later.

After DEAL opened at the start of 1986 I worked there four days a week and stayed home on Wednesdays so Anne could do her essays and correspondence. As it happened, most of those Wednesday afternoons were taken up with Penny. Penny continued to visit me at home, partly because the psychiatric hospital was a long way from DEAL and partly because Penny's screaming would have disturbed our other clients. One advantage of having Penny come to our house was that we were able to make her visit a social occasion. Penny would arrive about two o'clock and we'd work till about four, and then she and her parents and Anne and I would have afternoon tea. They provided a cake, we provided the coffee, and we would talk about life in general. As long as Penny was eating and drinking, she didn't scream—after all, she could scarcely scream and swallow—and it meant that Penny did participate in at least one ordinary social occasion each week, with ordinary adult conversation on politics, the theater, and so on. Anne was the first new friend Penny had made since her illness, and they teased each other unmercifully.

Over the next few months Penny's screaming reduced somewhat, but she still wasn't quiet enough to go out in public. She declared that her voice wasn't under her control. Her parents had taken Penny to a behavioral psychologist once a week for seven years before bringing her to see me, but all his efforts had not reduced her screaming. The doctors and speech pathologists in both the acute and the psychiatric hospital had not found a remedy despite trying various medications and behavioral modification programs.

When we sought help from a neurologist Penny spelled, PLEASE CUT MY VOCAL CORDS. Though this seems drastic it was the only obvious cure for a problem that was having far more impact on Penny's current life than her lack of speech or her quadriplegia, and the neurologist went to consult with his colleagues as to whether they would be prepared to attempt to reduce the volume of Penny's screams by severing some of her vocal cords. We were of course confident that Penny would never speak again, and if the impossible did happen and her speech did return she would still be able to whisper. This was explained to Penny's family, but understandably they found the solution too final. Going ahead with the surgery entailed formally recognizing that their daughter's appalling disabilities were not going to change.

We pressed on in the hope that Penny could overcome the problem in some other way. I often wondered what the neighbors thought I was doing as the house reverberated with Penny's screams. The DEAL speech pathologist suggested that Penny's vocal cords might be going into spasm, which would be as hard to break out of as any other involuntary movement pattern. An alternative hypothesis was that Penny's screaming was an extreme example of perseveration. Perseveration is the involuntary repetition of a response after the original stimulus is gone, and it's frequently associated with neurological impairment. Fortunately, the remedy was the same regardless whether Penny had either or both problems. We had to find a strategy for breaking the pattern, ideally one that Penny could initiate and control herself.

Eating broke the pattern, but we couldn't just keep on feeding Penny like a trussed goose. Anne suggested chewing gum, and we tried that; some was swallowed, some was spat out, there was some success. Penny tried sucking water through a straw to break up the screaming pattern, and she swallowed a lot of water to go with the gum. Her parents sat out in the garden to get a brief respite from the continual barrage of noise. We experimented with facial moments to see if they could break the spell of the screaming. Slowly we made a little progress. This isn't the royal we. Penny and I were partners in all these efforts. I would talk to her about what I'd like to try and why, and ask her if she'd be prepared to give it a go. After all, I wasn't hitting a patella with a hammer to produce a knee-jerk. Without Penny's cooperation nothing was going to work.

We marked the triumphs—the first recorded laugh, the first session with no screaming (that took six months). I experimented to see if there were times when the screaming stopped; there were. Often it stopped if Penny was moved into a room by herself, when she became torpid. It appeared to reduce when demands on Penny were low and increase when they increased. When she was trying new equipment and when she was trying to communicate with her parents and not me, the rate and volume went up.

As far as communication went, our aim was to find a way for Penny to communicate more independently and more quickly. Spelling was laborious for her, and she had a low tolerance of frustration. I'M REALLY READY TO GIVE UP COMMUNICATING— IT'S FRUSTRATING BECAUSE IT'S SO SLOW. It was terribly slow— on a good day Penny would perhaps get out fifty words in an hour. Penny tried a yes/no box, a speech synthesizer that said yes or no depending on which of two buttons you pressed. Pressing the buttons with her hands was difficult. We tried various switch mechanisms in various positions on various limbs in the hope that she would be able to control one well enough to operate a scanner of some kind. They didn't work because Penny had so much difficulty initiating or starting a movement that she inevitably missed the target.

We tried a headband with a light pointer attached, with which Penny could activate sensors on a computer interface. After all, she was using a head pointer, so clearly she had the necessary movements. Yes, she did, but we overlooked one thing. When Penny moved to a letter on an alphabet board or keyboard she was able to stop her movement by dropping her pointer into the hole over the letter. She couldn't stop the light beam in the same way, so when she moved to a letter she just kept going.

We tried Morse code, in the hope that Penny might be able to spell independently and retrieve complete utterances by moving between two switches connected to a laptop computer with a speech synthesizer. It wasn't successful—again, initiation was the issue. Penny just could not seem to initiate the necessary movements without physical contact of some kind from another person. It wasn't as though she couldn't make the necessary movements; she could. Her partner didn't have to help her with the mechanics of the movement, just provide physical contact to get her going, like jumper cables to a flat battery.

Working with Penny frequently reminded me of *Awakenings*, Oliver Sacks's extraordinary account of the arousal of people whose ability to move and respond had become frozen as the result of an epidemic of encephalitis lethargica decades previously. Her problems with starting up were reminiscent of Edith T., one of the patients Sacks describes in *Awakenings*:

> At times when . . . she would be frozen absolutely motionless in the corridor, the simplest human contact would come to her aid. One had only to take her hand, or touch her in the lightest possible way, for her to "awaken"; one had only to walk with her and she could walk perfectly, not imitating or echoing one, but in her own way. But the moment one stopped she would stop too. Such phenomena are . . . usually dismissed as "contactual reflexes." . . . "I can do nothing alone," [Miss T.] said. "I can do anything *with*—with music or people to help me. I cannot initiate but I can fully share. . . ." (Sacks, 1990, pp. 60–1)

Penny's encephalitis had been a different variant to that of Sacks's patients, but apart from the screaming her presentation seemed very similar. Was there any chance she would respond to dopamine replenishment, as Sacks's patients had? This was canvassed, but the aftereffects of L-dopa that had been reported in the years since those first marvelous awakenings were a concern. The idea was put on hold pending further investigation.

Penny's parents bought her a new wheelchair. She didn't slip down in it and have to be repositioned all the time, but as it had no arms available to hang on to she grabbed on to the wheelchair tray instead, which pulled her trunk forward and made head pointer use difficult. Fortunately, her hand use gradually improved, though she still could not isolate and extend a single finger. In order to use a Communicator she held a rubber ball with a pointer embedded in it in her right hand and had her wrist or arm stabilized. Sometimes her muscle tone was so low that she even needed assistance to help her to hold the pointer, and on those days typing seemed like trial by ordeal for both Penny and her partner. She typed to family members sporadically, and more when she was at my place than when she was back at the hospital. It was as though she, and perhaps her parents, felt more comfortable with a safety net. After all, if communication broke down here they could always call on me to help.

Gradually Penny's face became more expressive. Her uncontrolled screaming was fading, and every now and then she was able to vocalize appropriately—to indicate she wanted the communication board, for example, when she had something to say. Perhaps because I saw her improving, we kept having arguments about her not working when I thought she should.

After about a year of regular visits we had an interesting afternoon with Penny's sisters. When they were out of the room Penny worked and screamed, and when they came in both her screaming and her output dropped. When questioned she reluctantly typed, I PICK WHO I SCREAM IN FRONT OF, and became even noisier when I insisted that she finish the sentence rather than have me guess the end. I told her off in no uncertain terms, and she relapsed into silence punctuated by resentful and *soft* grumblings. We were making progress, but slowly. She asked again about surgery on her vocal cords. She said she hated being treated like a child, and I told her that if she didn't behave like one she wouldn't be. Given that many people patronize and infantilize anyone with a severe disability, this was only partly true.

In retrospect I am not at all sure that my reactions were appropriate. When we're dealing with disabled adults with difficult behavior we tend to work on a "discipline" model, as we might with children. We control the interaction and we don't reward unwanted behavior because, the theory is, if we make life unpleasant the offender won't repeat it. The trouble is that people with severe disabilities may have lost some of the ordinary control mechanisms and may have a limited repertoire of automatic, almost reflex behavior, so ignoring behavior may not have the expected effect. If Penny was hungry and I said, "Hang on, we'll have afternoon tea when you've finished this sentence," then she became distressed and screamed for half an hour. Ignoring her screams had no effect on their duration—indeed it was generally necessary to intervene with a drink to enable her to break the pattern and stop. It was difficult to see that stimulating her to repeat unwanted behavior would reduce the likelihood of the same behavior occurring the next time she was hungry. There seemed a good chance that, given her preexisting problems with disinhibition and perseveration, each repetition would simply entrench the behavior further.

It goes against the grain for us to reward "bad" behavior, but if the behavior is genuinely uncontrollable it may be the most sensible thing to do. It would have been interesting to see how Penny's behavior would have responded if every time she vocalized, someone asked her what she wanted, used her board to get her answer, and acted on what she said.

As it was, that approach wasn't an option because the psychiatric hospital refused to recognize her communication at all. The hospital speech pathologist had some years previously asked Penny to eye-point to a picture board, and she hadn't; if she hadn't managed to get Penny using a communication system, it couldn't be done, and consequently we couldn't be doing it. At the end of 1987, after several frustrating episodes in which the psychiatric hospital had refused to allow Penny's parents a say in their daughter's care on the ground that she was an adult, and had refused to allow Penny a say in her care on the ground that she couldn't communicate, Penny's elder sister applied for guardianship. Her case was that while Penny had the capacity to make decisions for herself, she had severe difficulties in communicating them and getting others to act on them. Penny supported the application, although she was depressed by it; I WISH I COULD DO THINGS MYSELF, she spelled. The Guardianship Board said that if she had the capacity to ask for a guardian she didn't need one and couldn't have one. This ignored the reality of Penny's situation—a quadriplegic with no means of communicating her wishes to those providing her care, and no means, other than screaming, of objecting to anything they chose to do. What she really needed was an advocate with the clout to make the hospital listen. In the lack of any such she fell back on the less powerful option of giving her sister a power of attorney.

At the time I was annoyed that Penny's sister hadn't been given guardianship. Interestingly, Penny herself cheered up perceptibly when the application was refused. She recognized the reality of her situation, and she'd concurred in the application, but the thought of giving up her autonomy had evidently depressed her more than we'd realized. Because Penny wasn't able to exercise her autonomy in any way, I hadn't thought it mattered whether or not she kept it. I'd told her that real power over her life, even if exercised through another, was preferable to theoretical but unexercisable control. Penny had reluctantly accepted the logic of that, and if the application hadn't been lost we might never have known how important that last remnant of personhood was to her. As it was, the Board's decision helped Penny cast off the weight of depression that had threatened to overwhelm her. Whatever else had changed, she was still in charge.

During 1988 Penny continued to come to my place nearly every Wednesday. By this time the DEAL therapy staff were quite reasonably putting pressure on me to stop seeing her. After all, Penny now had a means of communication, and while it was slow and she wasn't using it very much outside her visits, that wasn't our lookout. We had a waiting list and Penny was consuming a disproportionate amount of services. How could I justify continuing further appointments?

There was also Anne to consider. Anne had given up most of her Wednesday afternoons to Penny for the last three years. While she had become sincerely fond of Penny and her parents, no one could pretend that Penny's early visits had been other than painful. Then and later, Anne had sacrificed her precious communication time to Penny—the words Penny spelled were words Annie didn't get to spell, because the time and energy I devoted to Penny were no longer available for Anne.

Actually, I wasn't sure how I could justify the time either. The problem was, if I stopped Penny's visits that would leave her with no social contact apart from her family, nothing to do, and no hope of change. I couldn't bring myself to do that, and won a reprieve from my staff's criticism by setting up a formal program aimed at speeding up Penny's spelling overall and increasing her fluency with family members. We all signed a contract committing ourselves to the program, and Penny spent a lot of time typing "The quick brown fox jumps over the lazy dog" against the clock.

After three years' work Penny now vocalized only when there was an immediate cause of distress or frustration. Even better, she had worked out a technique of her own to damp down the continuous screaming. Rather than gulping air in and then exhaling it through her open mouth, she now often managed to bring her lips together, forcing the air out through her nose. If she was able to do this a few times it broke up the pattern; the controlled breathing, furthermore, had a generally relaxing effect, and you could actually feel the muscles in her arms loosen.

Not surprisingly, Penny still wanted to be able to go out in public. We started with short walks around the block, and when these went well we made short visits to local parks. Penny's parents bought a van which accommodated her wheelchair and made transportation easier. In January 1989 she ventured into a populated setting for the first time. Melbourne Zoo hosted a visit from two giant pandas, and Penny and Anne decided they'd like to visit too. The only loud noises Penny made all day were after we'd been waiting in the panda line in the sun for some time, and the only response from the public was sympathetic.

This success was very important for building up confidence in both Penny and her parents, who'd found this first outing very stressful. After this Penny's level of arousal, her cheerfulness, and her muscle tone all increased. Her hand skills improved, and she started to feed herself again. Her reach and grasp continued to improve (though it was all very variable, and a movement that had worked well at one session would often not seem to be available at the next visit). Now she wanted to return to social life and go to plays and films and get out of the hospital (which still didn't believe that she could spell). We set her some social goals—a quick visit to McDonald's, a movie matinee, shopping at some relatively unfrequented shopping center—and her parents worked their way through them. As her screaming had reduced so substantially, it was now possible to think of her attending a day center. An agency for people with cerebral palsy was approached and agreed to give her a trial in an adult group. She started part-time and gradually built up: three, then four, and finally five days a week. The extra stimulation, the therapy, and the contact with people who saw her as disabled rather than disturbed helped enormously. By the second half of 1989 Penny had recovered control of her facial expression and could smile again—indeed, she tended to laugh maniacally whenever she became excited, which while a great improvement on screaming was still disruptive. And then the surprises really started. Penny regularly attended a music group at the cerebral palsy center—she'd listen and beat time while others sang or played musical instruments. One day, completely unexpectedly, she started singing along. Denise West, a Spastic Society speech pathologist, arrived to find Penny belting out ABBA songs with staff and clients clapping and crying alternately.

It certainly isn't unknown for stroke patients to sing before they can talk, but Penny hadn't had a stroke, and she had last sung more than fourteen years ago. Her speech didn't come back virtually overnight, as Carolyn's had; initially she just said occasional words. By the end of the year she was talking sporadically—a few words every day, and every day some expressions that hadn't been heard from her since the encephalitis. At this stage she was very limited in the words she could use, and the things she could do with them. She was able to generate her own utterances, but she needed a prompt. Even so, when she was prompted she didn't just echo the prompt. When her mother said to Penny "Say hello to Rosie!" Penny said "Hi, Rosie, how are you?"

Interestingly, the vocabulary Penny used initially resembled that of a toddler rather than an adult. Denise West recorded that when she was asked to name pictures a cat was a "pussy," a train was a "choo-choo," a candy was a "lol lol," a horse a "horsie" and an egg a "googie." This was not only infantile, it was completely different from her typed vocabulary. Even though she had not recovered the ability to say everything she could spell, Penny immediately rejected the Communicator, both because she was so excited by the return of her speech and because she thought of non-vocal communication as a step backward.

Penny and her parents were coming round to exchange Christmas presents. I was worried how Anne would react. When they had first met, after all, it had been Anne who was the relatively able one, the one who could give Penny hints on communication techniques. And now here was Penny doing something Anne would give her right hand to be able to do, something which had been her dearest wish ever since she could remember. If she cried or sulked no one could blame her.

I showed Penny and her parents into the sitting room and went, with some trepidation, to get Anne. I needn't have worried. When Penny said, "Hello, Annie!" Anne just beamed. Her pleasure in Penny's good fortune was unforced and genuine. Apart from spelling "Wish it was me" directly after Penny had gone, she has never expressed any envy and the two remain good friends.

I paled inwardly. So it was possible. . . . Rose never knew how much I wanted to speak—not type, not spell, but speak with my own voice. I only had the fantasy for a moment, but it really hurt to return to my old choked throat.

Fortunately Penny was able to get intensive speech therapy at the cerebral palsy center. Soon she was getting out complete, appropriate sentences four or five words long. She was also getting out some less appropriate ones. Thoughtless hospital staff encouraged her to swear and make inappropriate comments like "Shut up." I was trying to discourage this, not out of prudishness but because at that stage Penny found it hard to resist bad linguistic habits. She had difficulty finding the right word and tended to get stuck on particular phrases, which meant that obscenities she'd indulged in earlier could pop out again at times she didn't want them. She went through a phase of swearing a great deal, and a stage of repeating stereotyped utterances—"good girl"—ad nauseum.

Ironically, Penny's speech at this time indubitably showed that she was aware but also appeared to confirm the views of those who had been skeptical about her spelling and the sophistication of her typed language. Her speech was initially limited and childish. She had problems spelling or reading aloud, or producing a spoken response to a written question. If her speech development had stopped at that point she may have been doomed to perpetual childhood. People who have restricted or immature speech may be judged more harshly than people who have no speech. It may be difficult to induce anyone to believe that Maria, who is mute, has hidden potential, but it's still easier than getting anyone to believe the same of Jana, whose utterances are short and whose vocabulary is babyish. Jana answers simple questions with "I don't know"; Jana says "yes" when she should say "no"; it's going to be hard to convince people that Jana is intelligent. Penny did all these things, and for some people her new speech only proved that I had overstated her capacities.

In May 1990, some six months after getting speech back,

Penny, her parents, and her sister Helen (she of the Roses Chocolates) visited our house for a belated birthday party. Penny was very sociable, with no swearing and no uncontrolled laughter, but she was holding a stuffed frog given to her by someone in the ward, and this combined with her limited range of utterances ("Oh dear me" was a particular favorite) made her seem immature. Nonetheless, she'd obtained more power. Previously we wouldn't have given her a third piece of cake no matter how clearly she'd pointed to it, but when she asked for it in speech we all leaped to her bidding. During the afternoon she greeted people, responded to what people were saying, and occasionally echoed what someone had just said. Her speech wasn't always clear (her parents commented that it was less clear than usual), and she occasionally made quite long statements which were too slurred to be intelligible.

Anne, who of course still couldn't talk despite Penny's earnest encouragement (at this stage she seemed to think that if Anne just tried harder she, too, would be able to speak), used her communication board to tease Penny. Penny was very with it; she would start laughing when Anne had spelled no more than the first few letters of the key word. She was clearly following extremely well—decoding Anne's spelling, which I was saying aloud letter by letter, and getting the message ahead of other people in the room.

After the cake was finished Penny's mother got out the Communicator and everybody left Penny and me together to see whether Penny would agree to use it. In the past Penny's use of the Communicator had varied from the extremely laborious to the merely laborious, and her typing had never been easy or fluent.

On this occasion she took the pointer from me, held it well, and moved her hand easily and rhythmically, far more relaxed than she'd ever been before. At one stage I was just holding her sleeve to support her against gravity. She started by typing, I REALLY WANT TO SPEAK BUT I CAN'T SAY EVERYTHING YET. Then WHEN WILL— When Penny typed I said the words aloud as she typed them, so when she typed, WHEN WILL, I said, "When will." Then Penny *said*, "*it all.*" She typed COME, I said,

"When will it all come . . ." and she said, *"out."* She typed CAN I EVER and said *"say"* before typing ALL THE WORDS I WANT TO SAY. CAN I READ WHAT I WRITE? "Can" meant "was she able to," that is, not "was she allowed to," because I had been showing her the tape as it had come out. I retyped that sentence with spaces in between the words—she'd been typing without spaces, for speed—and held up the tape with my fingers, positioned so that only one word was visible at a time. She read out, "Can—I—read—what—I—write" completely accurately. I then typed a sentence of my own without saying it aloud. The sentence I typed was BOB HAWKE HAS HAD AN OPERATION, and again I showed it to her a word at a time. She read it correctly and clearly. I was sure she hadn't said a word like "operation" for fourteen years. When she was reading aloud Penny's speech was far clearer than when she was talking spontaneously.

I asked Penny if she had more that she wanted to say. She typed EXTR and said, *"extra."* She typed WO, I said, "whuh," and she said, *"work."* She typed WI; I said, "wi." The word was obviously going to be "will," and she left it and completed the sentence by saying *"help."* "Extra work will help." Not only was the typing enabling Penny to get out utterances and retrieve words once the sequence had started, the words she said validated her typing beyond question.

She went on typing; HELL I WRITE BET; I said, "better." She laughed and looked up at me and said, *"than you."* She typed HELEN [her sister] IS BET . . . and completed it in speech, ". . . *er than you,"* with a lot of laughter.

I typed out on tape the sentence I AM A PIG for her to say out loud, showing it to her one word at a time, as previously. Penny could obviously guess that I had something up my sleeve here, so she read, *"I am,"* laughed, and said, *"going"*—it was time to go, and people were waiting.

I laughed too. "Keep reading."

"a . . ." I showed her the last word and she said, *"p—,"* broke up laughing, and said, *"pig."* Helen said she certainly was, the amount of cake she'd eaten, and then it was time for farewells.

The last thing I did before Penny left was to take that very inappropriate stuffed frog and throw it at her. She put up her hand and caught it, still laughing.

When Penny visited next in October her speech did not show much improvement. She still had a great deal of difficulty finding the words she wanted, and tended to fall back on stereotyped avoidance strategies such as "Don't worry about that." When answering a question she knew she was likely to get wrong, such as "What's the capital of Australia?" she buried her spoken answer, "Adelaide," in laughter. She then typed CAN-BERRA, the correct answer. The sentence structures and range of topics addressed in typing were still broader than those in Penny's speech. As on her last visit she sometimes said a word after typing the first couple of letters or completed a phrase orally after typing a few words. She listened attentively while I discussed word-finding problems at length and nodded agreement enthusiastically when I talked about the kind of problems I thought she might be experiencing.

Of course, the speech therapists at her day center were aware that what Penny said was not necessarily indicative of what she was thinking and that further development could be expected. Penny's speech problems are not uncommon in people recovering speech after strokes, and the etiology and general prognosis are well understood.

In November 1990 a report written by Denise West from the Spastic Society of Victoria said that Penny was able to talk about recent events but "she has difficulty in initiating language about past events. This does not mean that Penny is unable to recall past events, only that she needs questions and cues to 'trigger' her language and responses." Her spoken "yes" and "no" were not always reliable. "When tired or unwell it is Penny's head movements [nodding or shaking] that are the more reliable response as she may still perseverate on saying 'yes' and 'no'." That is, after correctly answering one or two questions "no," Penny might get stuck, and answer any following questions "no," regardless of whether that was the answer she really wanted. Imagine the frustrations—you're dying for a drink, and say, "I want a . . . a . . . a . . ." "Do you want a biscuit, dear?" "No." "Do you want a magazine?" "No." "Do you want a drink?" "No!" you hear yourself saying, though your throat feels like the Sahara in a particularly dry year.

Penny's speech was continuing to improve. On a naming test in mid-1991 she was initially able to name forty-two out of fifty pictures correctly. At the end of the test I got out the Communicator to see whether she could type some of the eight she hadn't been able to say, but in fact she didn't need to—the second time around she was able to name five out of the eight in speech. You know the experience of having a word, often a proper name, on the tip of your tongue—you know you know it, it's there somewhere, but you can't get it out right when you want to; and you know how if you stop consciously trying to search for it, often the word will surface minutes or hours later. That's more or less what was happening to Penny, except in her case the list of words she might have difficulty with was longer than yours, and included many of the most common words. After the test I asked her, "What do you think is the worst problem with your speech now?" Penny answered, "I can't control it. It just comes out." "Can you say everything you want to say?" "No, of course not." "Do people realize that you're thinking more than you can say?" "No. They think I'm dumb."

Soon afterward I videotaped an interview with Penny in which I questioned her about her life after her illness. The specifics of her memories were not always accurate, but she was definite about her memory for feelings. When I asked her, "Do you remember spelling things on the [alphabet] board with the head pointer?" she replied, "Yes, vividly." "How did you feel?" "Very loud. Glad—happy to be speaking again." Now at last I had an opportunity to ask Penny about some of the things she'd typed which had been impossible to clarify at the time because her typing had been too slow and laborious to permit extended questioning. Could she tell me what she'd meant when she'd said her screaming was energy? She didn't wait for me to finish the question. "Energy! And you believed me!" "You mean you were having us on?" "Yes! And you believed me!" she said through gales of laughter. "How did people treat you when you couldn't speak?" "When I couldn't speak they thought I was dumb [stupid]." "Could you understand what people said to you?" "Of course I could understand." "Sometimes you didn't want to spell. What was the problem then?" "I'd get lazy in my hands."

Toward the end of the year Penny moved into an ordinary house which she shared with three other women with disabilities. A psychologist's assessment prior to the move found that Penny had significant short-term memory and/or word-finding problems. As ever, in assessing memory and cognition through the medium of defective speech the psychologist came up against the chicken-and-egg question. In a memory task was Penny not giving the appropriate answer because she couldn't *remember* it or because she couldn't *say* it? The most heartening sections of the report were a finding that "she has good reading ability" and a comment that "Penny's behavior was impeccable."

At the time of the move Penny could still type more than she could say. We lost touch with her for six months because we spent a semester in the United States. When we returned, after the end of Penny's first year out of the hospital, her speech was equal to her typed language. Though she still had word-finding problems, I was finally able to say that the Communicator had nothing to offer her. Her most recent achievement had been regaining handwriting. This was legible but produced with considerable effort. Placing the words on the page was a problem—while Penny started at the left of the top line as you'd expect, her words sloped up at a forty-five-degree angle from the line and tended to run off the page. The slope didn't change when I put my hand over hers, and it seemed due to perceptual rather than purely motor problems. Because Penny needed to concentrate so hard on the process of getting the words on the page, she sometimes lost the thread of what she was writing and extra "automatic" words were included that she would not have used in spoken or typed language. For example, "I hope you are you well."

As a souvenir of our trip Anne had bought Penny a nest of wooden balls painted with scenes commemorating the five hundredth anniversary of Columbus's voyage to the Americas.

That hadn't been a big event in Australia and I was interested to see whether Penny could work out what event was shown. I showed her the ball which pictured Columbus's fleet. "Clippers," she said. "Look at the ship's names." "Spanish." "Yes. They sailed together." "Spanish Armada." "No. Think of another Spanish fleet." "Columbus." "Yes!" After this she went on to talk about syphilis and Indians and Columbus's birthday before moving to the present and talking about the recent resignation of the Canadian prime minister over the introduction of a goods and services tax. Whatever her long- or short-term memory problems, she was certainly doing at least as well on history and current affairs as the average Australian!

During 1993 she started going to a local primary school once a week to help the children with their reading and spelling. It was a useful educative exercise—as one little boy said, "I didn't know people in wheelchairs had any brains." From this time onward my contact with Penny has been mainly social. She comes to Anne's parties, we've been out to dinner and the theater, and we've met a few times to talk about her memories of her illness and her experience of disability.

I asked her how the hospital staff had reacted when she started to talk again. "They didn't want to believe it. When I got better it went against their rules—the doctors said I'd be a vegetable all my life and never recover. All the doctors said that."

She remembered things from when she was thought to be in a coma. She told a journalist, "The doctors used to say, 'Oh, don't worry about her, she's a vegetable.' They thought I couldn't hear or understand them but I understood every word they were saying."

I thought back to Penny's first visit here, when she screamed for two hours solid. She had no social relationships—her parents were seeing her at least once a week, but Penny had no way of responding to them; she would either shut her eyes and appear to be asleep or scream. It wasn't clear whom she remembered, what she remembered; most people didn't think she understood language. When she used a head pointer to type at that first visit, it was straightforwardly unbelievable. I think virtually nobody apart from me believed it, and every now and again I'd become unsure and think I must be imagining it, it seemed so extraordinary. Then I'd see her moving the pointer around the board and know it was real, but I could understand other people's skepticism. I can also understand people being absolutely terrified to think it was true, to think a functioning mind and an aware person survived inside that immobile screaming body.

Penny is the most challenging client I've ever had. She had more sessions with me than anyone apart from Anne. There have been many people for whom communication has been more difficult, but no one else's communication has been received with more intense skepticism. It was so hard—for most people, it was simply impossible—to think that there was any intelligence alive in there. And now someone who hadn't talked for fourteen years is talking. Never judge by appearances.

The handwritten message in Penny's 1994 Christmas card said "Great job we did together!" That "we" should include many people, especially her family and Denise West and the other Spastic Society staff. Penny's fortieth birthday party in 1996 affirmed her re-integration into the community. Held at her parents' home, the guests included her old school friends as well as friends she'd made since her illness. In many ways the evening was like a belated twenty-first with speeches and toasts. The center of attention was Penny, looking glamorous and laughing and joking as she opened her presents and read out the cards, and passed around the Roses Chocolates Helen had given her.

5

Getting the Message

Expectation is very important if speech isn't "normal." If pointing and coordination of eye movement are also impaired, it's harder to match sound and referent—a bit like Felix saying "wahla" with a vague hand movement after passing the pot holder—even if you do expect speech. The speech attempts of a baby with a disability are likely to be less clear than those of other infants. Without expectation, the attempt will pass unnoticed altogether. Presumably all young infants make some speech attempts which pass unrecognized—after all, there is a continuum between "wahla" and "koala," and between apparently generalized arousal and clear localization of interest—but the nondisabled infant develops quickly and isn't stuck with apparently undifferentiated sounds and movements for many years as a child with cerebral palsy might be.

In making sense out of unconventional speech, expectation is especially important at the early stages of the continuum. I often meet children with disabilities whose parents describe them as having no speech. With some children this appears to be correct; however, surprisingly frequently the child is getting out word (or even sentence) approximations which would be the pride and joy of any parent of a nondisabled eighteen-month-old. An interaction with a four-year-old whose parents thought he couldn't talk went:

"Hullo, Ben!"

"Uh-oh."

"That's a great T-shirt! How old are you? Are you three?"

"Nah," with headshake.

"Are you four?"

"Eh," with smile.

"Do you watch *Sesame Street?*"

"Eh," with arms waving.

"Who do you like best, Ernie or Bert?" (holding up pictures)

"Er."

"Ernie?" (It could be either.)

"Eh. Er-ees eh eh-in." (waving at picture of Ernie and his red engine)

Ben's parents tended to hush him whenever he opened his mouth, presumably because they found his sounds distressing or embarrassing. Given that virtually everyone he met, apart from his little sister ("She gives him toys when he makes noises and it seems to shut him up," his father said), believed his parents when they said he couldn't talk, how long was it going to be before he stopped trying?

The doctors had told Ben's parents that Ben had severe brain damage, which was true—his motor cortex was damaged, which was why he couldn't walk and why his speech hadn't become any clearer as he got older—and either the doctors or the parents had then made the jump to not expecting him to talk at all. As a result, his parents just didn't hear Ben's noises as speech attempts. The important role that expectation played showed when Ben's baby sister started making similar word approximations to Ben. Even if her parents couldn't understand everything that she was saying, they accepted that she was trying to talk and listened with attention. Nonetheless, despite the similarity in sound, they still didn't recognize that Ben was speaking.

Switching on to one person's speech approximations often makes listeners sensitive to a broader range of possibilities, and they become more receptive to atypical speech in general, but Ben's parents' negative expectations were apparently so strong that nothing could break through them. They certainly didn't hear what the speech pathologists and I heard when we talked with Ben. And that was the other thing, of course—we talked with Ben; they didn't. They gave him instructions and spoke around him, but they rarely addressed any comments to him, much less talked with him.

What does not being able to speak intelligibly mean to a child? It's an experience we all share, but most of us can't remember what it was like. What's more important—not being understood or not being thought to have anything to say? We all grow up in an interactive multimedia learning environment—if we can't interact, what does that do to our learning? We develop a sense of self and of our selves in the world as we act on the world, banging those blocks, calling "da-da" and having the big man come. We develop all our nonspeech communication skills—eye contact, pointing—through interacting with people, usually our parents. If this doesn't happen we are not just deprived linguistically—we miss out on acquiring the very skills which might clarify our speech attempts, if anyone was listening.

Not being able to walk is a very different problem from not being able to talk, and not just in the obvious functional differences. Not being able to walk is a nuisance, it may affect your self-image, and some people may behave awkwardly around you, but you're still a person, you're still you. If you can't talk, if you have never spoken, who are you? What do you think, what do you feel? Crude responses, crying and smiling, serve babies pretty well, though parents trying to find out what's wrong at three in the morning may not agree. They're not enough for toddlers, as anyone can attest who's seen a toddler almost bursting with the frustration of having something to say but not the words to say it in.

Babies understand more words than they say, and probably we do too. It's far from clear just how important speech is in learning language. There are enough examples of people who had no intelligible speech in childhood and who became successful writers—Christy Brown, Christopher Nolan, David Eastham, Birger Sellin—to establish that speech is not essential for the development of rich language. The numbers may be small not because only a small number of mute children develop language but because there are only a few whose language ever finds a way out.

Another obvious drawback of not being able to speak is not being able to ask questions—those endless streams of "what" and "why" questions which emanate from preschoolers. How do children learn if they can't ask questions? Again, there are enough adults who were not able to ask questions as infants who have achieved academic success to make it clear that questions aren't essential for learning, though they may well speed up the process by enabling children to fill in gaps when they become aware of them rather than having to wait till someone talks about that interesting thing over there. Some academically successful nonspeakers probably had parents who assiduously brought knowledge to them, but some certainly didn't. It may be that many toddler questions have more to do with making contact and getting adult attention than with the acquisition of specific information.

Being able to influence the behavior of others would seem to be central to the development of a sense of identity. Here nonspeaking children are at an enormous social disadvantage. Infants spend a lot of time saying "no," rejecting assaults on their persons or their egos. Children who can't say "no" and who may not be able to move away from unwanted attention or push away an unwanted object can either tantrum or accept whatever comes. If either response becomes habitual you've got behavior problems or extreme passivity. More subtle choices may be impossible. You screamed when the TV was turned on, so your father turned it off. Now you're screaming because you wanted to watch *Sesame Street*, not the sports show your father had chosen, and he's saying, "It's impossible to please that kid. She doesn't know what she wants."

Influencing people's behavior is important, especially for young children or children with physical problems who can't do things for themselves. As children get older, influencing the way people talk to them and about them may be just as important. After infancy I talk to you because you talk to me. Being an adult I may initiate an interaction with a child, but I'm unlikely to continue talking if I don't get a response. The other children you meet as a non-speaking child may not talk to you at all, and the ways you've got of getting their attention—screaming, taking their toys—become less acceptable the older you get. Tugging at adults' clothing is a time-honored way for toddlers to get attention—it's looked on differently in a twelve-year-old. So you either behave unacceptably, or you sit there doing your own thing and watching the world go by.

Not only can't you get people to talk *to* you, you can't get them to stop talking *about* you. All parents talk about their children. As the children get older they modify their parents' use of them as conversation fodder, at least when they're around: "Oh, *mom!*"; "Dad, shut up!" Without this feedback many parents don't stop talking about their children, and the topics they choose may be both unappealing and embarrassing. Afternoon tea with Ian and his mother always included an in-depth analysis of the state of Ian's bowels. Ian was sixteen but could neither move away nor voice an opinion. If he scowled and hit the table he was told, "Stop being a naughty boy now, and eat up your nice cake."

Every interaction we initiate sets up a feedback loop: I speak to you, you respond to (or ignore) me, I react accordingly, and so on. We notice the behavior of our conversation partners and we adjust our interactions accordingly, even if irrationally. Have you ever lost your voice and been reduced to whispering, only to discover that everyone whispers back to you? On the telephone this is reversed; talk louder in an effort to get the person at the other end to speak up, and they move further from the receiver and reduce volume. Whisper and they move closer and speak more loudly in an effort to get you to speak up.

In everyday life, if someone doesn't respond when you speak, you repeat what you said more loudly. If it's clear that you're being heard, but you're still getting no response, you may simplify your language or speak more slowly. There are three common groups that we do not expect to respond to ordinary speech—foreigners, the hard of hearing, and babies—and the adaptations we make for them may be applied to anyone who doesn't answer us, with the result that college graduates who can't speak may find themselves addressed in slow, loud baby talk! Some people born with obvious disabilities have never been spoken to in any other way.

Those who can speak, but whose speech is distorted, may be only marginally better off. The uninformed public, hearing the word approximations of babyhood and responding to the medium and not the message, perceive impaired speech as infantile, and children and adults who speak it risk being treated as an infant regardless of the evidence to the contrary. John Hickman has a Ph.D. in mathematics. His speech is affected by cerebral palsy, but is quite intelligible to anyone who makes a small extra effort to listen. When he received his master's degree a nurse who had looked after him when he was a child gave him a graduation present of a children's picture book.

All of us differ in our communication effectiveness. Most public speakers fit somewhere on the continuum between Martin Luther King and Dan Quayle. For people with communication impairments there is also a continuum. The articulation problems caused by one specific speech problem, dysarthria, common among people with cerebral palsy, cover the range. You may have had a conversation with someone with dysarthria. People with dysarthria have difficulty speaking intelligibly due to problems in controlling the muscles of the mouth and throat. Often they are able to make vowel sounds but have difficulty with consonants, many of which require lip closure or fine tongue movements. "Uh-oh, ow are oo?" might represent "Hello, how are you?" said by someone with dysarthria.

Mild dysarthria produces only occasional intelligibility problems. Often these will occur when the speaker says an unfamiliar proper name, because then there are no syntactic clues and predictability is reduced. Moderately severe dysarthria may necessitate frequent repetitions, but nonetheless the speaker can still generally be understood by sympathetic strangers when talking on everyday topics. Speakers with severe dysarthria may only be understood by people who know them well, or may only be understood when the listener knows what they are going to say.

That might sound absurd—how can you know what someone is going to say? and isn't the communication valueless if you already know what it's going to be? In fact, we all take part every day in a number of highly predictable interactions. What do you say when you're trying to get through a crowd; when someone holds the door open for you; when you sneeze? These situations are highly predictable, but the communication is nonetheless important because it reinforces social networks and establishes that the speaker is a member of the network.

At the end of the continuum, people with the most severe dysarthria may only rarely be understood, even by family members, and even in predictable situations. Volume control is often affected, so speech attempts may come out inappropriately loud. People with the most extreme incoordination problems may have their attempts at speech actively discouraged because they are thought to be making meaningless and disruptive noises. As with Ben, the expectation of their listeners will be an important determinant of communication success.

Intelligibility varies among speakers with dysarthria, and the decoding skills of their listeners also vary. Some people find familiar speakers with minor impairments hard to understand; others are able to understand strangers with quite severe problems. Experience helps—you get used to the most common articulation errors and the dysarthric form of common words, and process them without conscious thought, as you do regular speech. Consequently, speakers with articulation disorders are usually understood better by the people who know them well. The continuum of intelligibility is just that—a person's place on the continuum says nothing about his or her understanding or academic abilities, but is purely a reflection of muscular control.

Perhaps the most remarkable true story involving limited intelligibility due to severe dysarthria is *Tongue-Tied*, the autobiography of Joseph Deacon. Deacon, who had severe cerebral palsy, was admitted as a child to an institution in England and was thought to be severely retarded and unable to communicate other than through noises and body language. When he was a young man a new resident, Ernie Roberts, whose speech was clear, said that Deacon could talk and that he could understand him. There was initially considerable skepticism about this, resolved when a doctor asked Deacon to tell Roberts to come to the director's office at two o'clock in the afternoon and Roberts duly arrived.

Toward the end of his life Deacon, who was physically unable to write or type, wrote his autobiography with the assistance of three friends. He dictated it to Roberts, who was illiterate but could understand his words and repeat them to a second friend, who could write. Deacon then reviewed the handwritten text and relayed it letter by letter via Roberts to a third friend, who couldn't read but could operate a typewriter. Remarkably, the psychiatrist who wrote the introduction did not see the production of Deacon's book as evidence of his intellectual capacities but as an example of what could be achieved by a person who was severely mentally retarded.[1]

People with severe dysarthria can of course use compensatory strategies to enhance their communication effectiveness. My friend Rachel has athetoid cerebral palsy that is similar to Anne McDonald's, although her movement control is not as severely affected. She can walk, albeit with enormous effort, and she can talk, though her speech is often hard to understand. With her family she augments her speech by using sign language and drawing letters in the air. Out in the community she types her message on a pocket computer. None of these strategies help when she wants to use the phone, and as Rachel is a phone junkie this is a source of great frustration. She wants to be a sitdown comedian and often rings me up to try out her latest joke. A typical conversation went:

[1] Deacon was subjected to many IQ tests after writing the book. These have been described by psychologist David Ellis, who finally determined that both Deacon and Roberts were "not mentally handicapped" (Ellis, 1982, p. 488). Justice at last, although it would have been preferable if this conclusion had been published while Deacon was still alive.

RACHEL: Ow eh ee eye ol oh is uz i ake oo ay uh ite ul?

ME: What?

R: Ow.

ME: Are?

R: Ow!

ME: How?

R: Eh-ee.

ME: Try again.

R: Eh-ee.

ME: Nope.

R: Em

ME: N.

R: Em!

ME: M.

R: Ay.

ME: M, A—oh, many? (Predictable after "how")

R: Ehh! Ow ehee eye ol oh is.

ME: How many what?

R: Eye ol oh is.

ME: What!

R: *Eye ol oh is.*

ME: No, I'm not getting it.

R: Ee.

ME: E.

R: Ee!

ME: T.

R: *Ee!*

ME: C.

R: Nah! Ay, ee, ee, ee, ee, eh, ee, ay, eye, ay, ay, el, em, en, oh, *ee.*

ME: Oh, *P!* (Did you get it? Rachel said the alphabet A, B, C, . . . P, and then stopped. As long as I don't miss a sound we'll end up at the same letter.)

R: Ehh! Eh.

ME: F. (A lapse of concentration here—obviously it can't be F after P, but I'm concentrating so much on the bits I've lost sight of the whole.)

R: Nah! Eh.

ME: Sorry—S. PS?

R: Ehh. Eye ol oh is!

ME: Psychologists!

R: Ehh.

At this stage, given the predictable joke formula, I can work out the rest of the question. If you want to hear what it sounds like, try saying, "How many psychologists does it take to change a lightbulb?"[2] with your jaw fully extended and your lips never touching.

Then we go through the same routine for the answer. Can you imagine what this does to a punch line? A simple two-liner can often take ten minutes, and if I'm tired or distracted I may never work it out.

Obviously any such interaction can only succeed if the listener has the necessary skills and perseverance. To be sure of

---

[2] Only one, but the lightbulb has to sincerely want to change. I didn't say she had *new* jokes.

getting Rachel's message I need to give her all my attention, in a quiet room. Often I shut my eyes. Her signal-to-noise ratio is so low that decoding her message requires total concentration on each sound, which has to be analyzed with every bit of semantic knowledge I possess, then added to the previous string of letters or sounds while remembering the message to date.

At Rachel's end the effort is truly heroic—she has to be prepared to repeat herself endlessly, and use a whole range of clarification strategies, including going through the whole alphabet till she reaches the wanted letter, with her listener internally saying the letters along with her. She has to remember what she wanted to say for much, much longer than the rest of us, and she has to remember where she is up to in the sentence as well as where she is up to in spelling "psychologists." When she was younger, and would have spelled "psych" as "sike," there was often no hope of me working out the message, and she used to have to call on her mother to interpret.

The whole system depends on feedback—speak, repeat, confirm. Rachel and her partners have to have similar levels of literacy, and have to know the clarification strategies. Most importantly, both parties have to be highly motivated and prepared to expend considerable time and energy to enable communication to take place. (When I'm tired or busy I tell Rachel a joke and hang up while she's still laughing!)

Rachel is almost as close to the end of the speech continuum as you can go and still be able to get across whole sentences on a new topic you've initiated yourself with no body language. Rachel has a number of people who can understand her speech, but because she is so close to the end of the continuum, minor changes which wouldn't prevent me communicating can stop Rachel. Any background noise, at her end or mine, makes it impossible for me to decode her sounds. If either of us is tired we lose track of the message. Partner familiarity is important—if someone else answers the phone at my end, Rachel might not be able to ask for me, much less leave a message. Partner expectation is also important—I know that Rachel is intelligent and that she has a message to deliver, even if her jokes are terrible. I do not take the easy, or tactful, way out, pretending that I understand when I don't. Equally, Rachel is extraordinarily persistent and self-assertive—she does not either give up or accept misinterpretations, as many people with severe communication impairments have learned to do.

Of course, the intelligibility continuum does not stop with Rachel, and dysarthria is not by any means the only form of speech impairment. There are many people with just as much to say who can't get words out at all, or who say the wrong words. Some people whose speech is quite clear have just as much trouble getting their meaning across as people with dysarthria. Depending on the severity of their problems they may have to augment their speech with other strategies or even depend totally on alternative means of communication.[3]

Unfortunately, much nonspeech communication suffers from similar intelligibility problems to dysarthric speech. Speech intelligibility is affected by muscular incoordination interfering with accurate positioning of tongue and lips. The intelligibility of manual signing is obviously affected by muscular incoordination, as is use of a communication aid with hand, head pointer, or eye pointing. If the incoordination is very bad, it may not be possible to decipher any message, and it may not even be evident that communication is being attempted.

Between complete clarity and complete unintelligibility of nonspeech communication there's a continuum, as there is for

---

[3] Deacon's speech was understood by someone whose speech was comprehensible to non-disabled speakers. Sometimes people who have severe dysarthria understand each other and talk to each other, but in a closed loop, because no member of the group is understood by anyone outside the group. The existence of such communication is only recognized when someone with more standard speech or a communication aid joins the group, and passes on information picked up from the "nonspeakers" to people outside the group. One of the few joys of being perceived as a nonspeaker is that people talk in front of you in a way they wouldn't dream of doing if they thought there was any chance of you repeating what they're saying, so you hear all the gossip. You go back to the group with a particularly juicy story about who's doing what and to whom, and the group member whose communication is understood outside repeats it, causing great embarrassment to the original speaker. Virtually every center for people with cerebral palsy has a few notable examples of this enshrined in legend. An excellent account of the process is given in *Skallagrigg*, an extraordinary novel by William Horwood. (1987)

speech. Because the modes of communication used are less familiar than speech and may require special skills, such as knowledge of manual sign or the encoding strategies used with an eye-pointing board, dependency on communication partners is greater. It is probable that a relatively small number of partners will be available with the skills necessary to achieve successful interaction.

Interpretation is easiest when an individual is able to select letters, words, or icons accurately from a communication display or keyboard to construct an utterance which is either printed out or spoken clearly by an electronic aid. If the user can't make accurate selections, or if the aid used does not produce spoken or written output, intelligibility declines, moving through similar gradations to dysarthric speech—at one end of the continuum needing only occasional clarification, at the other intelligible only when the content is known; at one end usable with everybody, at the other intelligible only to family and friends.

With both dysarthric speech and nonspeech communication, different degrees of intelligibility are just that—they say nothing about the intellectual competence of speaker or aid user, but merely reflect the ease or difficulty with which an individual can get a message across. Mona's speech is less comprehensible than Rachel's, and she would not contemplate trying to tell me a joke over the phone. As it happens, her hand skills are good, she types accurately, and she has a law degree. If Mona wasn't able to control her hands so well, and if her communication aid use was as impaired as her speech, that wouldn't mean she was less intelligent.

In this age of electronic communication we should be particularly aware, as our faxes and E-mail disappear in the ether, that just because a message doesn't get through doesn't mean it wasn't sent. *Every human who is conscious and not in solitary confinement communicates something. We can only know the message we receive—we cannot know the message which was sent.*

6

How Do I Say I Love You?

In 1943 an article by Dr. Leo Kanner created a disability. If it had been possible to patent it, he would have made a fortune: Kannerian© autism™.

The article was titled "Autistic Disturbances of Affective Contact" and appeared in a short-lived journal called *Nervous Child*. Kanner said that since 1938 in his work as a child psychiatrist he had seen eleven children who seemed to form a special group. The children were physically normal, or nearly so. They had difficulties relating to other people and situations, they had delayed language or language difficulties, and they had an obsessive desire for the maintenance of sameness. Furthermore,

> Even though most of these children were at one time or another looked upon as feebleminded, they are all unquestionably endowed with good *cognitive potentialities*. They all have strikingly intelligent physiognomies. . . . The astounding vocabulary of the speaking children, the excellent memory for events of several years before, the phenomenal rote memory for poems and names, and the precise recollection of patterns and sequences, bespeak good intelligence in the sense in which this word is commonly used. (Kanner, 1943)

Kanner gave the condition the name "early childhood autism"—the first time the word had been used except to describe one of the rarer symptoms of schizophrenia. It was a powerful, persuasive, and well-written article, and it was the first of several thousand articles, books, and films on the topic in the fifty years since. What, though, did Kanner do?

The commonsense view is that he discovered autism. He identified a condition, described it, defined it, and differentiated it from other diseases in the same way that a naturalist might discover a new species. He noted a set of characteristics that generally occurred together, decided that the connection was not simply accidental, and made an implicit prediction that they would also be found together in other cases. Since then the discovery of tens of thousands of similar cases has, it would seem, borne out his thesis.

But if it was that easy, why hadn't someone else done it first? Other discoveries aren't really comparable. Newton wasn't the first person to observe that apples fell. He explained gravity, he didn't identify it. Koch discovered that tuberculosis was caused by the tuberculosis bacillus—he didn't have to convince people that tuberculosis existed. The question to ask is not "How did Kanner discover autism?" but "What were the questions Kanner was asking for which 'autism' was the answer?"

The first question was "How can the children of intelligent people be retarded?" This was a time when hereditarian theory was still riding high. Intelligent people should have intelligent children.

There is one other very interesting common denominator in the backgrounds of these children. *They all come of highly intelligent families.* Four fathers are psychiatrists, one is a brilliant lawyer, one a chemist and a law school graduate employed in the government Patent Office, one a plant pathologist, one a professor of forestry, one an advertising copy writer who has a degree in law and has studied in three universities, one is a mining engineer, and one a successful business man. Nine of the eleven mothers are college graduates. . . . All but three of the families are represented either

in *Who's Who in America* or *American Men of Science* or both.
(Kanner, 1943)

The second question, of course, was "What do I tell these
parents is wrong with their children?"

Kanner's article makes interesting reading. It is an achievement of the heroic age of psychiatry, and it would not be
printed in the current climate of academicism. A brief com-
parison with the other twenty papers reprinted in Donellan's
Classic Readings in Autism shows that Kanner's is significantly
longer and more discursive—thirty-nine pages, against an
average of seventeen. It is anecdotal—a good read, even for the
nonprofessional. A further feature of Kanner's article now
seems almost unbelievable. The other papers include an
average of fifty-three citations. Kanner's has not a single one,
and has no bibliography. No refereed journal would dream of
accepting it today.

Since Kanner's paper the needs of psychologists have
changed, and the criteria for autism have been extended; to
put it more precisely, autism has been redefined. For several
decades after Kanner, a diagnosis of autism exempted a child
from intelligence testing. By definition, the autistic child had
intelligence that was concealed by its affective impairments. If
the child was retarded, he wasn't autistic. In a culture that was
increasingly believing that IQ explained almost everything, this
represented a continuing anomaly. The protection given by the
old definition was removed in the sixties and seventies. Two
papers were published, one stating that children with autism
were not untestable (Alpern, 1967), and the second correlating
poor outcome and low IQ score (De Myer et al., 1974). Both
findings fitted in with the rising domination of the testing
system, and both were accepted without question. Children
with autism were given IQ tests, the scores were accepted as
meaningful, and the accepted meaning was that most children
with autism were severely intellectually impaired. To no one's
surprise, those children with autism who had always been seen
as high-functioning—children who could speak and who had
better hand skills—confirmed their supremacy by doing better

on the IQ tests than autistic children who didn't speak and who could barely feed themselves. There are, of course, other explanations for correlations between IQ scores and outcomes, explanations which have nothing to do with intelligence,[1] but if you believe that retardation is an explanation rather than a puzzle you don't have any reason to look for other explanations.

The generally accepted position on autism is summarized in a 1987 Australian article by Margot Prior.

> It was formerly believed that autistic children were normally intelligent children whose potential was not realized because of the severity of the emotional disturbance. Most autistic children are in fact retarded; at least half of them severely or profoundly so. . . . IQ is a good predictor of adjustment in the majority of cases. . . .
>
> Children who are untestable on intelligence or adaptive behavior tests have a poor prognosis. . . .
>
> Only a minority of children acquire functional language and even this is usually immature, deviant, inflexible, concrete, and lacking in communicative competence. . . .
>
> Behavioral methods . . . permit the learning of basic self-help skills, eye contact, and some co-operative behavior. . . .
>
> They are educable for the most part consistent with their level of intellectual ability, though there are always reports of a small number of unusual cases who surprise their caretakers by making major gains.

Before 1986 I'd only seen one child who had been diagnosed as autistic, a breathtakingly cute hyperactive seven-year-old with appalling behavior. His mother was a friend, and she asked me

---

[1] Employability, for instance, correlates with IQ scores among people with cerebral palsy not just because employment requires intelligence but because scoring well on an IQ test and being employable both require similar motor and communication skills.

if I could help her son to communicate (he was totally mute). I worked with Jonathan for several years, and by the time DEAL opened in 1986 he was able to type short sentences (although his willingness to do so was very variable indeed). Initially I held his hand while he typed (partly to stop him running away) but he had gradually moved beyond that, although at best he still needed a hand on his shoulder to maintain focus. Having only seen one of him, however, I didn't know whether his problems were typical of children diagnosed as autistic. The word about Jonathan's progress got around, though, and after DEAL opened we were approached by a number of parents asking if we would see their autistic children and try and find some way for them to communicate.

Seven-year-old Emma was brought to DEAL by her mother, Tracey, on the basis of a meeting with a friend at a church function. Tracey wrote later in an autism newsletter: "I tried hard for a fortnight or so to ignore her advice about attending yet another place that offered astounding improvement for our special child. Of late I'd preferred not to risk going through any 'false hope' withdrawals."

Emma was a beautiful child, tall for her age, with magnolia skin and lustrous wavy dark hair. She had been autistic since the age of one, and was now at seven described as functioning at a two-year-old level. Her IQ had been assessed as below 50. Her father had left her mother not long after Emma's disability was diagnosed.

Emma's speech was restricted to simple phrases, many of which were repetitive or echolalic and not used effectively for communication. Much efforts had been made to teach her sign language, but she was still only able to use six signs. Her comprehension was thought to be poor, just adequate for understanding simple instructions, and she had considerable difficulty with all self-help skills, such as dressing and bathing. She had disturbed sleep patterns, but wasn't hyperactive—left to her own devices, in fact, she just sat.

Emma was appealing in a way that many autistic children are not. It wasn't just her beauty (many children with autism are physically attractive) but her vulnerability. Unlike many of the children I saw, she didn't bite or scratch—she wept, and at the same time her muscles seemed to liquefy so that she couldn't do anything even if she had wanted to. Any pressure to perform—a slightly raised voice, say—reduced Emma to tears. It was almost impossible for me not to feel like a monster when my voice made tears roll from Emma's huge gray eyes down her alabaster cheeks. I felt I had to hug her, console her, assuage her misery. Sympathy, unfortunately, didn't help. Emma would certainly stop crying when I stopped asking her to perform, but the tears would start again as soon as I ventured another request. Tracey told me that many programs had foundered on Emma's tears as teachers found themselves unable to continue in the face of her misery. I felt like a child abuser but continued regardless. I had her mother's support, and if Tracey hadn't been able to harden her heart against the tears of her beloved daughter, Emma would never have done anything.

At her first visit in September 1986, Emma played appropriately with some battery-operated toys while I talked with her mother. When her turn came and I asked her to try some communication equipment she dissolved into tears, clasped her hands in her lap, and refused. I took her hand, despite her resistance, and made her push some of the buttons.

When given wrist support to compensate for her low muscle tone and to encourage her to move she was able to point with her right hand to named pictures on a toy called Touch & Tell, although she had some difficulty in extending her forefinger and pressing the display and had obvious eye-hand coordination problems. When asked to point to one out of two word cards she was again unwilling to cooperate. We set up a Vocaid, a communication aid developed from the Touch & Tell, with a sheet of letters and numbers which spoke when they were pressed, and she spelled out on request her name EMMA, MOM, MARK, SCHOOL, DOG, and in numbers her age and her brother Mark's age. On a Communicator she spelled her name, then I WOS TIPING. When asked if she had a message for Tracey, her mother, she spelled, TRACEY SIT UP. This was an echo of her mother's exhortations to her—an automatic repetition? an unexpected attempt at humor? Emma tended to point without looking, and it was necessary to inhibit her pointing until she was looking at the display. She burst into tears at intervals during the session.

It was a good start, and following it Emma had some success in her typing at home, although her work with her mother was very slow. She disliked the pressure at DEAL—when she acted up I called her a toad—and it was a long time before she stopped crying at least once a session. She could, however, be motivated by rivalry with DEAL's other young clients, competing with Jonathan to answer quizzes.

At the last session that first year she had loosened up sufficiently to spell out I CAN READ, I CAN FEEL, and I FEEL PRETTY. She discussed her mother's divorce.

STEPFATHER HATES ME. I MISS DAD, IM SORRY I MADE HIM GO.

No, her mother said, don't blame yourself, there were a lot of things.

I HERD HIM SAY IT WOS ME.

Emma used a borrowed Communicator to spell fluently with her mother over the Christmas holiday. She continued coming to DEAL for the next year. Her behavior improved, and she was able to communicate in less structured situations and with a wider range of people. An Education Department psychologist who attended one session recommended Emma for a normal elementary school placement. Her inappropriate and echolalic speech didn't disappear, but the number of appropriate utterances increased along with the typing. CAN I EAT ANOTHER BIS-CUIT I BADLY NEED TO DO A BIT OF WORK ON MY CANON [Communicator]. Her nickname for me was "special toad."

Wrist support was gradually faded to forearm or elbow and sometimes shoulder, and Emma gradually extended the range of her conversation. MUM LOVES ME SO MUCH AND IS SO SAD-DENED BY MY AUTISM SORRY TO BE DIFFERENT Despite our constant reminders she continued to try to type without looking at the display. In September 1987, a DEAL speech pathologist's report said "poor eye-hand co-ordination and low self-esteem and confidence ... mean that Emma needs someone to sit with her while she works, giving physical and emotional support and focusing her attention on the task in hand. . . . It is likely that Emma will remain 'choosey' about communication partners as each interaction involves what she sees as intrusion into her personal space."

By 1988, when Emma started primary school full-time, her echolalia and jargon had diminished substantially and she was able to be quiet on request. She worked well with her new school integration aide, spelling, TEACHER NICE. I AM GETTING READY TO LEARN. I HAVE NO CONCENTRATION. I LIKE DOING WORDS.

Shortly afterward Emma's family moved to the country, and when she came in at the start of 1990 I hadn't seen her for about eighteen months. Emma was in grade five, was about to celebrate her eleventh birthday, and looked lovely. She was far happier and more confident than she used to be. Tracey brought Emma's previous year's report—all subjects fine, apart from the ones such as physical education and handwriting that required a lot of motor planning. Her class teacher wrote that "Emma possesses an exceptional command of written language and produces sophisticated pieces of work" and "has exceptional skills of mental calculation." She could do in her head sums that the other kids used a calculator for, to the extent that they took their math answers to her for checking.[2] The music teacher found her "a delight to have in music classes. Her enjoyment of music is infectious." Her home class teacher summed up: "The opportunity to work with Emma has given both students and teachers a greater insight into the contribution that disabled students have to offer. The experience has been a very enriching one." More important still from my point of view, Emma was using her Communicator not just with her family and her integration aide but with the other kids in the

---

[2] That's the closest I've ever come to seeing "savant" talents of the kind featured in the movie *Rain Man*, and it isn't very close. The thing that interests people about savants, however, is how people who are so retarded can be so talented. If you believe, as I do, that the simplest explanation is that this is a reflection of problems with our definition of retardation, then the phenomenon is a lot less puzzling and perhaps less fascinating.

playground, and she had friends—kids who came and played at her house, or invited her to sleep over. For an autistic child to be popular is really quite something.

On the other hand, Emma still wasn't typing unassisted, and she still didn't look at the Communicator when she was typing. I had got rather tougher since last seeing Emma and I wasn't going to take this. Emma does have a real muscle-tone problem, being as floppy as a rubber band, and she does have real eye-hand coordination deficits (a sensory-motor program didn't seem to be helping much), but it was also true that one of the straightforward practical reasons for her eye-hand coordination problem was that she didn't try to look. She relied on the person who was facilitating her to make sure that the Communicator was in the right position in regard to her hand, and if she was clearly getting it wrong she expected the facilitator to help her. If Emma was supposed to be spelling CAT, for example, and she spelled CA, looked away, and had her finger stray toward the S, her facilitator would tend to adjust the Communicator so she hit the T she obviously wanted. I deliberately did the reverse; every time Emma gazed off into the corner of the room I moved the Communicator and repositioned it so that she'd make a mistake and have to look at it again. Her error rate went right up, and I insisted that she erase all her mistakes and redo them. This took a certain amount of pressure, and Emma dissolved into tears—she didn't often do this now, her mother said, but visiting DEAL must have taken her back to the old days. As she said, I SEEM TO CRY HERE BECAUSE THIS PLACE UPSETS ME . . . ITS A SAD PLACE.

Sad or not, it was good for her. I moved the Communicator around, shouting "Chase it! Chase it!" and stopping it in awkward places so she'd have to look at it. By the end of the fifteen minutes she was getting it right again. It was certainly quicker and more efficient if we didn't let Emma hit the wrong letters, but that meant that she didn't have to take responsibility for her mistakes and she didn't have to improve her coordination. It's a real problem getting children with autism to accept responsibility, and we often don't try—more than that, we don't let them take it. Integration aides often think that if their student makes mistakes it reflects on them. If a student's not keeping up the aide feels guilty and helps her, and if the student gets an answer wrong the aide points this out and lets the student correct it before handing it in. Naturally, the students take full advantage of this. I'm a great believer in no-fail learning in the early stages of skills acquisition, but once a student has the basic skills and confidence she could do with the bracing influence of a few failures; without them she will get into the habit of letting other people pick up the pieces.

I tried standing Emma up and holding the Communicator low (if you have a problem with low muscle tone it helps not to have to lift your arm against gravity), and by the end of the session I had Emma spelling out words with no bodily contact at all. Like many of DEAL's clients, she liked the human contact involved in arm support, and it was a wrench to be weaned so abruptly. This involved more tears.

The next day at school Emma spontaneously typed without any support. She continued to do so, provided that the Communicator was positioned low so that she didn't have to lift her hand against gravity.

We've done quite well with Emma's communication, but (whatever this book may seem to imply) communication isn't everything. There is also the issue of self-help skills. As Emma's mother said, "Periods start, you know childhood is over, and you ask yourself, 'If she hasn't learned to dress herself yet, is she ever going to?' " Emma's school is saying, "How can Emma be so bright and still not wipe her bottom after going to the toilet?" but she can't, or she won't. All the actions that we do on automatic pilot aren't automatic for her. She has a motor planning problem which may account for her inability to do things like orient clothing correctly. She also appears to have problems with motor memory—that is, she has difficulty repeating actions, even actions she has performed over and over previously, unless she's given a cue. She either hasn't been able to store the particular sequence of movements or she can't retrieve it at will. If we actually had to think consciously of each step in turn when we went to the bathroom we might have problems ourselves, but we don't—our bodies remember for us. Our water heater broke down once, and no water came out of the hot tap, on the right; for the entire week until it was fixed I would, every time I went to wash my hands, automatically take the soap in my left hand, turn on the right-hand tap, and get no water. I would sometimes even remember before I went into the bathroom, but if anything else at all came into my mind before I got to the basin I'd still use my automatic and wrong movement pattern. If it's that hard for me not to do something I know is dysfunctional it must be many times harder for these children. Closing the bathroom door, flushing the toilet—these things are for us automatic. For many children with autism they are not so, and making them automatic requires years of intensive and consistent nagging by parents and teachers. Equally, once a pattern has become automatic, it is extremely difficult to alter it.

Emma was smart, she was doing well at schoolwork, but in her independent living she was as handicapped as if she had cerebral palsy. She can walk, she can feed herself, and she can take herself to the toilet, but she can't dress herself, much less cook, clean, or iron. I suggested that her parents start yet another coactive dressing program, standing behind her and moving her arms through the routine over and over until she internalized the movements. "Start with just one garment and see how that goes," I said. It was the best advice I could give, but scarcely encouraging. It looks as though Emma might be functionally disabled for the rest of her life.

People like Emma require a whole new set of resources. In many ways it was easier when she was thought to be significantly intellectually impaired. You could institutionalize her in a place where people would do for her what she couldn't do for herself, and that would be that. When you're looking at providing for someone you know has ordinary academic and social needs,[3] but who's also going to need a lot of support, there's a whole new set of problems. In the future perhaps Emma could

---

[3] All students, of course, have social and educational needs, but if they can't communicate it's much easier to downgrade their program and provide child minding rather than schooling.

job-share with someone who's got good physical ability but weak academic skills. We need to consider some innovations, because otherwise Emma's future is very bleak, no matter how beautiful she is or how high she scores on an IQ test.

Emma's mother wrote about DEAL in a newsletter for parents of children with autism, and more parents asked us to see their children. Marco was thirteen when he came to DEAL for the first time in August 1987. A good-looking boy, with black hair and an olive complexion, Marco was tall for his age and solid with it. His father ran a fish-and-chip shop, and Marco liked the product. He was attending a school for children with intellectual impairments and had previously attended the same kindergarten as Emma, a kindergarten which had been set up just for children with autism. The standard practice was for children with autism to attend a segregated program, with a very high staff ratio and a strong emphasis on behavior modification, until they were considered ready to be "integrated" with other children or reached the age limit for the kindergarten program. A few children, the so-called higher-functioning, went on to ordinary schools, but integration for most meant placement in different segregated settings with children with other disabilities. Sorting was done on the basis of IQ scores—the name of the school Marco was attending told me that he, unlike Emma, had been assessed as having an IQ of 50 or above.

Our experience at DEAL is that if a person's speech is severely impaired then regardless of the diagnosis, handwriting is usually also severely impaired. Marco was a partial exception. He had far better hand skills than most of the people with autism who came to DEAL. He could actually write legibly, although his writing was immature for his age and looked more like the writing of a seven-year-old than a thirteen-year-old. He used to write shopping lists or lists of numbers, but nothing else. Marco's speech was mostly single-word utterances or short phrases, and sounded immature because he abbreviated words—"puter," say for "computer." He tended to perseverate on topics, saying the same thing again and again, and often replied to a question by repeating the last word said. Numbers were a particular obsession and he used to memorize and repeat the winning lottery numbers shown on television each Saturday.

Marco had in fact been motorically advanced as a child— he'd started to walk at the age of nine months, and his development had proceeded perfectly normally. Early photographs show a chubby handsome baby, with black curly hair, olive skin, and a wide smile. He'd babbled like most children, his language development and social development had been going well, and then he'd come to a stop.[4] As Marco put it later, I NEARLY TALKED RIGHT, BUT THEN I STOPPED.

Marco was finally diagnosed as autistic at about two and a half, by which time the smiling baby of the early photos had been replaced by a worried-looking toddler who often looked away from the photographer. He'd had speech therapy between the ages of three and five, but nothing thereafter.

By the time Marco came to DEAL in August 1987 many educational and not-so-educational talking toys were available. Some toys could be used as communication aids, and the ones that couldn't were still very motivating for most children and could be used to teach pointing and eye-hand-coordination skills. The one we found most useful was called My Talking Computer, which could be adapted for assessment. Marco loved computers and gadgets of all kinds, so when he came to DEAL the problem wasn't getting him to work but getting him to restrain his attention to the piece of equipment I actually wanted him to use.

Right from the start Marco's obvious problem was perseveration—the automatic repetition of a movement which is no

[4] This history is quite common in autism and is similar to the sequence in other disorders, like phenylketonuria (PKU), Rett syndrome, and Hurler's XXX syndrome. The cause of PKU is known, and on general principles it seems likely that problems which appear gradually in apparently normal infants are due to an excess or a deficiency of something important for normal development. Hurler's syndrome is a degenerative condition caused by a shortage of an enzyme needed to degrade the by-products of the metabolism of certain sugars. The by-products accumulate and at a certain level, usually reached between the ages of one and two, progressive changes in physical and neurological development start to occur.

longer useful. If he got a response—if he pressed a button on a toy, for example, and it spoke—he'd stick to that button, pressing it for minutes at a time, unable to move on and try the other buttons. If you gave him a multiple choice test he'd get his first answer right and answer every other question by pointing at the same spot. The easiest way of stopping him from perseverating was to pull his hand back as soon as he'd made a selection, holding him back until the next question had been asked; then you could actually see him switch his attention from the item he'd already pressed. His eye contact with the toy was good; unlike Emma, he kept his eyes on what he was doing.

Using My Talking Computer, Marco demonstrated good word-recognition skills. He constructed a sentence from a set of ten written words, with me pulling his hand back every time he pressed a word. My Talking Computer has a page displaying some thirty words, which can be used to compose a sentence or a story which the toy will then speak aloud. I asked Marco to make the longest sentence about one of the pictures associated with the toy that he could, and his sentence was "I see a yellow bird and a green tree and a flower on the grass." Not great literature, but fully grammatical, much longer than any sentence he was remotely likely to say, and including the little words, the articles and conjunctions, that Marco generally omitted from his speech, like many children with autism.

Marco went on to point correctly at named letters on an alphabet sheet and it seemed appropriate to try a Communicator. I showed him how it worked and went through the keyboard with him and asked him to type his name, which he did successfully. Throughout Marco had been saying "puter" at regular intervals and pointing at the laptops on the shelves. It was clear that he wanted to try to use one of the computers. I pretended not to understand and asked, "What do you want?" and he typed, I WANT TO USE SOME COMPUTERS. "Why?" BECAUSE REASON EXPLAINS EVERYTHING. DO YOU USE COMPUTERS? he asked me. "Yes," I said, "and what would you do with a computer?" He typed, USE IT MATHES[sic]. "Why do you like numbers?" I asked. NOT PEOPL. 11 IS MY FAVORITE NUMBER.

I got down another toy, called the Talking Teacher, which said the numbers and set Marco a range of sums. He enjoyed fiddling around with that. It was particularly good for his mother, Maria, to use with him, because there are only ten numbers and it was easy for her to facilitate him; his movement to the numbers was clear, and it was simply a matter of pulling him back and stopping him either perseverating on a particular number or pressing every number along the row.

It was several months before I saw Marco again, and at his next session he didn't behave nearly as well. He kept going to the laptops to get them to say his favorite numbers, and if his mother or I tried to stop him he'd become aggressive. At one stage he was so angry he threw a typewriter on the floor. In a pattern that was to become familiar, he behaved worse if his mother was in the room. Marco clearly loved his mother dearly, and it seemed that ironically this was the problem—he was more tense, and therefore more likely to lose control, in the presence of somebody he cared about than when he was with someone such as me with whom he had no significant relationship. Between bouts of resistance Marco typed sentences fluently, or as fluently as one can type using one finger, providing I was able to prevent him perseverating on his favorite words or favorite numbers. If standing up, he was able to type with just my hand on his shoulder. It's quite common for people with disabilities to find using a keyboard easier when standing up and typing with their arm at full stretch rather than having to lift it against gravity as they do when they're sitting down. Strength isn't necessarily lacking—after all, Marco was strong enough to throw typewriters around—but endurance is a significant problem. When trying to move the same muscles repeatedly, as is necessary in speech and typing, the signals seem to degrade progressively, causing the clarity of speech to deteriorate and keyboard work to become full of typos. If the problem is severe the spoken or written output quickly becomes unintelligible. Coordination is a related issue, and typing sitting down requires a large amount of coordination; you're using at least two joints (shoulder and elbow) and probably more (shoulder, elbow, wrist, fingers). Standing up and using a low keyboard you can lock your finger, wrist, and elbow joints and just move from the shoulder.

Marco's mother had tried to use a typewriter with Marco between appointments, but he had become obsessive about certain numbers and she had floundered. Marco was much larger than she was, and it was very difficult for her to restrain him from simply punching out his favorite numbers on the number keys.

In personality, Marco differed from Emma in almost as many ways as he could. While Emma was retiring, passive, and timid, Marco was offhandedly sociable, brash, and demanding. Emotionally fragile, Emma would burst into tears at the slightest criticism. Anything but fragile, Marco resisted criticism forcefully. After a session with Emma I often felt like Alice drowning in the pool of tears. After a session with Marco, I felt I'd done ten rounds with Mike Tyson (not because Marco had actually hit me, although he wrestled with me for control of the equipment, but because the battle of wills was so intense). In fact, Emma's tears may have been more effective in getting me to change my approach than Marco's resistance was. This had nothing to do with sympathy and everything to do with practicalities. Marco could work when he was angry, Emma couldn't work when she was crying, so it didn't matter if I upset Marco and it did matter if I upset Emma.

The following week Marco's teacher came to the appointment and Marco was, thank goodness, a different boy. He sat calmly in the waiting room while I talked to the teacher, and came in and sat down at the table as soon as I called him. No attempts to take the laptops off the shelves; instead, he typed out a reminder that he'd asked for a computer the previous week. I asked him if he would like to use one this week. He typed out, YES PLEASE, and so of course I produced one. The system I gave him was called a Trine communication aid; it was based on an Epsom HX-20 laptop, definitely an early-generation system, but for the first time he was working with a computer that could speak whatever he typed. It also had an onboard printer. The advantage, from my point of view, was that if Marco typed rubbish—strings of numbers, or his favorite obsession words—they would come up on the display, and if I was quick I could erase them before he made the computer speak them or print them. He typed, HOLD ME TO STOP ME DOING SILLY THINGS, which I suppose could be a definition of facilitated communication training.

I'd made up a special ABC chart with no numbers on it, and I gave it to Maria for her to try at home. Marco's teacher, having seen what he could do, was going to try to get him to use the school computers productively instead of simply using them to type his favorite numbers and obsession words. Before the end of the session I talked to the teacher about Marco's difficulty in inhibiting unwanted movements. Yes, she said, she knew what I meant. Her husband, who was a lecturer in computer science, had some of the same problems—if he started a movement sequence, he found it impossible to stop. "If he's started to shut the door of the refrigerator, he just has to finish the movement, even when he can see me coming over with a full jug of milk in one hand and a tray of ice cubes in the other." We all have different combinations of impairments, but we all have impairments.

By the next session Marco had done a small amount of spelling on the ABC board at home. His mother and father were both from Italian-speaking families, and Maria wanted to know whether Marco understood any Italian. To find out she wanted to say some sentences to Marco in Italian and have him type the English translation to me. Even if Marco did understand the Italian, of course, it didn't necessarily mean that he'd be able to translate it, but it was worth a try. If he was successful it would not only show that he understood some Italian but it would also show, my Italian being limited to *"ciao"* and *"arrive-derci,"* that he could produce language without any cueing from his partner. Maria said a number of sentences in Italian. After each sentence she asked Marco to type to me what it meant in English and he did so. She was satisfied by the demonstration; apparently his translations were very accurate (I had no way of telling, of course). Then I asked him to type the Italian for some English words—what's the Italian for "chair," and so on—and his mother said that while his word endings were a bit shaky, he did quite well.

At the last session before Christmas Marco and I had a massive confrontation over, of all things, the word "bread." "Bread" was one of Marco's obsession words—that is, he would type it repeatedly—and it was also, like most of his obsession words, an automatic completion word. If you asked him a question whose answer started with the letters of one of his obsession words, the answer you would get would be the obsession word, even if he was able to answer other similar questions correctly. For example, if you asked Marco why a car had brakes he would type, TO STOP, without difficulty. If you asked, "What do you press to stop the car?" he would type, BREAD. He presumably intended to type "brakes," but "bread" was, because he'd typed it so frequently, such a very well established motor sequence for him that it came out instead. Because "bread" was an obsession word, too, Marco didn't necessarily accept interference in his typing very amicably. The only strategy I ever found to tackle this problem was to work through it. I would give Marco a spelling list of words that started with *B* but did not have *R* as the next letter, so that the minute that I saw him going to *R* I would be able to pull his hand back and say, "No, not 'bread'; what's the right answer?" Once he was successfully handling words that started with *B*—"butcher," "baker," "bun"—we then went on to "brood," "brilliant," "brand"—words that started with *BR*, but where the next letter wasn't *E*. Sometimes Marco would still hit the E before I could stop him, but I could see it come up on the display and generally erase it before the full word was finished and spoken. I'd then hold his hand for a minute to inhibit him and say, "Okay, next letter," and he'd go on. Once he was handling words starting with *BR* we went on to words starting with *BRE*, and then *BREA* (and at this stage I was having to draw on the dictionary). While the process was effective, it was very stressful—I was continually interfering with Marco's typing, preventing him from completing what had become an automatic movement pattern, and on this occasion Marco ended up chasing me around the filing cabinets while I tried to field the equipment he was throwing at me. And, of course, once we'd worked through the entire sequence to "break" we then had to repeat the procedure with each of Marco's other obsession words. It wasn't a complete answer to the problem, if only because the obsession words still tended to surface on days when Marco was tired or tense, but it did help.

We lent Marco a Communicator to take home over the summer vacation—just as well, because we didn't see him again for a full three months. He and his mother were involved in a car accident, and he was brought to his next appointment by his father, Gino, while his mother recuperated. Marco talked about the accident, which had clearly upset him greatly, and typed, FORD WAS DODO   MUM WAS OK [as a driver]. Gino confirmed that the other car in the accident had been a Ford and had been in the wrong. Marco carried out an adult-level multiple-choice reading test quite well. He could point to the answers independently—with the complication, however, that he tended to say aloud any of the words on the page that he could say, whether the words were part of the correct answer or not. The answers he pointed to were correct, but if instead of asking him to point you'd asked him to say the correct answer he would have got a very low score.

I put a question that gently probed his ability to put himself in other people's positions. "Why do many snorers have black-and-blue ribs?"

Marco answered, REALLY I DON'T KNOW.

"Have a guess, have a guess."

IS IT BECAUSE THEIR WIVES HIT THEM TO WAKE THEM UP?

As character analysis this doesn't sound like Henry James, but people with autism aren't supposed to have any insight into character at all; it was recently suggested that they actually have an innate inability to imagine another individual's state of mind.

At this session, the first with his father present, Marco's behavior was excellent. There was very little of what I called rubbish speech (lists of obsession words, numbers), and only one episode of rubbish typing. He was calm throughout and stayed seated for an hour, the longest time he'd ever spent at the table in one stretch. Rubbish was an ongoing problem; sometimes even when Marco was typing appropriate spontaneous sentences an irrelevant phrase would come in out of the blue. At his school the teachers had, every morning, written, "Today is . . ." on the blackboard, and it occasionally surfaced in Marco's typing: I TODAY IS TUESDAY TRY TO BEHAVE BUT IT DOESN'T HELP.

Our occupational therapist had told me of a technique that was sometimes used with people who had perseveration following brain injury. The idea was to interpose an unrelated action between two desired actions—to break flow, to force the person to think, to break up the patterns. I'd watched the occupational therapist work with a girl who perseverated in pointing, and what the therapist did was to ask her to touch her nose after pointing to each selection. It had worked then, and what had worked with posttrauma perseveration might also work with autistic perseveration. You can't have people touching their nose each time they hit a typewriter key, however, so I put a red sticker on the Communicator's battery, placed it on the table between the keyboard and Marco and asked Marco to touch it between each letter. It worked really well—Marco learned the system quickly, and soon got into a rhythm. Suddenly I was no longer pulling his hand back after each letter—he was moving his hand back himself. I hoped that this meant he'd internalize the movement pattern more quickly.

Meaningful independent typing had initially been impossible for Marco due to his perseveration and his inability to prevent his obsessions intruding. Since coming to DEAL he'd had a facilitator to give him the impetus to pull his hand back, and this had enabled him to get out what he wanted to say. Up to this point, though, it hadn't improved his ability to type without facilitation. If Marco went up to a keyboard at school and there wasn't anyone there to slow him down, he produced the same strings of numbers and the same unrelated words that he had before. The technique of providing an alternative target made an immediate difference to how easy it was to facilitate him, and he immediately became more fluent in his Communicator typing both at the center and at home. His next session, a couple of months later, was the first at which he typed neither numbers nor obsession words.

Marco's special-school principal and his class teacher both attended his next appointment. His head teacher had previously been quite understandably skeptical about the whole business, but he'd become convinced of Marco's abilities after an incident at school. Marco had lost his temper, behaved atrociously, and thrown furniture around. His mother had been called and told that Marco had been suspended for several days and to come and take him home. On hearing these glad tidings Maria lost her temper and demanded that Marco tell her what on earth he'd been up to and what his excuse was for losing his temper. In front of the school principal Marco had typed out a full and accurate description of the incident and the events that had preceded it. He'd left his class with his teacher's permission, he said, to get a drink. The deputy principal had stopped him and sent him back to class. Marco didn't have sufficient speech to explain that he had permission, there was a confrontation, and he'd lost it.

During this visit Marco correctly answered questions asked in Italian by his mother and completed a crossword puzzle with his teacher. As he'd previously refused to do anything at all useful with the teacher, this put the icing on the cake for the principal. We'd found by this stage that it was often easier to get the children with autism using communication equipment with new facilitators if we provided highly structured activities such as crossword puzzles that required no original composition and that had no emotional component to them. They also had predictable answers, enabling the facilitator to see immediately whether the student was making a reasonable attempt at an answer or going completely off on a tangent.

This visit came about a year after Marco had first attended DEAL, and after that everyone's efforts were concentrated on finding a regular secondary school for him to attend. The language that he was using now and the work he was doing weren't up to his age peers in some respects (after all, he hadn't had the educational exposure they'd had), but they were so far above what he'd previously been expected to produce that it was clear that he was moving outside the range of special-school education.

At this time I started allowing Marco to use DEAL's Apple IIE. We had set it up with a simple speaking word-processing program called Talking Textwriter, but I'd kept him off it till then because I thought having his favorite words spoken and displayed in large print would probably bring out all his obsessive behaviors. But he was able to use it most successfully, and the output he produced at his first session (coincidentally, exactly a year after his first DEAL appointment) was extraordinary both in its sheer quantity and in the complexity of the vocabulary and sentence structure he was using—well up to ordinary conversational levels. Marco wanted to communicate without facilitation, and when the Communicator was positioned low down so he didn't have to reach against gravity he was in fact able to do some independent typing. Independence was, however, harder and more stressful, because without external inhibition he had to concentrate really hard to prevent automatic completions coming into his typing. His overall behavior deteriorated during the times he was trying to type without support. I MEAN TO BE GOOD THEN I GET UPSET AND FORGET. I THINK I'VE GOT A WAY OF GETTING BETTER. I TRY TO WALK AWAY BEFORE I LOSE MY TEMPER.

Marco was now using a keyboard successfully at school with his teacher, and at his next appointment he brought in an English assignment he'd done at school—a letter to the editor on the topic of the integration of people with disabilities into society at large. Marco's letter read in part, WE ARE ORDINARY KIDS AND WANT TO BE TREATED AS SUCH. PLEASE GIVE US A CHANCE AND I KNOW WE CAN SUCCEED. YOU MUST NOT BELIEVE THAT WHAT YOU SEE IS ALL THAT THERE IS TO SEE IN US. By this time Marco had started erasing his own automatic completions; if he typed BREAD for BREAK he would immediately erase the D and substitute K without any prompting from his facilitator. GLAD TO SEE YOU. HAVE YOU GOT ANY IDEAS OF WHAT YOU VERY MUCH WANT? I SHOULD LIKE TO GIVE YOU A PRESENT. Not a bad idea. He told me that he would be buying it with money he got from his grandmother and asked me if I had a coffeepot. Given the amount of coffee consumed at DEAL this was a somewhat superfluous question. He decided on a mug—YOU ARE GOOD TO ME AND I WANT TO GIVE YOU SOMETHING. I complimented him on a new top he was wearing and he typed, I NEED TO LOOK GOOD BECAUSE I'M DISABLED. I GET NEW CLOTHES ONLY IF I'M GOING SOMEWHERE SPECIAL. I'M KOOL IN MY RED WIND-CHEATER. OK?

Cool was all very well, but he knew what his priorities were. TO LEARN TO TALK IS THE MOST IMPORTANT THING IN MY LIFE. IT'S ABSOLUTELY IMPERATIVE THAT I LEARN TO CONTROL MY BEHAVIOR OR I'M OUT. AND I REALLY MUST SUCCEED.

Marco started at his local secondary school the next year. By this time he was fourteen and a half, a bit older than the other students in his ninth-grade class. It was an enormous step for him to move out of the protected environment of the small special school to a large high school campus. Fortunately, he'd been lucky in his choice of school, and staff and students couldn't have been more supportive.

I had a call from Marco's principal a couple of weeks after he'd started at the school. Marco had lost his temper rather badly, the deputy principal had been called, and Marco had kicked him. When the principal was called in to help sort things out, Marco kicked him too. High school principals are not really used to being kicked, at least not in Australia, and it wouldn't have been at all surprising if Marco had been expelled immediately. The principal wasn't even calling to complain about the student we'd been instrumental in sending his way. He was merely calling to see if we had any suggestions about how to handle such behavior. My response was purely pragmatic; given that Marco did have a real interest in how he looked, we should take advantage of it to tell him that if he ever tried to kick anyone again he would immediately have his shoes removed, which would both make him look ridiculous and ensure that if he did kick anyone he would do little damage. They implemented the suggestion, and fortunately it worked like a charm.

This incident apart, Marco's integration was surprisingly

trouble-free. Certainly there were times when he did lose his temper, but these became less frequent as he settled in. There was a lot of philosophical and practical support for integration in Victoria at that time, and so resources were there for Marco almost automatically; he was entitled to have a teacher aide with him all day, and the school also had a specialist integration teacher whose job it was to support all the kids with disability in the school and confer with home, class teachers, and everyone else in the school community. Marco's aides came to DEAL for training. They started off doing structured exercises such as crossword puzzles and picture captions, the same kind of thing that we'd found previously were useful in breaking the ice with new facilitators, and surprisingly soon Marco was participating in the regular work of the classroom. He obviously needed to do some catch-up work; as Marco's mother now had two young babies, that work had to be sandwiched in at school. Outside the classroom Marco was able to do some independent typing, but in the classroom he really needed the physical contact from his aides. There was more stress in regular school, and Marco found it difficult to inhibit his automatic completions without his aides to slow him down. As he became more confident, he did his math independently on a keyboard. He could also type one- or two-word answers independently but would always seek support for longer passages, reaching for his aide's hand and taking one of her fingers in the palm of his hand. He would then type with his index finger, carrying her hand around.

Despite the occasional confrontation, which became less of a problem as he matured, Marco was surprisingly easy to like. It may have been too much to hope that the other students, themselves in the throes of adolescence, would become close friends with someone who would unpredictably start reeling off lists of numbers or catchphrases from commercials, but they accepted his eccentricities surprisingly well. Once they got to know him most of his aides and teachers became fond of him, despite the difficulties his obsessions sometimes posed. The reason for this was his connectedness; Marco thought about other people, and while he was as egocentric as most teenagers, he worried about his family and his aides and his disability and the world at large. This pervasive anxiety was one thing he did share with Emma. Neither of them fitted the stereotype of the autistic child rocking in a corner, rejecting human contact, lost in a world of his own.[5] While Marco and Emma both had real problems with social fit, problems which were exacerbated by their speech difficulties, and both had routines which served to cut them off from the world on occasion, they were very conscious of other people and aware of being different. Unfortunately, awareness of a problem doesn't mean you can fix it, and wanting to be the same as the other kids didn't make them the same.

Nonetheless, everything seemed to be improving for them. The same could not be said for me. In the disability field each diagnostic group has its own set of professionals, who don't necessarily have much contact with the professionals working with a different diagnostic group. Therapists who work with children with cerebral palsy may never meet a child with Down syndrome or a child with autism. Even a child like Anne, who undubitably had cerebral palsy but was also labeled as mentally retarded and thus placed in the retardation system, would have no contact with the cerebral palsy professionals. Therapists who work with adults with acquired brain damage may never meet children with cerebral palsy whose physical problems are similar. Therapists who work with perseveration in patients with acquired brain damage never come across people with perseveration and autism.

DEAL's work, and hence my work, was directed to the specific problem of inadequate speech, and not to any specific diagnosis. There were advantages in this. Seeing people with

---

[5] While there must be some basis for this stereotype, none of the hundreds of children with autism that I have met have matched it apart from those living in institutions that provide an abnormal environment. While most of the people with autism I have met have had difficulty conforming with everyday social demands, and all have had some unusual habits, they have also all had strong relationships with at least one person. Typically the children who ran away from me or burst into tears when I approached didn't run to a corner—they ran to someone else that they knew. Indeed, so strong was the attachment of many of the children to their parents that they could only concentrate if their parents left the room.

many different diagnoses stopped us from getting stuck with the stereotypes of any particular diagnosis and gave us a chance to observe those common movement disorders, such as perseveration, which crossed diagnostic borders. Learning something about each disability and its associated professional system took time, of course, and this was one disadvantage. Another disadvantage, it turned out, was the number of people you offended. Nonspeech communication strategies were relatively new. When DEAL opened in 1986 most people in the state whose speech was inadequate had never been offered any form of alternative communication. Even if we did no more than find ways for these people to indicate yes and no, many of them were going to be doing more than they ever had before.

My experiences with Anne, Carolyn, and Penny had already shown me that doctors whose patients started doing more than they had been expected to do were generally underjoyed. As it turned out, the reactions of the retardation and rehabilitation fields were positively encouraging compared with the reactions of the autism establishment. Anne's case had raised the ire of the retardation bureaucracy, Carolyn's had got up the nose of the rehabilitation hospital, Penny was still battling the psychiatric hospital—but all this was merely dress rehearsal. Autism was sacred turf.

In mid-1987 I wrote to Margot Prior, the academic psychologist whose material on autism I quoted earlier, asking for help.

> Surprisingly, we are getting what appear to be quite unprecedentedly good results in establishing high-level verbal [meaning in words, not in speech] communication with people diagnosed as autistic. We are leaning towards a relationship between such neurological malfunctions as apraxia and autism, a relationship that would seem to be akin to the relationship you reported in 1985. I would very much appreciate an opportunity to discuss your work in this area. We are also attempting to set up a research program directed specifically at the DEAL findings, and I would greatly value your views on the direction of such a program.

I received a prompt reply:

> I view with some concern your venturing into the field of autism since autistic children suffer from such severe and global cognitive and communication problems which have been amply documented over the years in a veritable explosion of research.

I asked Prior to come and see for herself what our clients were doing, but she didn't; she told one of our speech pathologists that to visit and observe what we were doing was impossible because "it would give DEAL spurious credibility."

Despite the fragmentation mentioned earlier, DEAL nonetheless succeeded in bringing together professionals from all disability fields. A group of them formed what they called the Inter-Disciplinary Working Party on Issues in Severe Communication Impairment. Their aim was to close DEAL, and their basic argument was that what we said was impossible because

> the content and format of the communications achieved using assistance are inconsistent with informed expectations. Indeed, in some instances the communications defy rational explanation in terms of established psychological, medical, or educational theory.

My own personal view was that if the data conflicted with the theory it was the theory that had to give, but this plainly wasn't a view that the working party sympathized with. They wrote down all their criticisms of DEAL and sent the resultant paper to the Victorian government.

People with cerebral palsy, the working party said, couldn't communicate at a sophisticated level—they couldn't rehearse words before spelling them, they'd had no phoneme experience, and they had decreased sociability. People with acquired brain damage often remained in a persistent vegetative state, when they had no means of understanding and what looked like purposeful movement was in fact only primitive reflex activity. People with autism had severely and chronically impaired language comprehension and eighty percent of them were mentally retarded.

Part of the role of professionals working in the area is to help families to come to terms with limited hopes for their child. . . .
Sudden and rapid cures promised in a field where we know they are not possible can be very damaging and undo years of hard work and hard won adjustment.

Sudden and rapid cures like Anne's, Carolyn's, Penny's, and Marco's, presumably! Not one DEAL client has ever been cured. The most that we can ever do is give people a more powerful communication strategy than they had previously. Sometimes, as with Penny (who had not yet started to talk by the time of the working party report), we do a lot of work for very little apparent gain.

The Victorian government had got the working party's report, and felt it had to do something about it. The buck was passed to the Intellectual Disability Review Panel (IDRP), an agency which it had just established to handle disputes over the provision or denial of government services. The panel was asked to report on what the working party had called "assisted communication" and to determine the validity and reliability of such communication.

The panel eventually tested six DEAL clients, one of whom was Marco. Two testing strategies were used, each with three clients. One was a laboratory-style arrangement in which all ordinary conversation or interaction was precluded. The clients were asked prerecorded questions through headphones while their partners also wore headphones, through which they heard either different questions or white noise. Only one client passed that test. The other test was more similar to everyday conversation. Panel members spent time with clients and gave them presents; later the clients had to use their communication aids to tell someone else what had happened and what they'd been given. All three clients passed this test.

Marco was tested in February 1989, a few weeks after he had started at secondary school and some eighteen months after starting to communicate through spelling. His performance reflected accurately his strengths and weaknesses, behavioral as well as communicative, at this stage of his development.

Marco didn't find meeting two strangers any problem—after all, he'd just coped perfectly well with a move to a new school. He accompanied them happily to the shopping center across the road from DEAL, where they all had coffee. Marco was given a black T-shirt and bought a chocolate Easter egg with their money. He also got twenty cents' worth of M&M's from a coin-in-the-slot machine because, as the psychologists tactfully put it in their report, he "persisted in his request until he succeeded."

On their return to DEAL the psychologists said they'd given Marco something and asked me to find out what. "So what did they give you?" I asked. "Coffee," he said aloud—correct enough, but because he'd spoken it rather than typing it this provided no validation of his typing. "Tell Rosie on the Communicator what else you got." Marco then independently used the Communicator to type 20c M AND MS and CHOCOLATE. After CHOCOLATE he typed, FREDDO FROG, one of his stereotyped phrases, very quickly, instead of EASTER EGG. Because he was typing independently I couldn't slow him down, which meant that automatic completions and stereotyped language were likely.

"Okay, but we gave you something else as well. Tell Rosie about it."

At this point Marco reached for my hand and carried it around while he typed.

SCARF

"Did they give you a scarf, Marco?"

NO

"Then what did they give you?"

SOX

"Did they give you a pair of socks, Marco?"

NO

And so on through a list of different items of clothing until he finally got T-SHIRT. This performance is typical of people with word-finding problems, who get into the correct category, then have difficulty in naming the exact item, but recognize that their incorrect attempts are wrong.

"What color was it?"

BLUE

"Was it blue?"

NO

"What color was it?"

BLUE

"Was it blue, Marco?"

NO

"What color was it?"

RED

"Was it red?"

NO

"What color was it?"

MAUVE

"Was it mauve?"

NO

"What color was it?"

BLACK

"Was it black?"

YES

Black was the correct answer, but it had been the long way around. "Blue" was one of Marco's obsession words, but even if it hadn't been it might still have come out, given that its initial letters are the same as "black." Typing "blue" a second time despite knowing it was incorrect indicated how hard it was for Marco to break out of his automatic completions. The psychologists reported that "he typed *B* and *L* and hesitated for some time before completing the word 'blue.'"

Told that the test was over, Marco relaxed and conversed with the psychologists, who asked him why he took my hand.

I GET NERVOUS . . . CONFIDENCE . . .

"Why are you nervous?"

WE ALL GET UPSET IF WORK IS HARD . . .

"What was hard about today?"

GETTING MY THOUGHTS OUT.

As the session was winding up Marco took my hand again and typed his thanks to the psychologists for the T-shirt and, as they put it, "apologized for his insistent behavior in trying to obtain the M&M's." The psychologists had not tattled on Marco, and his detailed apology for the incident was evidence of his social and linguistic skills as well as a validation of his ability to type his own thoughts.

The panel reported in March 1989:

> The validity of communications using the "assisted communication technique" was demonstrated in four of the six clients who participated in the two studies. . . .
>
> Most of the clients who participated in the studies had had their communication and intellectual functioning doubted by others over a long period. Three of the four clients whose communication was validated are currently attending regular schools, whereas they had been previously assessed as suitable for Special Schools or Special Developmental Schools. . . .
>
> In summary, . . . it appears that the use of the "assisted communication technique" has greatly contributed to their progress in regular schools.

DEAL's funding was safe until the next change of government.

Marco stayed at school till he was eighteen and had completed eleventh grade, after which he joined his father in the fish-and-chip shop. His school was so happy with his progress that they made a videotape, *Alpha, Beta, Canon,*[6] to show new staff and other schools how integration could be a positive experience for students like Marco.

The last scene of the videotape shows Marco being interviewed at home. In the background Marco's baby sister is calling over and over for her "bluey and her dummy" (if she had a disability, we'd say she was perseverating). His mother is facilitating and saying over and over "In a minute, dear!" to the

---

[6] Canon was the manufacturer of Marco's Communicator.

baby. In the foreground his baby brother is trying to pull away the Communicator. Real life is intruding, but Marco remains totally focused on his typing. His last answer says it all.

"What does your Communicator mean to you?"

IT'S THE MOST IMPORTANT THING IN MY LIFE.

7

Can You Read Without
Moving Your Lips?

If you can, then you're reading differently from every European before Saint Augustine, according to legend the first European to read without moving his lips. The written European languages were developed and taught as representations of spoken language, whose spelling varied with the dialect and conventions used by each writer. Instead of seeing meaning in little marks on a page, most readers translated text into speech and got the meaning from that. The new technology of the printing press (which removed book production from the hands of individual scribes), the resulting availability of widely read standard texts (such as the King James version of the Bible), and finally the codification of spelling in dictionaries, combined to establish a standard written language that would be relatively unaffected in presentation by changes in the spoken language. Once a word had a conventional spelling which didn't change from place to place and writer to writer, it was possible to recognize its shape and understand its meaning directly, without having to sound out each letter. Readers could take in language through their eyes and not through their ears.

The language of sign, the language used by people who are deaf, is another visual language. Sign language was first regularized into anything like a standard form in eighteenth-century

France, but gestural languages had developed previously wherever there were communities of deaf people.

Two important lessons provided by the deaf community are that the acquisition of written language can be divorced from the acquisition of speech and that visual language can be acquired from exposure in the same way as aural language. These are lessons we have been slow to learn. Two centuries after the abbe de l'Epée taught his first deaf students to read, the accepted wisdom is still that speaking must precede reading as walking must precede running and that literacy can only be acquired from formal teaching.

Not so. Language is language is language. The experience of children brought up in a signing environment indicates that visual language can be acquired as quickly as aural language. The main reason that in the past children haven't learned to read at the same time they learned to speak, or even before, may relate as much to the differing rates of exposure to spoken and written language as to any intrinsic difference in difficulty. After all, decoding aural language has the problem that sound doesn't stop still—what's said is past. Babies can't replay utterances. They have to make sense of the words on one hearing, and if they don't understand they have to wait for other similar utterances and gradually accumulate enough information to allow decoding to take place. Written language has the enormous advantage that it stays still longer. The label on the milk carton stays around, and so does a page of a book or the alphabet frieze on the wall.

My first exposure to professional skepticism came at the age of four. My grandmother wanted to sign me up at the local library, and the librarian told her that according to the rules (this was the bad old days) membership was restricted to children who could read—children, that is, aged six and above. "But," my grandmother said, "Rosemary can read." The librarian refused to believe it. I wasn't going to school, so I obviously couldn't read. Next week my grandmother took me into the library after I'd finished kindergarten for the morning, handed me a book, and told me to read it to the librarian. I did, and I was allowed to join the library as their youngest borrower.

This precocity had nothing to do with intelligence. It was due, rather, to my somewhat unusual circumstances. I was an only child, and I lived on a farm with my father and grandmother. My father was away all day working the farm. My grandmother was approaching seventy. She couldn't get down on the floor with me for games, and so she kept me amused by reading to me. She read all the children's books in the house to me, over and over, and after a while when Grandmother was too busy to read to me I took out the books and read them myself.

Nobody taught me to read. I had normal eyesight, normal eye-hand coordination, and the ability to turn pages—the prerequisites for taking advantage of the print in my environment. I saw a lot of written language in circumstances in which it was meaningful, and I learned to understand it. Because I could speak, people knew I could read.

The youngest reader to come to DEAL was Theo, who was three—a little boy with spastic quadriplegia and a severe visual impairment corrected by glasses as thick as the bottom of a beer bottle. He had been a premature baby and was a survivor of neonatal intensive care, one of a group of children with multiple disabilities we had always assumed (somewhat thankfully in the light of their daunting physical and sensory impairments) to be severely intellectually impaired. Claims by his mother that her speechless, near-blind, quadriplegic three-year-old could recognize words were met with general skepticism. There was no doubt about it, though. In answer to questions he fist-pointed independently and accurately to words printed in letters two centimeters high and shortly thereafter started to spell. He went on to regular primary school, where he was reported to be a real problem for his teacher—not because of his impairments, but because he was academically advanced for his class.

Realizing that his speech was likely to be severely impaired by his spasticity and the need for neogastric feeding in his early months, Theo's mother had taken particular care to ensure that he had maximum exposure to written language despite his visual impairments. She made sure that he had appropriate glasses, and that the glasses were put on; she made sure that he had books with appropriate-size print, and that he was positioned so he could see them; she read to him and turned the pages. Without her special care he probably wouldn't have latched on to written language, because with his particular problems he would not have been able to pick up the incidental print surrounding him in the way that other children could.

Historically, reading has been seen as a special skill separate from the acquisition of language, as such—a skill which had to be taught. A bumper sticker doing the rounds at the moment says, "If You Can Read This, Thank a Primary Teacher." Nonsense. Most children in my society—urban, comparatively affluent, late twentieth-century—will learn to read at least something, whether or not they have anything to do with a primary teacher. Our society now provides everyone with an enormous amount of involuntary exposure to written language. A child with no interest in books, a child who refuses to open a book, is still going to be bombarded with commercials on the television, advertisements, signs; every time she opens the refrigerator she'll get a reading lesson.

When I was four there was no TV in Australia, you went to the grocer to do your shopping, and staples like sugar and flour were ladled out of unmarked bins into brown paper sacks. The explosion of supermarkets during the 1950s enormously increased meaningful print exposure. If you were going to get the right packet of cereal—the one that had those cute little plastic figures in them that everyone was collecting—you had to know what those labels said. Since then readership of newspapers and magazines has increased enormously with increasing affluence, and even households that don't buy any and don't read books are still bombarded with free newspapers, catalogs, and junk mail. Most advertising material is ideally suited to learning to read. You get a picture of the object for sale, and the words that go with it. Children think it's great, and because it's expendable it is often given to children who wouldn't be given books, either because of their age or their disabilities.

All right, then, why doesn't every child learn to read? A small percentage of children have specific neurologically based reading impairments, in the same way as a small number of children have specific speech impairments; but in the main, children who don't learn to read simply haven't been motivated to read, haven't had enough exposure to written language, or have had their acquisition of literacy skills impeded by poor teaching. Most speaking children come to written language as a second language—their essential communication needs are already being met by speech, and print may be seen as an optional add-on of no particular interest. After all, it does require close attention. You can play and talk—you can't play and read.

Children with severe disabilities are especially likely to have their access to books restricted. If they have unremedied visual impairments they may be unable to read regular print. If they have mobility problems they may be unable to get to the bookshelf. If they have hand-function problems they may be unable to pick up books and turn the pages. If they have speech impairments their parents may not read to them, if only because, like Ben, they can't ask for a bedtime story. If they live in an institution there are probably no books. For some of these children television may be the major source of print exposure. They are the real beneficiaries of such programs as *Sesame Street*. Their range of activities is restricted, they are seen as perpetual children, their disabilities may prevent them from complaining, moving away, or changing the channel, and as children and as teenagers and even as adults they may be sat in front of children's television every afternoon. Some DEAL clients have watched virtually every *Sesame Street* program ever made, and between those, game shows, and commercials they've had an exposure to written language which would just not have been available to them in pretelevision days.

Many people with disabilities who come to DEAL show a pattern of knowledge and ignorance that tends to confirm the hypothesis that they've acquired written language through incidental exposure. *Neighbours* is Australia's most popular TV soap. Now "neighbours" is a word that in my childhood frequently used to come up in spelling championships, and in the finals, at that. It breaks a variety of rules, and it's a word whose spelling is impossible to guess. Of the scores of clients who gave *Neighbours* as their favorite program over a four-year period only three spelled it wrong. The clients who spell "neighbours" correctly weren't spelling champs either. Some of them had rather poor spelling skills, and produced a lot of phonetic approximations such as "woz" and "hurd." It's my guess that these people have absorbed what spelling they can from limited print exposure, and are making up the rest.

After I'd seen a lot of clients at DEAL who had acquired some word recognition and spelling skills without special teaching, clients who in many cases did not seem particularly clever, I went back to Anne and berated her for having me on. She must have known how to read before I started work with her, I told her, and rather than telling me this she'd pretended to allow me to teach her. Not only that, but when we'd come to write *Annie's Coming Out* she'd perpetuated the myth. To my surprise and initial disbelief she declared that I *had* taught her to read—she had picked up some of the letters and some words from *Sesame Street*, but her exposure to *Sesame Street* had been so erratic that she knew the alphabet song but not the shapes of all the letters (especially in lower case), and there were a tremendous number of basic words she had never seen at all. Then I started to think. There were no books or magazines around St. Nicholas, and she couldn't have turned the pages if there had been. She'd been lying on the floor of a hospital, she wasn't getting junk mail, she never saw inside a refrigerator, she certainly didn't go shopping, she occasionally and unpredictably saw the television. She was telling the truth. You can learn to read without a teacher, but you can't learn to read if you don't have meaningful exposure to print.[1]

---

[1] It's not clear how much exposure is needed. After all, any hearing child isn't learning *language* from the print alone, but joining it together with whatever language has already been learned from the surrounding speech.

It was for this reason that Brian worried me. Brian was diagnosed as having significant intellectual impairments. He had major word-finding problems, and could not read aloud. He had major motor-planning problems, and could not write. When he started to learn to type with facilitation in his midforties and appeared to show some spelling ability, his mother was understandably skeptical. She told me she'd prayed for guidance because, while she didn't believe Brian's facilitators were making up his typing, she was sure he could not be literate. He could not read aloud or write, he had never attended school, and he had no obvious interest in books or magazines. He had no significant exposure to print except on television, and while television might have taught him to spell "neighbours" correctly it would not, his mother said with some justification, have taught him to spell "through." All the suggestions I propounded, such as listening to his siblings do homework, were exploded. His mother had not even read him bedtime stories, as he didn't appear interested. In the absence of assistance from Brian, who was not around to be questioned, I could not answer his mother. To learn to read and spell conventionally you need significant print exposure. Brian had not had significant print exposure. Therefore, Brian could not read. We continued chatting about Brian and his problems, and Brian's mother continued to produce evidence that he could not have learned to spell. That "through" really worried her and was starting to worry me.

If Brian didn't like books, what did he like? Music, and in particular hymns. While his speech problems precluded him from singing the words (he sang a made-up language, in tune), he was able to match the sung words with the text in front of him. His most cherished possession, his mother said, was his hymnbook—but, she said, he still couldn't find the hymn unaided. Given that Brian was bedeviled by perseveration, which meant once he started turning pages he could not stop, this wasn't surprising. His mother used to find each hymn and give him his book ready opened.

"Do you sing the Twenty-third Psalm?" I asked Brian's mother. "Yes, of course." "Can we try a chorus?" And there we were, at 6:30 on a Friday night,[2] belting out "The Lord's my shepherd, I'll not want" until we reached "E'en though I walk *through* death's dark vale, yet shall I fear no ill" and the penny dropped. Her question had been answered. Every Sunday for forty years Brian had attended church, seen the same hymns, and heard the same words. No wonder he loved his hymn-book—as well as whatever religious and musical significance he attached to it, it had given him a way into the world of print.

It is truly amazing how quickly someone who has preexisting language can learn to read if she has enough exposure and enough motivation. Anne started to spell in May 1977. By the end of the year, as well as *The Double Helix,* she'd read Luria's *Man with the Shattered World,* a neurological case study. Ironically, the deprived circumstances in which she was living may have contributed to this unusual rate of progress. When I went home at night I would stick photocopied pages of whatever book she was reading around her crib. Like all the hospital residents, she spent most of her life in her crib—she was in bed by 4:30 in the afternoon and lay there until 7:30 in the morning. As she required no more sleep than any other sixteen-year-old, and as the lights were on for much of this time, she had many hours to look at whatever was left on the bars and absolutely no distractions. She was more fortunate than many of the other residents in that she could wriggle and turn over, so that she could move around and see any page stuck anywhere, given enough time (and time was the only thing there was no shortage of in St. Nicholas). The image of Anne's crib stuck around with copies of Luria remains with me, and does seem in retrospect to have an extremely high improbability index. No wonder everyone thought I was crazy.

---

[2] Crossley's law—the most interesting discoveries always occur after 5 P.M. on Friday evenings. For confirmation see chapter 11.

8

When All You Can Do Is
Wring Your Hands

Bella used to sit bolt upright on a sofa at St. Nicholas with her legs crossed. She didn't appear as much withdrawn as anxious. She would gaze at people intently with a deep frown creasing her forehead, but she also had a shy warm smile and beautiful big eyes which would lock on to yours. She had the reverse of eye avoidance; once Bella made eye contact you couldn't leave—she gripped you with her eyes, in a way she couldn't with her hands. She could walk, if two people supported her, but she couldn't feed herself, she couldn't do anything much—anything, that is, other than wring her hands; her hands had calluses from her constant wringing. At the time I interpreted her hand-wringing as evidence of distress at her environment, though the fact that she kept on wringing her hands even when she was smiling and appeared happy didn't really gel. She was a very pretty child (except for her distended stomach—Bella swallowed air until she looked six months pregnant). When I saw her I'd stop and play hand games with her to try and break the wringing pattern. I had to help her play along, but she'd show pleasure. Sometimes it took half a minute after we'd stopped before the wringing started again—never longer than that, no matter how long I sat and played. I didn't understand what was wrong till many years later, after I met Tara.

When I first met Tara in the early eighties she was nearly

twenty. She was lying on a divan on the patio of her parents' house. Vivien, her mother, had heard about Anne, and thought that Anne's methods of communication might help Tara. After all, Tara could do a lot more than Anne; she could walk (unsteadily, and with some difficulty) and feed herself (with a spoon or her fingers, messily), and Anne couldn't do either. Tara couldn't talk, though, which was why Anne and I were there.

Tara was totally unresponsive. Her face was expressionless—she didn't make eye contact or avoid it (and a purposeful avoidance of eye contact at least indicates awareness). If she was interested in anything I was saying to her or showing to her she managed to conceal it brilliantly. It wasn't clear how much speech she understood. She did not spontaneously do *anything*. It was all most embarrassing. I had no suggestions to make about Tara's communication; before there can be communication there has to be a will to communicate, and Tara wasn't showing any. Anne was as embarrassed as I was. She found the situation very difficult, and she thought Tara's parents were probably making comparisons. Tara could clearly use her body better than Anne, but Anne looks at you when you speak to her, laughs when you make a joke, smiles when she's cheerful; she's a person with whom one can interact, she's obviously *there*, and it wasn't at all clear that Tara was. We made some kind of tactful excuse, made some obvious suggestions about offering Tara choices, and got away as soon as we decently could.

Five years later, in mid-1987, DEAL had been running for more than a year. We'd found light under several surprising bushels, we had more equipment and better techniques, and one of our speech pathologists who knew Tara suggested that Vivien might bring her in for another go. (We've sent out a number of these recall notices over the years, when either a new communication technique or new communication technology has become available.) The form Vivien filled in then listed Tara's diagnoses as severe intellectual disability, autism, cerebral palsy, and epilepsy. The epilepsy was absolutely certain—Tara has severe epilepsy that's never been totally controlled. Tara's gait was unstable and she had a small amount of spasticity in her legs, so yes, cerebral palsy would fit. But severe intellectual disability? With the other handicaps she had, how could anybody tell? Autism? Tara didn't interact much, but then she didn't do anything much. She certainly didn't have any of the antisocial behaviors often associated with autism though she did rock.

Tara's major problem seemed to be motivation. She could feed herself, but even when she was eating a meal (and she enjoyed her food) she sometimes needed a physical prompt to reach for the next mouthful. Virtually the only other spontaneous hand movement she had was a continuous washing motion in her lap, rubbing hand against hand. Hand-wringing was a very dominant pattern. Tara's mother described how Tara would sometimes stop feeding herself to wring her hands, even though she was clearly hungry and in fact had her eyes fixed on the piece of food she'd been reaching for when the wringing intervened. On the rare occasions when she did try to do something else with her hands she had a significant intention tremor—her hands shook—making it hard for her to make accurate movements.

We wanted to see if Tara could point. The first step in assessment was to separate her hands (to give her something to point with) and to stabilize her arm (to inhibit the tremor). Her face was still virtually expressionless, but with this amount of assistance she was able to work her way through a number of tasks on the Talking Computer toy that showed she could recognize pictures, shapes, and written words. I finally asked her to make as long a sentence as she could from a display of written words on the Talking Computer. She beat Marco's record of fifteen words by composing, I SEE THE SMALL CAT AND THE BIG DOG BY THE GREEN TREE AND THE RED CAR. Touching the last word she smiled delightfully, the first smile I had ever seen from her.

From her second visit Tara went on to show reading and spelling skills. She answered one question, for example, by spelling out, MOTIVATION IS PRESENT, BUT I CAN'T MOVE. As a child Tara had been given a lot of exposure to flash cards and books, but because she couldn't talk it had been unclear how much she was taking in. She often sat with a magazine on her lap, but she had difficulty turning the pages. It wasn't clear that she was interested at all, much less whether she was looking at the words or just the pictures.

On Tara's second visit to DEAL we tried a head pointer. This was slightly easier for Tara than using her hand, but it was tiring and slow and she needed to have her head steadied to achieve any worthwhile speed. With my hand on her shoulder, which stabilized her trunk and gave her more proprioceptive feedback but had no direct influence on her head movement, she typed more quickly than without any physical contact. It was not simply that the stabilization made Tara more accurate; it also appeared to provide some of the oomph Tara was lacking. She moved more quickly and she kept going longer. Between her epilepsy and the drugs she took for it, however, she was effectively narcoleptic, falling asleep uncontrollably. Every now and again she would suddenly drop off to sleep with no warning. We spent about half of every session waiting for her to wake up again.

It was clear that Tara had severe initiation problems. She had almost as much difficulty in moving as Sacks's patients in *Awakenings*. Until now all anybody had expected from her was that she would lie on a divan doing nothing, and the fact that she wasn't doing anything wasn't remarkable. Now she was commenting on life around her, and the fact that she wasn't otherwise interacting with her world was more remarkable.

If you can move your eyes reliably you can spell out words on eye-pointing boards, but Tara seemed to have apraxia of gaze; her eyes would get stuck in one position. If you can work one switch reliably you can work a computer, but Tara couldn't work a switch reliably—she couldn't get her muscles started to perform the necessary movement in the time allowed. We kept on experimenting with different arrangements of switches, head pointers, and hand use, trying to work out what would be easiest for Tara. She used her head pointer to spell out GO AFTER HAND, so we took off the head pointer and tried her hand again. She still couldn't reliably extend a single finger, so she had to use a pointer. We cobbled together a pointer stuck into a foam-rubber ball.[1] Tara could hold it, but even with me supporting her arm she just couldn't make the pointer go where it should. She had virtually no movement from one side of the communication display to the other. I'd ask her to point to the far left side, and nothing much would happen for a while. After a minute or so there might be a slight movement, and I'd help her arm over. Then I'd ask her to point to the right side, and nothing remotely functional would happen at all. If Tara hadn't already used the head pointer to spell, and if she hadn't through that spelling already shown good comprehension, I would probably have thought that Tara simply didn't understand what I was asking her to do.

We crept through IM SORRY GIVE U. I didn't need much encouragement. When Tara started moving her hand and the pointer toward her mouth that was all I really needed to demonstrate the full extent of her incapacity to function, and I was quite ready to give up altogether. I thought, "Oh, all right, Tara, that's it." People like Tara give you very little facial feedback, they do look dull, and it's very easy to lose confidence in their abilities, particularly if your negative visual impressions are reinforced by inappropriate behavior. If Tara had sucked the pointer I really would have wondered if I'd imagined the spelling.

Tara didn't suck the pointer, or even put it in her mouth. She lifted it up, changed its angle, and put it down clearly and forcibly on the P. For the rest of the session Tara spelled relatively quickly by taking the pointer back to her mouth between letters and directing it on the downward movement.[2] I CAN DO IT I LIKE TYPING.

It was fascinating. Tara had only one purposeful repeatable hand movement, and that was feeding herself, a movement she had been taught coactively as a toddler. What she was doing was almost a textbook demonstration of apraxia. MOTIVATION IS PRESENT, BUT I CAN'T MOVE. Tara appeared to have no

[1] Penny later used this pointer successfully. Her engineer father refined the design, and eventually Penny used it for her first independent typing.

[2] Everything is relative; using the head pointer she could get out five words an hour, with the hand pointer she got out twenty.

paralysis that would prevent her moving her arm from side to side, and the way she used the pointer once she worked out this novel technique made it perfectly clear that she understood what I was asking her to do, but she simply hadn't been able to do it until she made use of the one functional motor program she did have involving her hand. She could take her hand to her mouth and put it down again to pick up another piece of food, and she was able to direct that movement.

In 1989, when she was twenty-five, Tara was finally given a name to put to her handicap. She was diagnosed as having Rett syndrome. Rett syndrome is an uncommon degenerative condition of unknown cause. The syndrome was first described by Dr. Andreas Rett, an Austrian, in 1965, but it wasn't until 1983 that articles on the syndrome were published in English-language medical journals. It affects only girls.[3] The girls appear normal at birth and for the first six months or so thereafter. Their hand use, social responses, and initiation are normal, and they hit their first milestones on time. Then skill development stops, they appear to lose interest in playing, and their muscle tone often becomes very low. Repetitive hand movements, especially hand washing or wringing movements, take over from the wide range of hand movements of the typical infant.

As the cause of Rett syndrome is still unknown and there is no specific remedy, the late diagnosis made no practical difference to Tara. It's a moot point, in fact, whether the diagnosis of conditions like Rett syndrome—conditions whose outcomes are bleak and for which there is no cure—actually helps parents at all. Parents of children with disabilities have said to me that a certain diagnosis, even a pessimistic diagnosis, is preferable to uncertainty, but I don't know which way I'd go. Still,

---

[3] Hypothetically this suggests an abnormality on an X chromosome, specifically an autosomal X-linked dominant, which is lethal in male fetuses carrying the abnormality. It says nothing about the cause of the abnormality, which may be a fresh mutation. With all conditions of gradual onset one can hypothesize that the infant has too little or too much of something—a digestive enzyme, cerebrospinal fluid, a neurotransmitter—whose absence or excess gradually produces impaired functioning.

when I heard about Rett syndrome it did explain a lot about Bella—even if I still didn't know what lay behind those beautiful wide brown eyes.

Fortunately, Tara's parents were keen amateur filmmakers. They had a full and detailed visual record of Tara's life, starting even before she'd left the maternity hospital. Real life isn't a movie, and at first Tara's parents didn't notice that she was deteriorating when she stopped progressing—they thought she'd just hit one of those plateaus that babies sometimes have. She was still bright and responsive, and till she was one and a half it wasn't obvious that she wasn't doing as much as other children of her age. But slowly her milestones got further and further behind, slowly the purposeful use of her hands stopped and the characteristic hand-wringing started. When all the pieces of film showing Tara growing up were edited together you could see, heartbreakingly, the changes. The beautiful baby, the infant playing and babbling, the sociable one-year-old watching other children playing (with the knowledge of hindsight you notice the restricted hand movements, the start of hand-wringing), the passive but still smiling two-year-old, the generally unsmiling older girl whose hands never seem to be apart.

The course of the Rett syndrome is very variable. After the age of one there's often a major regression. Those girls who have a few words of speech at this age usually lose them. Eighty percent develop epileptic seizures. Their appearance and behavior may look increasingly autistic as they lose eye contact and facial expression, and their play becomes restricted to a few repetitive actions or disappears as the hand-wringing takes over. Tara's hand-wringing wasn't ever as bad as some of the other girls, who wring their hands every waking minute, wring them until they bleed. Between the ages of two and ten, seizures tend to get worse, not better, and in those years girls with undiagnosed Rett syndrome are usually assessed as being severely intellectually impaired. Their muscle coordination is generally affected, and if they are still able to walk it will be with a jerky gait. Breathing disorders are common—Tara often has breath-holding attacks when she seems to "forget" how to breathe out. They have weight loss, despite excellent appetites—Tara eats very well and is quite thin. Many of the girls develop scoliosis or curvature of the spine—luckily, Tara's is quite mild. Overbreathing, teeth grinding, grimacing—all these symptoms fitted Tara. After the age of ten the deterioration generally stops, but the lost skills are only rarely regained. Some girls never lose the ability to make eye contact at all and are responsive throughout, but those who do lose it are said to regain it at this stage. Tara's parents had worked hard on her eye contact when she was still a child. While she didn't actively avoid eye contact and often gazed with unmoving eyes at a person, it was hard to feel it was *contact*, partly because of her usual lack of expression. BECAUSE I CAN'T CRY, OTHER PEOPLE DON'T THINK I AM FEELING PAIN, Tara said.

Early articles about Rett syndrome all described the girls as having severe intellectual retardation associated with communication malfunction, severely impaired speech, and severely impaired understanding of language. Nowadays the received view of intellectual functioning tends more to the "not proven" verdict—while most of the Rett girls have severely limited speech and movements, there is an increasing recognition that these external expressive problems are not necessarily a reliable measure of understanding or processing. Current research is seeking ways for the girls to communicate and interact with their environment that do not require them to use their hands.

In our experience the receptive problems of girls with Rett syndrome have never been as severe as their extraordinarily severe expressive problems, problems which make accurate detailed intellectual assessment virtually impossible. Tara doesn't speak at all, but her understanding of language shows no obvious defects. We can't say for certain that her receptive language is unimpaired, because the extreme laboriousness of her communication makes it difficult to justify carrying out the barrage of tests that would be necessary to find out.

Tara had shown us some of her abilities, but that didn't mean that everything was plain sailing. Her mother had back problems, which meant that Tara had gone to live in a large residential center for people diagnosed as intellectually impaired and that she attended the institution school. I visited the institution to discuss Tara's programs. There were immediate difficulties. The teachers there had been taught to work with people who were intellectually impaired, and they knew Tara had to be intellectually impaired—after all, she lived there, didn't she? The "school" program did not allow for any academic work at all, and the circumstances of residential care did not even allow for choice making. Tara's central problem, however, was that she'd decided, in order to reduce her dependence on facilitation, to go back to using the head pointer, and the very real difficulty she had in moving her head and controlling the head pointer made her communication very slow indeed.

In the institutional environment there was just no way that Tara was going to be able to use her head pointer to communicate by typing. It would still be possible, though, to set up opportunities for her to practice using the head pointer in other ways, all of which would improve her control of her head movements. With the pointer she could hit the keys on an electronic piano, she could paint, she could play games, she could do craft work, she could do a whole host of activities that did not involve assessment and that would enable her to practice the physical skills she needed to type without having to be worried about failing. Would you ever have learned to ride a bike if you'd had someone standing behind you giving out pass or fail grades for your every movement? The teachers seemed to have some difficulties grasping the concept of an activity that couldn't be scored, but I had to leave them to it.

On my next visit to the school six months later the reports were most discouraging. Her teacher said, "Oh, we've tried Tara with the head pointer two or three times a week just like you said, but we haven't got very far." Well, I said, why don't we try it now, and see whether there's anything else I can suggest? Tara was brought out, she was fitted with a head pointer, and the teacher held a picture of a cup in front of her.

"Point to the cup, Tara." Tara didn't. "Point to the cup, Tara." Tara moved her head away. The teacher put her hand on the head pointer and bobbed it down to the picture. "Yes, that's right, Tara, that's the cup."

What, I asked, was the point of it? "What do you mean, the point of it?" *Why* was Tara supposed to be pointing to the cup? What did she get out of it? "You said she had to practice her head-pointer work, so she's practicing it by pointing to things." Yes, but what was in it for Tara? What conceivable reason could anybody have for pointing to a picture of a cup? It had no purpose and no possible gain. I'd left a sheaf of activities that Tara could do with her head pointer; why couldn't she do them? The other students were picking out dried flowers and using them to make Christmas cards. Why couldn't she do that? Tara could use the head pointer to point out the flowers she wanted, couldn't she, and then someone could hold out the card and she could dab paste on it with the head pointer, and there'd be some purpose to the activity.

"Yes, but I don't think it's appropriate for her to do activities until she's shown she can use the head pointer." I could have throttled the teacher, but instead I explained that there just isn't a before and after with this kind of work; you learn it by doing it, and as you do more you learn to do it better. Tara and I then played a game of two-up using the head pointer—a no-fail, fun, motivating activity—and her head control improved even during the course of one game.[4]

"Anyway, I don't see why she couldn't use a keyboard with her hands. Her fine motor skills are excellent." Tara's fine motor skills are *appalling*. "She can feed herself." Yes, she had that skill trained for years, and she can do it, with difficulty. But if she wants to move her hand laterally she can only do it by lifting it to her mouth in a feeding movement and putting it

---

[4] Two-up is the traditional Australian army gambling game. Traditionally it was played with pennies which had the (British) monarch's head on one side (heads) and the Australian coat of arms, including a kangaroo and an emu, on the other (tails). The spinner would toss two pennies up in the air and the diggers would bet on their fall—two heads, two tails, or one of each. What Tara and I played was really One-up. She pointed to heads or tails on a card to make her bet, and I tossed a half-dollar coin. If she'd picked right she got one point, if she'd picked wrong I got one point. First to ten points got to keep the coin.

down further over. Had the teacher ever really *looked* at Tara? What she meant was that Tara's fine motor skills were reasonable for a one-year-old, which is how she saw her.

Tara had been made to point to the same picture of the same cup ten times a day two or three times a week for six months. I wouldn't have blamed her if she'd sworn off head pointers for life. I had to ask whether by telling the school about Tara's abilities I'd harmed her more than I'd helped her.

The school had a good staff ratio and lots of resources, but they were systematically demeaning their students. Any problems with Tara's motivation were Tara's fault, not the teacher's. Whether the teacher realized it or not, she was setting up Tara to fail. The procedure she was using was designed not to teach Tara how to use the head pointer, but to enable enough crosses to be put in enough boxes to ensure that Tara's failure with the head pointer was thoroughly documented so that the program could be stopped. She appeared to be afraid of Tara showing her anything she didn't know. It was astoundingly perverse teaching practice, but then she didn't really see herself as a teacher but as a child minder.

Toward the end of 1991, as part of a campaign to obtain more appropriate educational services for Tara, her parents arranged for a psychologist to assess her. She used her head pointer to respond to questions from the Weschler Adult Intelligence Scale (WAIS). Testing must have been extraordinarily slow. In three sessions of two hours each Tara only completed three subtests. However, her responses were good and the psychologist inferred that her intellectual capacity was of average level.[5] This seems reasonable; she greeted the introduction of a puppy to her unit by spelling, I HAVE BAD BALANCE — DOG OF UNSEDENTARY NATURE CAN CAUSE ACCIDENTS.

---

[5] How meaningful such test results are is always a matter for debate. Whether you accept IQ tests or not, however, you must still question a system that demands that people do standardized tests, regardless of whether they belong to the population on which the test was standardized. Even if you believe that the WAIS is a worthwhile test, it was unquestionably designed to test people who can talk and who have no significant physical impairments. The ultimate absurdity may be the production of a Braille version of Raven's Progressive Matrices, the "tartan-matching test," for use with people who are blind.

Around this time Tara's school was transformed into an adult education center. More stimulating programs became available, at least until the budget cuts of a new government took hold a couple of years later. Tara's parents, who took her home several times a week, also did everything in their power to enrich her life with music, talking books, and excursions. In 1994–95, with her mother's support, Tara successfully completed twelfth-grade history and English courses at a community college. She needed help to get books from the library, to turn pages, to get to classes, to take notes, to contribute in class, and to do assignments. Her answers were short and couched in her characteristic style, as if she were writing a telegram and being charged by the word. Writing about herself in an English assignment, Tara said, "I educate people about being apraxic. Cognitive abilities can be masked. Doing things is harrowing. I'm trying enabling actions by hypnotherapy. Aim: control of one finger." (The hypnotherapy was an interesting idea of Vivien's which was not successful. The limited goal was realistic—normal control of one finger would have given Tara access to almost anything electronic—computers, speech synthesizers, page turners, phones, and so on.)

At the end of the day people with severe initiation problems like Tara may be more functionally impaired than people whose physical impairments at first sight seem far more severe. While a spinal quadriplegic, for example, may have obvious practical difficulties in getting up in the morning, he's no more likely to have trouble getting going than the rest of us. He would be unlikely to have epilepsy, and would avoid the side effects of anticonvulsant medication which complicate Tara's life. He may have only a small amount of movement, but that which he has got he can make work for him, starting and stopping movements when he wants to. Consequently, he can operate on the world around him, typing or using a computer in a way Tara can only dream of. Socially, of course, he has the enormous advantage of having normal speech and normal facial expression. It is obvious even before he speaks that he is aware and with it.

Tara can walk, but finds it difficult to get up from a chair, so she may actually move around less than if she had a motorized wheelchair. If she had an environmental control system she probably would not be able to use it, not because she wouldn't understand it, but because she could not get the right movements to happen at the right time. For Tara the first step really is the hardest—it's the first step, or hand movement, or head movement that she needs help with. Once started, she can keep going till one of her involuntary movements intervenes; for as well as lacking voluntary movement, Tara also has to contend with the problems caused by involuntary movements, the hand-wringing and nap attacks. For any activity other than passive watching, even turning the pages of a book, she needs someone with her to keep her going. Until we know more about the neurological bases of initiation and inhibition, and how to adjust the settings, virtually all we can offer to Tara is a better view.

9

What's the Product of 3 Times 21?

It's hard to read a poem to yourself—
You cannot hear the words.
You have to imagine the sound, the rhythm.
The sense is there, the feeling lost.

Imagine writing a poem without being able to read it aloud.
It's like playing a record in a soundproof room—
It's going round, but no-one on the outside can hear.
If I was deaf, would it be the same or different?

Almost no one who knew Jan, the fourteen-year-old author of this poem, believed she had written it. She has Down syndrome. People with Down syndrome don't write poetry. People with Down syndrome can't learn to read. That's what everyone believed when Jan's parents were growing up. It's probably what the doctor who delivered her believed.

Down syndrome is the name given to the cluster of physical and neurological impairments caused by certain chromosome abnormalities, most commonly a third copy of the twenty-first chromosome, trisomy 21. The physical effects of the chromosomal abnormality are variable—about forty percent of babies with trisomy 21 have heart defects, up to sixty percent have correctable visual impairments—and these effects may include almost every part of the body.

The syndrome was first described in 1866 by Dr. Langdon Down. Down argued that many congenital "idiots" (a quasi-technical term in his day, not just a term of abuse) exhibited anatomical features absent in their parents but present as defining features of "lower" races. He found idiots of the "Ethiopian variety"—"white negroes, though of European descent." Others approached "the great Mongolian family." "A very large number of congenital idiots are typical Mongols." The term "Mongol" has gone out of use in most countries, but the prejudices inherent in the term remain.

Jan is a pretty, shy, slightly built girl. When she first came to DEAL she was almost fourteen, but her short stature and her sweet little dress and pigtails made her look much younger. Her mother, Laura, must have been in her mid-forties when Jan was born and was now about sixty, and her father was probably nearer seventy. Jan lived on her parents' farm and traveled to and from a nearby small town to attend a special school for children diagnosed as intellectually impaired.

Jan's shyness made it very hard to assess her speech. At first she wouldn't answer questions at all, and when she did her speech was so soft that it was almost inaudible. Her parents said she had some reading and spelling skills—she could write a few words and phrases by herself, she could copy written material, and she could read aloud. With some coaxing, I got her to read a few lines from a children's book, and her reading was slow and halting but reasonably accurate.

Jan was very interested in DEAL's communication equipment. She went to the typewriter of her own accord and began typing quickly without assistance. Like most people with Down syndrome she had low muscle tone, but despite this she appeared to have few problems with her fine motor skills—she looked at what she was doing and she was able to use her hands and fingers well. All that came out, however, was a few words she'd practiced typing a lot previously: MUM, DAD, JAN.

I wanted to see what she would do if she was slowed down, but

for a timid girl Jan was surprisingly determined about her independence. I finally got her to accept some help—I held on to
one end of a rod, she held the other with her left and best hand
and typed with one finger. The resistance I provided slowed her
down very substantially, and the quality of her output increased
as her speed fell. I gave Jan a picture of a cow and asked her to
write me a sentence about it. Instead she typed, THIS TYPING IS
HARD. I HAVE TO THINK. That was, of course, the aim of the
exercise. Previously Jan had simply been repeating some over-
learned motor patterns, almost without conscious thought.

Jan was one of those unlucky children in whom shyness and
fear of failure combined to give the appearance of stubborn-
ness and stupidity. She was so afraid of getting things wrong—
afraid with good reason—that she preferred not to try them at
all, so afraid of giving the wrong answer that she preferred not
to speak at all. This got her in trouble constantly. Unfortunately, Jan had severe word-finding problems which limited her
ability to get her meaning across and restricted her to very
simple utterances.[1] While she could read aloud—the written
word on the page cued her, and she was able to retrieve the
spoken word with an effort—her reading aloud was bedeviled
by the same word-finding problems which affected her spontaneous speech, preventing her reading with any fluency.

While I was talking to her mother Jan spontaneously and
independently typed MUM DAD COW   DAD IS COW. We both
laughed, and I said, "No, dad is a *bull*", whereupon Jan spontaneously typed, MUM IS COW. She then typed DAD IS and went
for the B, stopped short, and typed JAN, her most fluent word—
the word that was most likely to come out in typing, though

---

[1] It is commonly presumed that the vocabulary of children with Down syndrome is limited to what they can say, rather than that they know words but
can't get them out. One way to tell whether expression accurately reflects
vocabulary is to reverse ordinary procedures—instead of assessing the children's language through their speech, assess their understanding of your
speech. Instead of holding up a picture of a kangaroo and asking a child to tell
you what it is (an excellent way of revealing word-finding problems), you present a number of animal pictures and ask the child to show you the kangaroo
(if the child has sufficient pointing skills to make reliable choices). If you do
both kinds of tests with the same list of words you can see if there are any
words the child knows but can't retrieve or articulate easily.

not in speech, any time her concentration lapsed or she hesitated. I held out the stick, she took it and typed, DAD IS BOOL. It was almost like aphasia of the fingers. Gradually Jan relaxed and became more willing to work with me, and more willing to allow me to hold on to the end of the rod and slow her down.

Five months after her first visit Jan came in carrying a copy of *Peacock Pie*, a collection of Walter de la Mare's poetry. A number of the poems are old favorites of mine, so I read them aloud to her:

> 'Is there anybody there?' said the Traveller,
> Knocking on the moonlit door;
> And his horse in the silence champed the grasses
> Of the forest's ferny floor;
> 'Tell them I came, and no one answered,
> That I kept my word,' he said.

Jan's parents were limited in their ability to read to her because they were not native English speakers. Laura said *Peacock Pie* was Jan's favorite book; she'd bought it herself. Jan wanted to type out a poem from it, and while she was doing this I got some other anthologies out.

While Jan finished her copy-typing I again discussed the nature of Jan's speech problems with her parents, who were anxious to cure them with speech therapy. While speech therapy may have helped Jan's articulation, her best hope for overall improvement in speech and communication seemed to be via written language. When Jan was typing she sometimes typed the first couple of letters of a word and then said the whole word—that is, she was cueing herself from written language in the same way as Penny had when she was recovering her speech. This self-cueing was a very powerful way of helping Jan get out more words immediately and in the long term might also increase her spontaneous speech. Regular reading aloud might also help. In word-finding problems, as in many other things, nothing succeeds like success—the more times that a person succeeds in retrieving a word, even with a cue, the more likely it is that the word will be retrieved spontaneously next time it's needed.

Her parents saw Jan's problems differently from me. They thought she was saying everything she wanted to say, that the only explanation for her not saying more or for giving inappropriate answers was ignorance and that her communication problems were solely due to poor articulation and lack of volume. Her slurred soft speech certainly didn't help Jan get her message across, but making her speech more intelligible wasn't going to fix all her communication problems. It was hard for her parents to accept that.

By now Jan no longer needed to hold on to the rod to slow down, and could type short messages with just my hand on her shoulder. When she finished copy-typing her favorite poem she typed, I LIKE POETRY   CAN I WRITE

"A poem?" I hazarded.

Yes. And she typed:

> Better a mother who cannot love
> Better a car that cannot move
> Better a boy who cannot walk
> Than to have a voice that cannot talk.

Jan's parents were quite pleased with the poem, but I don't think they realized that Jan had written it.

On the next visit Jan brought in another anthology. Again she'd bought it herself. I read and discussed a few poems. Very early in the session Jan indicated that she wanted to write another poem and quickly and confidently typed the poem quoted at the start of this chapter on the word processor. She was familiar with computers from school, and especially liked being able to see what she'd written on the screen and correct mistakes before they were printed. Her low muscle tone meant that she had little endurance, and after the first line I held her sleeve lightly, supporting her against gravity. By this time she'd lost her reluctance to accept assistance, recognizing how much more she could do with it than without it. She'd clearly composed the whole poem before coming. Apart from helping her with punctuation and layout I contributed nothing.

Jan's next visit was her last for the year. Again she brought in an anthology, this time one of her brother's old English text-books, and again I went through several poems at her request. She had some poems she particularly wanted me to read aloud—she showed them to me in the index—and some diffi-cult poems that she wanted me to explicate. One was "The Ballad of Patrick Spens," which has a lot of dialect words in it:

> O laith, laith were our gude Scots lords
> To wet their cork-heel'd shoon;
> But lang or a' the pay was play'd
> They wat their hats aboon.
>
> And mony was the feather bed
> The flatter'd on the faem;
> And money was the gude lord's son
> That never mair cam hame.

I could understand her wanting help!

By this time Jan could type original sentences without physi-cal contact, but that was sitting next to me with my reminders to slow down exerting a brake and Jan using one finger. When she typed by herself she liked to use two hands in imitation of regular typists, and as she found it difficult to control one hand it was impossible for her at this stage to control two.

She wanted to write another poem and again did so on the word processor, a machine which had plainly inspired her at her last visit.

> Using a computer to write poetry is like using
> Hand-made writing paper for the grocery list—
> It is more sophisticated than the message.
>
> Whatever happened to pens?
> No-one will ever be sold a manuscript of my work.
> Can I ever go back to my first ideas?

> Quality presentation may hide poor content.
> Does the software live up to the hardware
> In poet as in computer?

She tired quickly, and I held her sleeve for most of the poem.

One of the more creative explanations offered by my critics for the unexpected output of people who type with facilitation is automatic writing. It is suggested that people like Jan type one or two letters at random and then their partners "automatically" make these letters into a word. Having got one or two words by this procedure, the partner then "automatically" completes a sentence. It's an interesting notion, and may even be correct in some cases, but among the questions it doesn't answer is the question of individuality. Jan regularly wrote poetry. Of the hundreds of communication-aid users I have partnered over the years, perhaps a dozen have written poems while I was their partner. These have all been of varying styles and standards. Anne, required to write a poem for an English assignment, found the task extremely difficult and struggled for days to produce some passable doggerel.[2] Why do my automatic completions produce poetry when I sit next to Jan and not when I sit next to Anne?

Because her parents thought that Jan did not fall into the category of someone who needed to work with a communication aid, this was the last time they brought her to DEAL. During the next year I visited Jan twice at her special school. In June she used a Communicator well, joining in a discussion involving her teachers. What the teachers said, however, wasn't encouraging. Being her own worst enemy, Jan was said to have rejected any slowing of her typing (as she had initially with me) and because of this her production at special school had been little more than her usual stereotyped utterances. She was doing some original typing, but not very much. Jan just hadn't had enough practice at independent keyboard use, and the self-monitoring techniques that I'd been teaching her hadn't

---

[2] On the other hand, some reviewers of *Annie's Coming Out* were unkind enough to point out that Anne's prose was better written than mine.

been practiced enough to become ingrained. The only positive news was that Jan's teacher reported that her speech was more fluent in everyday situations.

When I came back again in November I was shown into a meeting with Jan, her special-school teacher, and her parents. Her parents made it clear that they didn't think Jan should use any form of augmentation for her speech because "she can say everything that she needs to say." Her teacher went along with them. And Jan sat there mute throughout. She wouldn't or couldn't speak, and we were sitting in such a position that I couldn't just bring out a Communicator and give it to her.

I argued as best I could. I told her parents truthfully that Jan was as talented with language as any child I'd ever taught. I told them that her poetry was exceptional for a student of her age, that she had real talent that she could use only if we gave her the equipment and the skills she needed. Nobody (Jan aside) believed a word I was saying. Her father, her mother, and her teacher saw the person that they had always seen, the person that the textbooks told them that they should see. They saw a girl who was doing well for someone with Down syndrome. I was saying that Jan was not just doing well for someone with Down syndrome but that her writing was exceptional for any child, and that was not believable. Her parents thought I was sincere, but they didn't think that our "great work" could possibly extend to their own daughter. *Their* daughter has an extra chromosome.

I hope Jan's story has a "to be continued," but at the moment there's no sign of it. I haven't seen her for years. What has happened to her talent? Is her head full of poems that she can't tell anyone, that she can't type because the stereotyped words get in the way?

Her parents were told to have realistic expectations; Jan's teacher was told what could reasonably be expected of someone with Down syndrome in her special-education course. Jan has been gagged by the limited expectations imposed on people with Down syndrome.

Down syndrome is usually diagnosed at birth (if not before, through amniocentesis). Depending on the age, training, and experience of the diagnosing doctor, the parents may be told within a few days of the child's birth that their baby is severely, moderately, or mildly retarded. The other professionals with whom the parents come in contact are also likely to have a definite opinion on the intellectual attainments to be expected from a child with Down syndrome. Their views will vary depending on their experience or the reference sources they consult. Generalist reference sources may be quite out of touch with more recent developments. The *Oxford Companion to the Mind* (Gregory, 1987), for example, says that intelligence is "limited to an IQ of between 20 and 60" and "most die young."

Views on the extent of the intellectual impairment have changed significantly since the syndrome was first delineated in 1866. A 1986 article said that

> Up to the early 1900s people with Down syndrome were typically viewed as being *profoundly* mentally retarded. Surveys of children and adults during the first half of this century classified most people with Down syndrome in the *severely* mentally retarded category. Kirman's (1944) review suggested that the majority of Down syndrome children fell in the *moderately to severely* retarded range, with 2–3% achieving at the *mildly* retarded level. In the 1960s there were reports of up to 10% of cases being *educable* or *mildly* retarded. By the mid-70s it was suggested that perhaps as many as 20–50% of older children and adults with Down syndrome were in the *mild* range, with a small number even achieving within the normal range. . . . (Clunies-Ross, 1986)

This revision is the equivalent to a jump of something approaching 40 points in mean IQ scores over a sixty-year period. What will we be saying in 2006?

What we're dealing with now, however, is the prejudices parents and professionals have acquired over the past thirty years. If you hear something long enough and often enough it becomes part of your worldview, built into the structures you've erected to order and control your experience. If something occurs that contradicts one of the beliefs that have formed your worldview it's not easy to handle it, especially if accepting it entails dismantling an entire structure. Rather than risk seeing the walls come tumbling down when you try and replace part of the foundations, you protect yourself by ignoring the discrepancy. You refuse to come and see the contradictory evidence. You see the evidence but find reasons to dismiss it. You reshape the evidence to fit your preconceptions.

If the divergence between expectation and reality is large enough you see the evidence but don't process it into memory. People who observe a child showing some unexpected capacity sometimes come away with no memory of the event. If reminded of it they are genuinely surprised and say they must have nodded off. Shown a videotape in which both the child's performance and their reaction to it are evident, they become confused. Some observers are happy to be shown that their recollections were wrong; it may be that their amnesia was due to the incompatibility of the new information with their preexisting memories, rather than to intrinsic negativity about the child. Other observers have such strong negative expectations that it is virtually impossible to change them. They didn't see the child do anything unexpected. Shown the videotape of the child performing in front of them, they try to rationalize it away—it was a trick of the camera, or the light. Ask the child to repeat the performance and the observer needs the bathroom or has to make a phone call.

One common misconception is that the parents and professionals associated with a disabled child will accept any improvement with open arms. If the parents have painfully "come to terms with limited hopes for their child," have in fact abandoned hope for their child's development, and have made plans and placement decisions accordingly, it may be as hard for them to accept later good news as it was initially to accept the bad. If the professionals had a role in developing the negative prognosis given to the parents or if they have provided services to the child based on that prognosis, they may also be threatened by any suggestion that the child has more potential than they thought.

Communication at a previously unexpected level may be

especially likely to cause distress because it not only challenges expectations but almost inevitably entails immediate changes. Your child, your patient, your student, is not the person you thought you knew. Requests, jokes, criticism, questions— coming from a teenager or adult for the first time, they're all threatening. Think of the difference between the average teenager and one who can't ask for money, can't use the phone, can't object to anything you do, and can't swear! Not every parent who's used to living with the latter welcomes a move toward the former. You have to interact with this individual in a way you didn't before, you have to consider his wishes, ask his opinion.

The first person with Down syndrome for whom I tried to find a means of communication was Heather, a young woman in her twenties who was brought to DEAL early in 1986. At that stage I hadn't done any reading on Down syndrome since taking my teaching diploma in the mid-seventies, when the texts had said that people with Down syndrome typically had IQ scores below 50. This undoubtedly influenced my approach to Heather. At the time there were few portable communication aids for people who couldn't read or spell. I didn't even offer Heather any reading tasks because I didn't want to embarrass her. The lack of appropriate low-level communication equipment for people like Heather in fact prompted me to ask a local firm to develop a small, simple speech synthesizer, containing eight utterances, along the lines of "I'm hungry," which would be spoken when Heather pressed a picture of, say, food. Meanwhile there was nothing for Heather, who totally refused to use any communication aid without a voice.

While Heather was waiting for her new eight-utterance voice, a literacy program was established for other people at her center. Seeing what the others were doing, one day she reached for an alphabet board and started to spell. Later her elderly mother told me that Heather, the youngest in a large family, had always been in the kitchen when the others did their homework, and they'd always spelled out messages to her using magnetic letters on the refrigerator. "I always knew Heather had plenty in that small head of hers but couldn't tap it."

However, Heather had learned over her twenty-three years to manipulate the people around her pretty well, and one of the ways that she did it was by playing dumb. She'd found out that you had a much more peaceful life if people didn't think you could do very much. I'm sure that a lot of children would drop out in the same way if they could, but their parents won't accept their excuses and their teachers write "Can do better" on their report cards. Heather didn't have that problem—she had Down syndrome, and people had been perfectly prepared to accept that she *was* dumb.

Heather needed persuasion to give up her coping mechanisms. She had a job in the hostel laundry, but for quite a long time after she started to type she refused to type at work. The supervisor was in a very difficult situation. She didn't know whether she should berate Heather for not typing, because she didn't know how much Heather could do. Heather was certainly not about to show her; she knew very well that she was going to have a much easier existence if the supervisor never knew what she could do. I was brought in to troubleshoot—the traditional hired gun. When she saw me walk through the door Heather's face was a picture. After typing a few words to the supervisor under direct orders from me she then went on with a great grin on her face to type, LAY ME OUT—I'M DEAD. She'd been found out, and she knew it.

If I'd been aware of what was happening elsewhere with children with Down syndrome I wouldn't have been so ready to write off Heather. Because most children with Down syndrome have significant problems with speech, some countries make early intervention with sign language as much a priority for infants with Down syndrome as it is for infants who are deaf. These programs, which start at the age of six months, not only produce the immediate benefit of being able to communicate in sign, but produce very significant improvements in speech among the children who participate. Research having shown that visual memory is a strength for many children with Down syndrome, reading programs have been developed to take advantage of this, and it is now not uncommon to find children with Down syndrome reading at or above the level of their school classmates. However, until this is common knowledge, many children with Down syndrome will not be challenged to perform. Fiona's experience is typical. Petite and pretty, Fiona always wore trendy clothing, and liked getting her ash blond hair permed. Her mother provided foster care to temporarily homeless infants, and Fiona often came to appointments accompanied by a new little baby. She loved looking after all the children, but always had a particularly soft spot for those with Down syndrome. Perhaps she saw herself in them.

When Fiona started coming to DEAL she was twelve and a half and in fifth grade at her local elementary school, though most of the academic work she was given was around the second-grade level. She was old for her class because she'd started school late due to health problems. She'd had heart surgery and needed to wear glasses. Her hearing was normal, but she'd had ear infections as a youngster. If you asked Fiona a question sometimes she'd reply in perfectly clear speech, sometimes she'd reply in speech which was hard to understand, and sometimes she wouldn't say anything at all. (This variability in speech is common among people with Down syndrome, who often have variable muscle tone and variable hand skills as well.)

During assessment Fiona's main problem was a tendency to burst into tears like Emma. If she felt unsure of an answer or unsure of the situation she would cry. If she was asked to do something that she hadn't done previously she would cry, and would be totally unwilling to attempt the task. Her usual response to being asked a question was "I don't know." Fiona could be asked a question such as "What animal gives milk?" and she'd say, "I don't know." She had Down syndrome, it is expected that there are lots of things that kids with Down syndrome won't know, and it had been assumed by everyone around her that when she said she didn't know this was correct. She was thought to have only very limited written-word and letter-recognition skills and minimal counting abilities.

We looked first at Fiona's speech. When she was asked to name pictures of well-known items—and you could recognize what she was trying to say even if her speech wasn't totally clear—it became evident that she had a significant word-finding problem. Out of fifty pictures she named thirty-five correctly in speech. To a number of the pictures, including pictures of common things like an elbow, she gave her stock response of "I don't know." Fiona could point to her elbow, she knew what an elbow was, and her response was not due to ignorance but to an inability to say the word quickly enough. Whenever that happened she said, "I don't know." If she'd had more fluent spoken language, or had been older, she might have said, "I know what it is, but I just can't think of the word." That, however, required not only more maturity but more speech than Fiona had at her command. Her errors were typically associated words—that is, related words that were stimulated by the image—or words for things that were similar visually. The picture of a tent produced "camping," a cup "coffee," a flag "Australia," and a picture of a crutch produced the response "needle." In that picture the crutch appeared to have a large eye at the top. She obviously knew that the crutch wasn't really a needle, because she went on to say, "under shoulder." People who've had strokes often have similar difficulties with naming tasks.

Some children with Down syndrome write well, but those whose speech is significantly impaired usually also have problems with handwriting. Fiona's writing was worse than her speech. She was left-handed, and left to her own devices would start on the right-hand side of the page and move back toward the left. The most common problems affecting the handwriting of children who can't write without a model to copy are motor planning and motor memory. Motor planning is required to start each letter in the correct place and start moving in the correct direction. It overlaps with motor memory, in that you obviously have to recall the movements necessary to produce a letter to know where to start it. Motor memory enables us to recreate a sequence of movements, such as riding a bicycle. It seems to be a particularly enduring form of memory, possibly because it is renewed each time the sequence is performed. Motor memory is involved in all actions we repeat regularly. Fiona didn't have the problems with everyday activities that were so incapacitating for Emma, but she did have major problems recalling and recreating sequences of fine movements, such as the sequences needed to speak or write a word.

At Fiona's school the expectation was that she would produce written answers. Like all of her problems, her difficulties with writing were seen as the unavoidable corollary of Down syndrome. In one sense they were, of course, in the same way as my deteriorating eyesight is the unavoidable corollary of advancing age. Unavoidable doesn't mean irremediable: I got glasses. Fiona needed a remedy for her handwriting, and if it wasn't remediable then she needed a replacement for it.

Typing might have produced an alternative to writing, but while Fiona could type out a small number of words that she had practiced often, and could laboriously hunt and peck to copy-type, she was unable to type a sentence spontaneously. If asked a question she would head to the first letter of the expected answer but would then go off the rails. When she was trying to type without a model she had problems with impulsivity (moving too quickly, leaving out letters and losing the thread like Jan typing with ten fingers) and perseveration (which in her case meant getting stuck on one letter and hitting it a number of times). Like Marco, Fiona also had a problem with automatic completions to words. Asked "What animal goes 'meow'?" she'd type, CA, but then put R to give CAR.

Ironically, for children like Fiona the ability to write or type *with* a model often produces, rather than alleviates, problems. If a child can't write or type at all, people are prepared to believe there might be a physical problem. If a child can write or type with a model but not without, the obvious explanation is that the child has the necessary physical skills but can't spell. Like many obvious explanations it's an oversimplification.

Typing evades many of the problems of handwriting. The motor-planning and motor-memory demands are minimal because there is no need to re-create the letter shapes. If you have the hand skills to push typewriter keys, even with one finger, all you need to do is recognize the letters you need and hit them in the right order. That's fine, if you're not impulsive and don't perseverate. Fiona was and did. Without a model, she was unable to stop herself speeding up and she found herself hitting keys before she'd had time to work out what came next and redirect her movement. Instead of erasing her mistake she would get stuck and hit the wrong key repeatedly. When she was copy-typing, she did so letter by letter, looking back to the original after every letter, thus both slowing herself down and breaking the pointing pattern, preventing perseveration.

When I held Fiona's sleeve and pulled her back so she had to push against pressure to get to the keyboard, two things happened. Her accuracy improved (she didn't wobble, she didn't get typos), and her typing slowed down, enabling her to compose original sentences. While a lot of her words were phonetically spelled, it was clear that Fiona had a rational and consistent code for the representation of spoken language, and her output was probably not much different from that of other children in her class.

Asked to type the names of another fifty pictures, Fiona identified forty-nine, though her spelling wasn't necessarily orthodox. Apart from whatever difference there is neurologically between recalling written and spoken language, producing written language is expected to be slower and so you get more time to think. You can look at the letters on the keyboard and perhaps cue yourself with the initial letter of the required word.

Given a sentence to complete, "The baby pulled the cat's tail—what happened next?" Fiona said, "I don't know," and typed, MOW WAS MY TALE SED CAT—an attempt, we presumed, to get out something like " 'Meow! That was my tail!' said the cat."

Tears really came in when we tried to assess Fiona's reading skills. I asked her to read an extract at the fourth-grade level. She declared that she couldn't do the task, burst into tears, and was reluctant to have anything to do with it. For Fiona, reading and the assessment of reading were associated with reading aloud. This meant that she really did have major problems with these tasks, and in fact failed at them consistently because of her speech problems. Reading aloud does not necessarily correlate with comprehension; it is a translation between modes. If the mode that you're translating into is severely impaired, as Fiona's speech was impaired, the process will obviously fail.

Fiona had been failing even basic math at school. Again, that turned out to relate very much to her expressive problems. She had difficulty saying the correct answer, even if she knew it. Because Fiona's word-finding problem often caused her to say words associated with the word required it was thus extremely likely that if she was asked for a numerical answer any of the numbers would pop out, just as any letter would pop out if she was asked to name an indicated letter. It was then of course assumed that Fiona didn't know the answer. This is a perfectly sensible explanation, and the burden of proof is certainly on anybody suggesting that it isn't correct. In fact, however, it turned out that her errors didn't mean that she didn't know the correct answer, only that she couldn't say it. She would have been better off not saying anything at all. She had realized this herself, and so ended up saying "I don't know" and "I can't do it" all the time.

It eventually became clear that Fiona could handle the concepts being taught in mathematics, but she did have a problem getting out the answers. In handwriting, her motor-memory problems created difficulties; there were frequent confusions between numbers, particularly 2 and 5. Such confusion is very common in children just learning to write, and is only a cause for concern when it persists to a point where it significantly affects academic performance. The sheer effort of getting numbers onto the page distracted Fiona from solving the math problem itself. Our eventual strategy was to get Fiona doing math on a number board. When she was asked a question she was able to point completely independently to the number or numbers that made up the answer. It acted as a good prompt for speech; she would often point to the correct number on her number board and then say it. After having used the number board for some time Fiona occasionally even said the correct answer immediately without touching the numbers on the board first.

Three months after the start of the assessment we finally got Fiona to do a reading test. I enlarged a text on a photocopier so that she could see it from a distance, and I left it without comment on the table in front of her while I went to get some equipment, leaving her with nothing else to do but look at it. I'd memorized the associated questions so that I could ask them without referring to the test sheet. Under these circumstances and with me holding her sleeve she typed the answers to a fifth-grade reading comprehension test, and her performance was fine.

Gradually we got through Fiona's tears. When I asked, "What about doing some reading?" or "What about doing a crossword puzzle?" Fiona wouldn't say "I can't" or "I don't want to" but "Okay." Indeed, after six months when I said, "Now, I've got something *really* hard for you today," she'd say, "Oh, I can do that." This may have been due to two things; she was experiencing success, able to show for the first time that she could do the tasks that she was set, and she had confidence that the task was going to be presented in a form in which she did have a reasonable chance of doing it.

With other children we had some success using spoken cues to elicit speech, but Fiona's speech really wasn't cued either by being given the starting sounds of words, or by the use of word pairs such as "knife and . . ." or "cup and . . ."[3] It was very difficult for her to get the words out, she knew that, and so she tended to freeze when asked to do it, which didn't improve the situation.

To find out whether Fiona could produce an extended narrative I gave her a picture of a man giving something to a robot and asked her to make up a story about it. She typed,

It was the first time Len had met a robot. He didnt know how to behave. He was worried that hed get it angry and really it would go crazy. He put his hand out but the robot did nt shake it. He expected the robot to speak the robot said Hullo Len in a gastly voice. Len said hullo and made a cup of tea. He offered the robot a cup but the robot wouldnt have

---

[3] Whether a particular cueing strategy works for a given person depends on the nature and location of the brain dysfunction which is affecting his speech. Two people whose speech seems very similar may not respond to the same cueing strategy, and the nature of their responses provides clues as to the type of impairment they have.

any because it would rust its insides. Len gave him a micro chip instead.

Not great literature, but fine for a thirteen-year-old. Fiona's use of unexpected words is sometimes reminiscent of Jan, but she has never shown any inclination to write poetry. Six months after Fiona started coming to DEAL, when her pointing skills and her self-confidence had both improved, I gave Fiona a Peabody Picture Vocabulary Test.[4] Before asking each question I put Fiona's index finger on each picture, to ensure that she had scanned all possibilities and to ensure that there was a pause between questions, reducing the chance of impulsive or perseverative responses; otherwise, she had no facilitation. She obtained a raw score of 143, and her standardized score was well above the average for her nondisabled peers. The last plates that she got correct were "edifice" and "rapture."

Fiona's family gave her complete support. Her mother had always paid for Fiona to have extra tuition outside school hours. Her tutors visited DEAL along with staff from her school, and during her final year of elementary school everyone incorporated into their lessons the typing and multiple-choice strategies that we were using. The results were good, everyone's expectations rose, and Fiona blossomed.

One of Fiona's strengths was that with multiple-choice work she could mark the boxes independently with a pencil, provided that, again, the administration of the test was slow and that she was aware that there was an expectation that she'd do well and not muck about. Using multiple choice she completed seventh-grade reading exercises without difficulty. She read for pleasure and was crazy about Babysitter Club books. Unfortu-

---

[4] The PPVT is a rather out-dated vocabulary test. Its only virtue, from my point of view, is that it requires no speech and can be answered by people who only have a crude pointing response. For each item the person undertaking the test is given a set of four line drawings and asked to indicate the drawing which shows the word the examiner says. While there are many possible explanations for low scores including poor eyesight, poor hearing, poor pointing, and experiential or linguistic differences, a good score always impresses school principals, and can help change attitudes to a student with communication impairments.

nately, her typing had not yet become totally independent; while she could now type satisfactorily with just her partner's hand on her shoulder, if all physical contact was removed she was able to type only the first few letters of an answer before speeding up and losing it.

Despite Fiona's success at elementary school, all the problems of negative expectations resurfaced when she moved to secondary school. The teachers were kind, but they really wanted Fiona to be able to do the work in exactly the same way as the other students. If she couldn't, that meant she was retarded and she shouldn't be doing it at all. If she couldn't write, then she shouldn't be doing subjects that required writing, and some teachers tried to exclude her from their classes. In mathematics more adaptations were allowed and Fiona continued to use her number board. She answered questions by pointing clearly and independently to numbers. These were then transcribed by an aide, and she coped well with the regular math syllabus. At the end of the year, however, she was not allowed to move on to the next year's syllabus, and at the end of the next year, despite a successful repetition of the previous year's work, it was said she had no potential to progress any further.

Since then Fiona has participated in some research conducted by Stacey Baldac and Carl Parsons from the School of Communication Disorders at Melbourne's LaTrobe University, which aimed to explore the issues involved in testing people who use facilitated communication. I was Fiona's facilitator, and she did well, successfully describing pictures I had never seen. Her answers did, however, show the interference of the same word-finding problems which plague both her speech and her typing. For the first picture, for example, Fiona started by typing BED. I asked her, "Is that a picture of a bed?" "No," she said. She then typed BET, and BEG, and BEAST, and negatived each of them when I said it aloud. She typed, A GREAT BIG AUSTRALIAN BE ... but couldn't finish it. Finally one of the researchers pointed to something in the picture (which was concealed from me by a screen) and asked Fiona to tell me what that was. She typed SAND, and I was able to guess that she was looking at a picture of a beach. Once we'd broken through that impasse she was able to describe the details of the picture with no difficulty.

Fiona's mother and her tutor were still frustrated by her school's attitude. Fiona was doing more advanced work outside the school than the school would even allow her to try. She couldn't prove the school's expectations wrong because they wouldn't allow her to attempt any tasks beyond the level which they expected of students with Down syndrome. Fiona herself was angry. When we were talking about the problem and I asked her if she had anything to say she almost threw herself at the keyboard and typed, at speed, and without corrections or punctuation, the words which clearly she'd have spoken if she could:

> Getting off the train I saw a man in a wheelchair. He wasn't able to talk and he used a computer. Why do they have ramps for wheelchairs if they don't let [in] people like me— [who are] told [we are] stupid. After all access isn't about walking [but] about being in everything. I want to be in class with all the other students. After I get better at following all the work I want to do exams so I can do a childcare course. I like children but I need to get a certificate to work with them. A trial would be good. What about work experience in a childcare center? Now I've finished but don't just laugh. I really want to do this. Really seriously I want a job with children. Better to work than get a pension. Now that's all [Punctuation and capital letters added].

We linked Fiona's school up with a school where another DEAL client with Down syndrome and very little speech was a successful senior, and last time I heard from Fiona's mother she said things are now going better. Fiona's family is supportive, and her ambition to work with children seems both reasonable and realizable.

Many people with Down syndrome are doing or have done things which challenge the accepted wisdom about the inevitable effects of trisomy 21—writing books, graduating from college, holding down regular jobs, driving cars, even winning gymnastic contests. Accounts of people with Down syndrome who didn't fit the pattern have appeared regularly over the years.

Under the unlikely title "The Sage: An Unusual Mongoloid," John Buck, a psychologist, discussed the case of Benjamin Bolt, who had been "committed to a hospital for the mentally deficient in the early 1940's" after the death of his parents. Mr. Bolt, who was in his forties, was described as "about as defective a Mongoloid as one could expect to find locomoting without active assistance." Nonetheless his "courtly acknowledgment" of Buck's introduction "would have done justice to a seasoned diplomat." Mr. Bolt, who had been educated by his mother, did not have significant impairments of speech or hand use and had little difficulty convincing Buck that he did not belong in a state hospital. Buck describes in some detail the tests he administered.

> His answer to the third Similarities question (In what way are a dog and a lion alike?) is noteworthy: "They are in two different classes; the lion is in the cat class, and the dog is in a class by himself." Then, after a brief pause, he added as if in afterthought, "But of course they are both carnivorous!" (Buck, 1955, p. 457)

It still took several more years for Buck to convince the medical administration that Bolt should be allowed to leave the institution. Buck concluded his account by saying,

> For many years the term "Mongolian idiot" was freely used in the literature. Later it was conceded—grudgingly, to be sure—that Mongoloids under optimal circumstances might even function with the efficiency of morons. Then Pototzky and Grigg reported two Mongoloids whose intelligence might be termed "borderline."
>
> This changing trend and the case of the Sage [Benjamin

Bolt's nickname in the institution] compel one to speculate
that before too long it may well be demonstrated that Mon-
golism need not inevitably be accompanied by mental retardation. . . . (Buck, 1955, p. 481)

And this was forty years ago!

Part of the difficulty in changing the stereotypical view of
Down syndrome may be due to Down's original invention
of the term Mongol, which carried with it overtones of
inevitability and permanence. Inherited racial characteristics,
after all, cannot be changed. A racist approach may still be
operating in the community at large. Individual differences
between children with Down syndrome are often overlooked
because of their superficial similarities of appearance, and the
similarities between children with Down syndrome and other
children are often ignored. A ten-year-old with good speech
and writing skills had been attending her local elementary
school without any extra help, and was not by any means
bottom of her class; her teacher recently asked DEAL for a
book on how to teach children with Down syndrome. Her student isn't "children with Down syndrome," she's a child who on
the face of it doesn't have any disability except other people's
prejudice against her face.

What academic achievements are possible for most children
with Down syndrome cannot be known until the first group of
students who have had their expressive impairments addressed
since infancy and who have attempted the regular syllabus at
regular schools has proceeded through the regular school
system. They will be the first group for whom the playing field
has been leveled. If they are not held back by the prejudices of
their teachers, doctors, and peers, they may show us that trisomy 21 produces a variable range of physical and neuromotor
problems, which, like cerebral palsy, may, but does not necessarily, include learning disabilities.

A few years ago I spoke about the surprising competencies
we were finding in people with Down syndrome to an academic
whose speciality was Down syndrome. He said, "Yes, I know
what you mean. Last year I gave a five-year-old Down girl a set

of standard intelligence tests, and she scored an IQ of one hundred and fifteen." Wonderful, I thought, here was some supporting evidence, so I asked him where he'd published this. He looked at me somewhat oddly. "Oh, I couldn't publish it. People would think I was crazy." Just to round off the story, I was telling it to another researcher shortly afterward, and he said, "That's interesting. The highest I've ever had one of my Down subjects score is ninety-nine." That's how stereotypes persist. Anomalies that would test the system are simply discarded as inconvenient.

10

Eat Now, Pay Later

While I was at school I always read the disease-of-the-month section in my grandmother's *Reader's Digest*. One article in the late 1950s or early 60s explained how mental retardation could be prevented if each newborn had a drop of ferric chloride applied to a wet diaper before the baby left the hospital. It was exciting because it combined so many desirable elements: a real benefit for a large number of people, a cheap, simple, definite diagnostic procedure, and a straightforward remedy.

Phenylketonuria (PKU), the condition which causes ferric chloride to turn green, is a disorder of amino acid metabolism affecting the processing of the essential amino acid phenylalanine, and damages the brain of a developing infant through the accumulation of the toxic by-products of abnormal metabolism. The disorder is caused by an enzyme deficiency and occurs in roughly one baby in ten thousand. If the condition is undetected, phenylalanine in excess of that which the body needs accumulates in the blood instead of being broken down into harmless metabolites. Excessive phenylalanine in an affected baby's blood is likely to impair brain development. The abnormal levels of phenylalanine in the urine and blood of babies with PKU could be picked up by the diaper test (and now by giving every newborn baby a heel-stab for a blood sample). The promise of the discovery was that if the baby's diet could be controlled for a few years—if anything containing phenylalanine could be avoided, as you'd remove milk products from a child with lactose intolerance—the damage would be avoided and the child would be normal.

In fact, it was never that easy. The discovery was undeniably a breakthrough, but some caveats eventually emerged. PKU was responsible for only a small percentage of mental retardation. The urine test missed some babies. Phenylalanine is almost ubiquitous, occurring in nearly all sources of protein, which meant that the wonder diet which was to prevent brain damage involved eating your protein in the form of an expensive gray sludge that in the early years smelled nasty and tasted repellent. Once PKU is diagnosed the baby's family and doctors have to perform a dietary balancing act. Too much phenylalanine causes brain damage; but it's still an essential amino acid—too little of it and the baby also suffers brain damage. An infant with PKU will be damaged if it gets *any* more than it needs, but it must get enough. Unfortunately, phenylalanine is very common—it's not just a matter of dropping one or two items from the diet, or counting calories.

A baby with PKU has to have a diet in which the exact quantity of phenylalanine is known. In its most extreme form this means an extremely restricted diet containing a high proportion of that specially formulated gray sludge. (This can be made into a drink, which improves its palatability somewhat, but it's still never going to make it to the menu at Maxim's.) A baby which knows no better may tolerate this, but it's much more difficult for older children who see their families and friends scoffing ice cream and peanuts with every sign of enjoyment. The children may have to be virtually under guard until they reach an age where they can fully comprehend the effects of any dietary infringement—no McDonald's for them, and no birthday cake or Christmas turkey. The refrigerator and food cupboards may have to be locked to prevent potentially disastrous sampling. The indulgent grandparent who says "just one won't hurt him" has to be educated or restrained.

After all this, there are still problems. Some children will still suffer damage from too much or too little phenylalanine, and a small percentage of children have a variant of PKU which is not helped by the diet at all. There is still debate about the age at which it is safe to terminate the diet, and current thinking is that lifelong restriction of phenylalanine may be necessary. Certainly women with PKU must go back on the diet if they intend to become pregnant, or else run the risk of having a baby with more severe disabilities than their own, due to the effect on the brain of the fetus of the toxins their bodies produce.

Nonetheless, these days most children with PKU develop normally and have no obvious impairments. With all its difficulties, PKU screening of newborns stands as the best example of successful screening for congenital defect, though all we've done is find a way to stop the damage, not a way of fixing the underlying disorder, or repairing any damage which has already occurred.

Back to the sixties. Introducing a new treatment for any condition is always difficult, and PKU was no exception. There were inevitable delays while the products required for testing and treatment were manufactured and distributed, while medical staff were trained in the new techniques, while the tests became automatic and reliable, and while the diet was being developed. At the start everyone was learning by doing. While this was going on, children with PKU who had been born before the tests were getting worse—should they be treated, or should they be "let go" on the ground that their disease was too far advanced for the new treatment to be successful?

Fred was unlucky to have been born early in 1960, shortly before universal, reliable testing for PKU was available in Australia. Thirty-five years later his mother, Laura, can still remember the date of her son's diagnosis (September 1, 1961) as well as she remembers his birthday. Fred started eating the special diet in December. He didn't die, as many untreated children did, but the diet was started too late to prevent his brain being damaged. Laura describes how on their occasional visits to the PKU clinic today the children in the waiting room (who all appear perfectly normal) stare at Fred and ask questions about him and why he's there. An appropriate answer might be "If he wasn't the way he is, you wouldn't be the way you are." Fred was a pioneer—one of the first generation of babies with PKU to be diagnosed and treated. He showed us the way. The children in the waiting room don't have the disabilities Fred has partly because the medical profession learned from Fred and other babies like him.

Fred was the first client with PKU to come to DEAL. Nothing about his appearance or history gave any cause for optimism. I was watching through the front window as he was helped across the road from the parking lot by his mother and an attendant, and my heart sank. He was in his mid-twenties and around average height. His balance was obviously impaired, he had difficulty moving one foot after the other, and he looked quite out of it. He wore a motorbike helmet to protect his head, which meant either he had epileptic fits and fell over a lot, or he was a head banger, or both. And he obviously couldn't talk or write, or he wouldn't have been coming to DEAL.

Laura gave me a brief account of Fred's history. He lived with his parents and older brother and was at home virtually all the time because, as had been the case for most of his life, no school or adult center could be found that was prepared to take him. He was considered too difficult—too difficult for a special center, that is, not too difficult for his mother to look after twenty-four hours a day. His vision and hearing, as far as anyone could tell, were good. He could walk by himself, but was unstable and tended to fall over; he was currently being treated with Dilantin (for epilepsy) and chloral hydrate, Melleril, and Mogadon (as tranquilizers, to calm him down), and it wasn't clear how much of his balance problem was due to neurological impairment and how much to the side effects of his medication.

Fred had a very small amount of speech, occasionally getting out one or two words which Laura understood. He sometimes tried to say longer sentences, but these weren't comprehensible. He pointed at things he wanted, and had just begun to learn sign language; he used the sign for "bed" but no others. Nobody really knew how much he understood. He bit his hands (and, it turned out, would try to bite mine) and hit his hands on his teeth, making his gums, which were puffy and soft from the Dilantin, bleed. He wore a helmet because he banged his forehead on anything handy if he was upset and because he hit his ears unless they were covered. Despite the bashing and the helmet it appeared that Fred's hearing was okay—it hadn't been tested because he was impossible to test accurately with the helmet on and impossible to test at all with it off. As well as covering his ears the helmet came down low in front and often seemed to obscure his vision. Fred's upper jaw and palate were deformed, which affected the clarity of his speech. He was thought to be severely mentally retarded.

During my discussion with Laura, Fred was banging his head on the floor noisily. I looked him over. While this kind of behavior is not always voluntary, and it is true that people with behavioral problems may have attacks of aggression or rage that they can't control, it is also true that with them as with us most things are done for a reason. When people with severe communication problems want to manipulate someone's behavior they can't argue, or wheedle, or order. They have to use their bodies to get their message across. Sometimes they do it with grace and subtlety through the medium of deaf sign; sometimes they mime or point to what they want. Sometimes they vocalize and wait for other people to work out what they want by asking questions or following their eye gaze. Non-speaking children who can walk may indicate that they want a drink by leading an adult to the kitchen sink and placing the adult's hand on the tap. Problems occur, regardless of the strategy used, when the want is more abstract. If it's something to do with feelings, or something in the future—"Don't forget my Coke when you go to the store!"—the child may get frustrated and angry. Nonetheless, very few of them ever do what Fred was now doing. They may cry, grumble, throw a tantrum, or knock things off the table, but they rarely attack themselves.

The exception to this, as to many other things, is the group of children diagnosed as autistic. They quite often bite their hands, and some are head bangers. There are a number of conditions with known causes which give rise to problems similar to autism. Fred looked autistic, and if it was still impossible to test for PKU he would certainly have been diagnosed as autistic (raising the possibility that other cases of autism might be caused by metabolic disorders as yet unrecognized). Our autistic clients used or abused their bodies more aggressively and to less obvious purpose than our other clients. Sometimes the self-mutilation had no obvious trigger, and sometimes the trigger was clear but the aim of the outburst wasn't.

But however strangely they may behave, people with behavioral disturbances only want to hurt themselves as much as they feel they need, but not more. John, an autistic client, was a case in point. When I first saw John biting his hand I was very impressed. He was biting the inside edge of his hand, on the fleshy base of his thumb, holding it palm side down and pushing it into his mouth like a sandwich from which he wanted to take a large bite. He had done it so often that his hands had thick semicircular calluses where his teeth went. Like most people, I found this behavior profoundly distressing. It was awful to think that you had provoked a child to hurt himself like this. John would glare at me across his hand sandwich and if he was very annoyed with me he would shake his head and growl. I tried to do better, to avoid the detested activities, to reduce the pressure. Eventually we reached an accommodation—if I didn't make John do things, he wouldn't bite himself. Equally, he wouldn't do anything.

By the time we had reached this impasse I had seen a lot of other hand biters. Surprisingly enough, they nearly all bit themselves in the same place. There had to be something in this. There was only one way to find out what was going on. I bit my hand in the same way, closing my teeth at first tentatively, then gradually increasing the pressure until I was grinding away like John at his worst. And I found it doesn't hurt nearly as much as you'd think. This part of your hand is concerned with grasp, not touch—today it tolerates the pressure caused by holding and swinging a golf club; millions of years ago it tolerated the pressure caused by swinging from branch to branch. Our fingers are exquisitely sensitive to pain, but our palms aren't. And the calluses on John's hands just meant his biting hurt less, not more.

Next time John came he found my demands had increased again. He tried his hand sandwich, but I wasn't impressed anymore, which made him so angry he took a bite without proper care and attention and bit his fingers, which did hurt. His face was a study. He did give up biting his hands, though, at least when he was around me. This was fairly typical. Sometimes when I showed clients that the game was up by duplicating their hand biting they would laugh and drop their hands. They didn't necessarily give up the hand biting completely, at least not immediately, because over the years it had become an automatic action which it took them a long while to unlearn, but whether they stopped biting themselves or not my life and conscience were considerably easier. I could go on applying pressure without feeling that I was causing appalling pain.[1] I was ready for Fred.

After more than twenty years of practice Fred had developed a few techniques all his own. When he banged his head on the floor he put his hand between his head and his helmet, thus increasing the noise and decreasing the pain. When I saw this, I pretended to laugh at him, while counting aloud how many times he banged his head in each burst. He began with strings of about a dozen, but when he saw that they weren't having the desired effect he slackened off. When he only did six in one burst I told him it wasn't enough and asked for ten, like push-ups, which he did, implying both that he could control his head banging and that he could count. At this point I asked Laura and the attendant to wait outside, because it seemed that Fred could be playing to the gallery, and that some of the joy might go from his performance if the audience dwindled.

When he was finally sitting at a table Fred rejected the picture recognition task I started with and indicated the keyboard equipment on the side table. I usually checked that clients

---

[1] Of course, this is not a universal answer. There remains a small but very distressing group of people who really do hurt themselves badly and who are not able to desist from doing so. Some specific patterns of impairment include painful self-mutilation. Sufferers of Lesch-Nyhan syndrome, a metabolic disorder which in other respects is similar to athetoid cerebral palsy, compulsively bite their hands and lips despite the distress this causes them.

could recognize pictures and then words before attempting spelling, but as we seemed to be going nowhere I broke with the usual sequence and brought over the Vocaid (an early speech synthesizer, which pronounced each letter aloud in a robotic voice as you pressed it). I asked him to spell his name, and to my considerable surprise he did, before leaving the table for another bout of head banging. This time he seemed to be genuinely distressed, and I asked him why. Back at the table he spelled the first clear sentence of his life: I CANT TALK.

He selected the letters with the index finger of his left hand. Because he had a severe tremor he needed his arm stabilized. At DEAL we have a wide range of communication aids, toys, and games on the shelves, and Fred kept gesticulating at various pieces of equipment he wanted to try. I said he could have anything if he spelled it, and he spelled out the names on two of the boxes—DIXIT and TALK N PLAY—and then sat quietly while I showed him both. When he said he wanted to go home we went back to Laura and his attendant.

Anne, who was visiting DEAL, used her alphabet board to comment that Fred had been hiding his intelligence. Fred watched, smiling, and when I gave him Anne's board and asked for a two-letter good-bye he pointed to CU (See you) very nicely.[2] As he walked out it was noticeable that he was walking taller. His mother was quite impressed.

So how had Fred learned to read? In the deep sense that is impossible to answer—how did any of us learn anything? In the superficial sense of where did he get the necessary print exposure, Fred was always looking at whatever magazines and papers were available. His parents thought he was looking at the pictures, though that didn't seem to match his behavior with television. He didn't like the actual programs on television and refused to watch them, but he did like commercials. He would come into the lounge room while they were on, returning to the kitchen table and his magazines when they were finished and the program started again. His parents thought he liked

---

[2] Anne's board had some common words—"be," "see," "are," "you," and "why"—printed above similar-sounding letters to speed up communication.

the noise and color, but there had been a fair bit of both in *Get Smart* and he hadn't been interested, so I hypothesized that it was the written language in the commercials that attracted him. Was there anything else that especially interested Fred? Well, yes, there was, though his parents had always found it quite inexplicable. When they were watching public television, with no commercials, Fred would come in at the end of programs and watch the credits, and if they were watching a movie he would stay for the titles and come back for the credits. It all fitted together—Fred was a print junkie. Somehow he had become hooked on written language as a youngster. Commercials are particularly suited to beginning readers because they repeat the same text again and again, text which is often spoken and displayed simultaneously.

Finding that Fred could spell and providing some explanation for how this might have happened certainly didn't solve all his problems. At the start of his next visit Fred refused to walk in the door at all. He carried on so much on the footpath that we had to seat him in a spare wheelchair and trundle him in with that. Once inside he spelled out I WANT TO GO HOME on the Vocaid before throwing a tantrum which lasted for more than thirty minutes, during which my main concern was to keep him and the wheelchair in the middle of the room so he could not bang his head on the walls or pull equipment off the shelves. Telling him he was behaving like a two-year-old seemed to have a good, if temporary, effect, and I used it so often that I was soon able to abbreviate it to "Two!" in a warning tone to correct or prevent inappropriate behavior without appearing to nag. Bringing out a laptop computer also had a beneficial effect, and Fred spelled out ANNIE IS CLEVER and I HATE YOU. He said he'd like to work with his attendant, but when she came in he did nothing. We both went out and left him alone for five minutes, after which he was calm and spelled very well on a Canon Communicator. IM SAD I CANT TALK. I asked him about head banging—why? I GET ANGRY. Is there anything in particular that makes you angry? LAWRENCE. I asked Laura who Lawrence was; Fred's instructor at a center he attended one afternoon a week was called Mr. Lawrence. He spelled GOODBYE on the Canon Communicator before leaving.

On his next visit Fred was angelic. Laura and his attendant stayed in the room and he used the Communicator like a champ, spelling out I'M SICK OF BEING A BABY. I NEED HELP. Not surprisingly, he showed low self-esteem—I [k]NOW IM RETARD[ed]. I CANT STOP MYSELF HITTING MY HEAD. I NEED TO HURT MYSELF. IM GASTLY [*sic*]. At one stage when I was talking to Laura he got on the floor and hit his head (but softly), but he sat back up at the table on request. Before finishing he did some spelling with Laura and the attendant—HI. ILL[I'll] TRY MUMY I LOVE U

Laura called a few days later to say that Fred was using the ABC board I'd given her well with her and with his attendant. He'd told his brother to GO TO HELL when he'd asked him to spell something! Fred was using it for short periods a number of times a day. Laura still couldn't quite believe it, though, and was worried that she might be cueing him when she stabilized his arm, though she kept telling herself that Fred used spelling (spelling fridge "fridj") that she wouldn't. I reminded her of the extreme difficulty of getting Fred to do anything that he didn't want to do.

By the time Fred came next he'd already been spelling sentences to Laura and the attendant and spelling out single words for what he wanted to his father. He tried out a Speechpak, a laptop computer with speech synthesis, and was most impressed. I LIKE IT HOW MUCH DOES IT COST I NEED IT NOW. When Fred said "now" he meant *now* too. When I told him he couldn't have one straightaway and that we'd have to try out a couple of other cheaper alternatives he became frustrated, distressed, and tried to hit me and himself. It was hard to get him to sit at the table and use the keyboard. "Why are you so upset?" VOICE DOESNT WORK I WANT MY MEDCINE I WANT MY MEDCINE It turned out that Laura hadn't given him his nine o'clock dose, which accounted for some of his aggression. He left the table at intervals to lie on the floor and wail. Because he was behaving like a baby I treated him like a baby, which was not appropriate behavior on my part; it's very difficult to balance the respect appropriate to an adult with the control needed by someone like Fred. Fred's intrinsic behavior problems may well have been exacerbated because no one had known how much he could understand, so he hadn't been expected to take responsibility for his behavior or to improve as he got older. On this occasion he sat back up at the table again and spelled IM SORRY I GOT UPSET.

As Fred started typing longer sentences another physical problem appeared. After he'd typed a couple of words, sometimes after he'd typed no more than a couple of letters, muscle tone would build up in his arm, which would become fixed in extension—that is, it stuck straight out—so Fred could no longer bend his elbow and could no longer reach the lower rows on the keyboard. When that happened his partner had to help him bend his arm and bring it back to his body. It was very frustrating because it made typing both harder and slower, and meant that Fred could only get out a few letters at a time without assistance.

After all those years of not being able to communicate his thoughts, Fred now could; and he found that his dreams hadn't come true after all. He could communicate, yes, to some people sometimes, but he wasn't cured—he still had severe physical handicaps, he had neurochemical abnormalities that affected his behavior, and he had the poor social skills of someone who'd missed out on almost every ordinary socializing experience since babyhood. Communication was about all he could do. He still wasn't living the kind of life other people lived. Like many clients, he was now blaming all his problems on his lack of speech. TALKING IS WHAT I REELY WANT TO DO IWANT TO TORK I WANT TO TORK LIKE OTHER PEEPLE I BELEVE MY PROBLEMS ARE DU TO NOT BEING ABLE TO TALK IM DOING BETTER SINCE IVE BEEN ABLE TO SPELL. His spelling was variable at this stage, a mixture of standard and phonetic, with different spellings of the same words in consecutive sentences. Before he went home after each visit I would show him the conventional spelling of the words he had spelled phonetically.

Fred was, he suggested, worse off than Anne, who was more

physically handicapped. MY LIFE IS WORSE THAN ANNIES SHE CANT HIT HER[self]. HOW DOES SHE COPE WITH NOT TALK[ing?] LAST TIME I SAW HER SHE SEEMD HAP[py] In between bursts of aggression he worked well. I gave him a written sentence comprehension test that had been designed for adults who had lost speech, and he scored nine out of ten.

As time went on Fred had new problems. Some people didn't believe he was communicating at all; IM SICK OF PEOPLE SAYING MY TYPING IS MUM. People who did believe he was typing didn't necessarily change the attitudes to him they'd developed over the years; IM SICK OF BEING TREATED LIKE IM STUPID I WANT ROSIE TO SPEAK TO GUS[3] TO EXPLAIN THAT IM OK MENTALLY — HE STILL TALKS TO ME LIKE IM A BABY. The desperate wish to talk remained and occupied most of each session at DEAL. OTHER PEOPLE TALK I NEED TO TALK JUST BECAUSE IM DISABLED DOESNT MEAN I SHOULDNT BE ABLE TO TALK I HATE NOT BEING ABLE TO TALK He seemed to think that there was a cure somewhere we were keeping from him. If there wasn't, that just meant we should work harder and find one.

A few years later there was good news and bad. Fred had taken some correspondence courses. He had more control over his behavior and was getting out and about a lot more, always accompanied by his indomitable mother. Fred still had no close friends, not because he did not want friends—he did, desperately—but because people able to accept Fred, or even people prepared to go out with him and tolerate the stares of the public, were rare. Here Fred's own prejudices got in the way. He was attending a friendly adult center half a day a week. It could have been more, but Fred did not fancy the company of people diagnosed as intellectually impaired, as he and the center's other clients all were. He participated in the same snobbishness as the rest of us, preferring the able to the disabled, preferring the society of those he perceived as his equals to those he perceived as his inferiors. He did not see that it was

---

[3] Gus was his brother's family nickname. It was this utterance that finally made Laura sure that Fred really was spelling.

exactly this preference on the part of the able which would ensure he remained friendless.

Fred discussed his prejudices with me. A point which he found particularly telling was that a year or two ago some agencies from whom he was now receiving services hadn't wanted anything to do with him because they saw him as too severely retarded. How many of the people attending the adult center could also have abilities they have been unable to show? Put like that, Fred could see that he was judging other people with disability in exactly the way he had complained about others judging him, and he did decide to give them the benefit of the doubt and increase his attendance.

On the downside, Fred seems to be losing neuromuscular control (again, this could be in part the result of the medication he has to take, rather than an integral result of his PKU), and is now using a wheelchair nearly all the time. An incident a few years ago does seem to indicate that Fred may have reduced pain sensitivity. He and Laura were off to demonstrate against funding cuts to services for people with disabilities when he slipped on his front steps. They went on to the demonstration regardless, with Fred in his wheelchair. At lunch some four hours after his fall he spelled out that his leg hurt. Investigation showed he had a fractured femur, not a condition most people tolerate for four hours without comment. If it is indeed the case that Fred feels less pain than most people that could help explain the severity of his self-injurious behavior.

Fred drew me a new bottom line. DEAL had many clients with more severe physical impairments than Fred; we had many clients who had severe behavioral problems; we'd not, however, had a client whose initial overall presentation was more negative. Fred's diagnosis, as well as his presentation, went against him. All the textbooks say that untreated or late-treated PKU leaves people severely mentally retarded. Fred certainly has severe disabilities—as with Anne, there can be no argument about that—but does that mean severe mental retardation? Who's measured Fred's intelligence? We certainly haven't. Are Fred's impairments similar to those of other people with untreated PKU, or is he different, for better or worse?[4] We only see people who don't have functional speech, so our sample may be skewed. The two other people we have seen with untreated PKU did not have physical problems as severe as Fred's, but they both had similar behavior problems, they both had been institutionalized as a result of their behavior, and they both had been labeled as severely mentally retarded. Both were also able to communicate by spelling and one went on to type without facilitation. In 1991 Fred joined a discussion group at the day center and was asked to try and write something about happiness. Laura commented, "I would like to change it a little but it is his, so be it."

I LOVE MUM GOD AND MEDICINE
IT IS MY WORLD
MY LIFE IS DIFFICULT
WITHOUT THESE I WOULD BE NONEXISTANT
HAPPINESS IS BEING ABLE
GOING PLACES TO SEE THINGS AND KNOW
I LOVE GOD WITH MY THOUGHTS
I CAN'T DO
CALL OUT TO GOD TO HEAR ME
I COULD DO MUCH MORE FOR MY HAPPINESS

The last time I saw Fred at the adult center he was charming and responsive. He seemed happier, despite his increasing physical impairments.

---

[4] PKU comes in several forms. There's a relatively benign variant which causes fewer problems even when untreated. Even people with "classic" untreated PKU are not all the same; Fred, though not exceptional, is more damaged than many.

11

The Trouble with Babble

Most people who seek help for communication problems want to talk more, but there are a significant number of people who wish they could talk less. These are the people whose speech works against them. They talk too much, or can't say what they mean, or echo what you say.[1]

One of the familiar aftereffects of stroke, for example, is not being able to say what you mean. My uncle Jim had a classic left-hemisphere stroke—that is to say, the blood supply to parts of the left hemisphere of his brain was temporarily impaired, and cell death occurred. When he recovered consciousness it was discovered that he couldn't move the right side of his body or speak. As he recovered he gradually regained some movement on his right side. At first he fed himself awkwardly with his left hand, then awkwardly with his right hand. Finally he held the knife in his left hand and the fork in the right, reversing his previous dominance. Eventually he learned to walk again using a four-pronged stick. Long before this stage was reached his speech started to come back.

Surprisingly, the frustration of having no speech did not

---

[1] Or say what they don't mean. The most extraordinary example of this is possibly Tourette syndrome, a neurological disorder whose sufferers may swear compulsively.

compare with the frustrations of having erratic speech. Uncle Jim had been a great storyteller. When his speech came back he tried to take the stories up again, but the right words wouldn't come. He'd ask about his grandchildren, but the name he'd say wouldn't be the name he'd meant, so Aunt Jean would be telling him about George when he really wanted to know about John. At the table he would start to ask for the salt and be stuck for the word and have to mime shaking. Starting into one of his favorite stories he'd say, "Now, during the war, when I was in Melbourne, no, not Melbourne, Sydney, no, not Sydney, Brisbane . . ." By the time we'd discovered he meant Port Moresby the impetus for the story had gone. Old friends were offended when Jim got their names wrong. They thought his memory had been affected. It had, but not in the sense we usually think of. He still recognized his friends, he could remember all they'd done together, but he couldn't put it into words because he couldn't retrieve the words he needed.

Uncle Jim's problems were relatively minor, but they still frustrated him, irritated his family, and affected his social life. Some of his friends felt uncomfortable and stopped dropping in. Uncle Jim took to avoiding social situations where he was likely to meet people he didn't know well (he stopped going to the pub, for example). By the second Christmas after his stroke Uncle Jim's speech had returned to the extent that a stranger meeting him would not realize there was anything wrong. The family, though, could see differences. Jim didn't put as much detail into stories now; he'd avoid using names, saying "Give my regards to your sister" instead of "Give my regards to Mary," and when he was tired his nominal aphasia would return and he'd muddle the names of things and people. There were lasting social changes, as well: he'd had a few shocks to his self-esteem since his stroke, he'd had to come to terms with the change in the way people approached him once he had a disability, and his speech impairment had forced him into a listening role. Jim seemed happy enough, but he never recovered his previous ebullience. A relatively minor speech impairment had a deep effect on someone who'd made his way in the world, who had an established position in society and in his family, and who had social strategies to cover up or compensate for difficulties.

Jim's speech went through three stages after his stroke: nonexistent, unpredictable, and finally, almost normal with a residual word-finding problem. Children who suffer similar brain damage before birth or in early infancy will usually have their speech development affected, and their speech may plateau (temporarily or permanently) anywhere along the continuum between these levels. They don't, however, have Jim's advantages. Firstly, children who have never been able to speak fluently have not had a chance to establish themselves. They have not had the typical infant's experience of controlling the world with their speech. Never having been certain what words will come out when they try to speak, they may feel their speech controls them. Secondly, those around the children do not know what kind of potential for language they have, or what kind of understanding underlies their obviously abnormal speech. Children whose speech does not progress may never experience normal interactions.

Because our judgments of intellectual capacity, both formal and informal, are strongly tied to speech, a child who says the wrong words, who gives "silly" answers when asked questions, is likely to be seen as stupid. A child who can never find the word he wants, or a child who cannot make his tongue do what it should, can come to associate speech with tension, embarrassment, and failure. Because the child is a child, he does not have the strategies—the gestures, the time fillers, the "It's on the tip of my tongue" explanations and evasions—that Jim used when he couldn't find the right word. Children with severe speech impairments often develop behavioral problems. These may simply be a result of the frustration inherent in not being able to say what you mean, but this frustration may also be exacerbated by the reactions of the people around them. In many children, too, the speech impairment is part of a broader disability such as Down syndrome or autism, so it is more likely to be seen as the unavoidable corollary of a global disability than as a specific, potentially treatable, speech problem.

Ralf was a thin man of medium-tall height; exactly how tall

was hard to say because he was always hunched over. He was twenty-nine, labeled as intellectually impaired, and looked a classic Forrest Gump. He had very thick glasses and peered at people through them while he talked. Ralf could talk; it was, in fact, his most noticeable characteristic. He talked and he talked and he talked. The original assessment from his day center said:

Speech
Long spells of irrelevant, interruptive, and childish conversation—subject fixations—seems compulsive but can be completely quiet. Speech is reasonably clear and construction and expression quite complex and correct.

Social Interaction
A great deal of offensive attention-seeking and manipulative verbal behavior. Interested in others, gets on OK with people apart from extreme irritation generated by aforementioned behavior.

The report summed up by saying:

Ralf's conversational patterns and presentation make him irritating, unpopular, and unacceptable in social situations.

There's a lovely word for talking too much; it's called logorrhea—like diarrhea, only with words. Ralf had it worse than anyone else we'd ever seen. Throughout our first meeting Ralf talked continually. He didn't just talk about the weather either. He used the kind of speech that might be expected to hold the attention of teachers and caregivers. "She's hitting me! My teacher's hitting me! Let me alone, you! I'll belt you! Let me alone! It's a tricky one, you know. I'll show you! Watch out!" in a singsong tone, again and again, every time he was touched in any way whatsoever, even if someone brushed up against him. Were these echoes of someone else's complaints? Had he been at a school where he was hit? His file didn't say.

Ralf wasn't DEAL's first talker; if he had been, he wouldn't have got to first base. We would have said, "Right, his speech is clear, he's obviously got all the structures, his problems must be psychiatric or intellectual and in either case don't come under the heading of severe communication impairment. He sounds *stupid.*"

Ralf had no history of cerebral trauma, and he'd never had a full neurological examination. (Few people with developmental problems, and very few people who've been diagnosed as mentally retarded, ever do.) He was epileptic, which in the circumstances suggested brain damage. If he'd had head injury his speech disturbance wouldn't have been so unusual—a familiar symptom of brain injury is uncontrolled talking; what the Russian psychologist Luria described as "a flood of uncontrollable verbal paraphrasias." Fortunately, we'd already seen people like Marco at DEAL—people with autism who had bursts of forced repetitive speech which didn't appear to reflect their thoughts or their intentions accurately. We were aware of the possibility that Ralf had more to say than he was saying and went on with the assessment. It was difficult to interrupt Ralf's flow of speech to get a question in, and I didn't necessarily get an answer if I did. Despite this I got him to do a few simple math questions on a Vocaid. He had an intention tremor and I steadied his arm while he pointed. There was a gap between his spoken utterances and his typed messages. When I asked Ralf the time he said, "I don't know" and then "past two," but when I asked him to type it he typed 2:20, which was correct. I wrote down the number ten and asked him, "What's that?"

"I don't know."

"It's a number. What number is it?"

He typed, TEN.

If I asked him questions that had a specific right or wrong answer he'd usually say, "I don't know." If I gave him another crack at answering he often gave an approximate answer in speech. If I helped him to type it, he usually got the answer right. However, it was very hard to get him together enough to give a typewritten response. There was the constant accompaniment of his complaints—"Stop it, I don't want to do this, go away, you're hurting me"—which all seemed to lead him down new tracks (particularly if anyone responded to them) he'd have to follow.

We didn't get into anything substantive at that first session, but when we saw him again he got straight onto a Communicator. TRYING TO TALK IS HARD TYPING IS TOO SLOW STOP ASKING QUESTIONS WHO ARE YOU? WHY DO YOU TALK TO ME AS IF I CAN UNDERSTAND? His chatter was still disconcerting, and I was still unsure whether it was better to respond to his speech or just look at the message on the typewriter.

During Ralf's third session I brought out the Talking Teacher and put on a Missing Letter game. A word would flash up with a gap in it, and Ralf would have to type the missing letter. He scored 99 out of 100, despite talking nonstop, saying stereotyped, repetitive phrases like "Stop looking at me" that had absolutely no relation to the words flashing up on the screen. The only time he had any difficulty was when the word flashed on the screen was "letter–__." That word appeared to be complete, it didn't have a gap in it, and despite every hint I could think of Ralf couldn't see that the word was "letters."

By this time it was clear that it was better not to acknowledge Ralf's speech at all unless it was original and appropriate. If I responded to Ralf's "You're hurting me!" by saying, "I can't be hurting you, I'm not touching you," that resulted in a whole lot more speech, not necessarily clarifying the point, whereas if I just didn't reply, Ralf's utterances would probably die out. I started shushing him. I found that saying "Sssh" or putting my finger to my lips was far more successful than saying "Be quiet," possibly because the words triggered more speech. He took up shushing himself—so we'd have a burst of disconnected stereotyped speech, then Ralf saying to himself, "Shhh, shh."

When Ralf articulated original sentences, sentences that really were what he wanted to say, he spoke much more quietly, and while his articulation wasn't completely perfect, the rhythm of what he was saying was much more normal. As Ralf's typing became more fluent he showed that he was fully aware of the effect his speech had on other people. It distressed him, but he couldn't help it. SHALL I GET BETTER? I WANT TO STOP TALKING. YOURE A BIT WISE ABOUT TALKING—ONLY SHOW ME

HOW TO STOP TALKING I DONT WANT TO TALK ALL THE TIME
He was somewhat perseverative about this, but his concern was
understandable. His speech was his most significant disability.
STOPPING TALKING IS HARD   IM LAZY ABOUT STOPPING TALK-
ING TALKING IS HARD TO STOP   I STILL TYPE SLOWER THAN I
TALK   I EXPECT TO SAY LESS BUT MAKE MORE SENSE.

Ralf's problem was that to the casual observer his speech provided apparently conclusive evidence that he was either severely intellectually impaired or severely psychologically disturbed.
This being the case, he had trouble convincing people that his
spelling was genuine. He could see the difficulty; I REALLY
NEED TO BE ABLE TO TYPE BY MYSELF. He wasn't at that stage
yet. We changed his support to having him hold one end of a
rod while his communication partner held the other. I REALLY
TYPE BETTER WITH THE STICK. He could see where it was
leading: YOU ENJOY LOOSING US[2] ON THE WORLD.

Over the next two years Ralf's speech did improve. He was
able to shut himself up more often, and was able to say more of
what he wanted when he was talking. He'd always been able to
sit without talking in his yoga relaxation classes, when everyone
else was quiet; he could now be quiet when he was typing and
when he was in his training center's communication group or
current affairs class. JUST FOR A MINUTE I CAN STOP. I found
that when there was a pause, if I talked to Ralf as I would to
anyone else, in a soft voice, talking not just about his own problems but about what had been happening to me or what was
going on in the world, I could see a different person. The compulsive talking stopped, the obsessive eye contact stopped, his
facial expression relaxed and normalized, and I was often able
to have a completely sensible real conversation with him in
speech—unless he was excited or distressed about something,
when all his stereotyped sentences came back. As he said, I
THINK OK, BUT I CAN'T KEEP TRACK OF WHAT I SHOULD BE
DOING.   MY SPEECH GETS IN THE WAY.   I'M TOO READY TO
TALK—I CAN'T INTERRUPT MYSELF.   DO YOU THINK I'M GETTING
BETTER? (punctuation inserted)

[2] Letting us loose.

Even though Ralf could now occasionally speak novel sentences, he still depended on typing for most communication more complex than "hello" or "good-bye." His typing was particularly slow, even by our standards, because of his intention tremor. He had to have a guard over the typewriter keyboard to stop him hitting more than one key at a time, and he could only type with one finger. But as he said, TYPING IS SLOW, BUT I CAN SAY WHAT I WANT. Even when the compulsive speech didn't take over, he still couldn't necessarily say what he was thinking with his voice. Often he didn't even like to try, because trying to talk was quite likely to start the whole routine up again.

Now when training center staff talked to Ralf on adult topics as if he understood he would sit quietly, listening, and participating either by using his typewriter or by the occasional appropriate spoken comment. He conversed about things in general. He joined in discussion groups. He wrote some short poems for a literature assignment.

MOST OF MY THOUGHTS ARE LIKE BEAUTIFUL FLOWERS;
MOST OF MY THOUGHTS ARE LIKE QUIET BIRDS FREE.
BUT SOMETIMES MY THOUGHTS ARE HELL AND HORROR
AND I NEED A FRIEND TO COMFORT ME.

And:

A DREAM IS A CHANCE TO BRIGHTEN DARKNESS;
A DREAM IS A DELIGHT—DON'T LET IT GO.
A DREAM IS A LIGHT IN A DIM DISTANT HEAVEN—
DON'T EVER LEAVE YOUR DREAMS TO DIE LIKE BIRDS IN THE
    SNOW.

He still had a problem convincing some people that he comprehended what was said to him. I DONT THINK PEOPLE WILL BELIEVE I CAN THINK WHILE IM TALKING. I DONT MAKE SENSE, AND PEOPLE THINK IM SENSELESS.

Having people doubt his understanding stressed Ralf and brought back the logorrhea. Presumably Ralf had neurological damage that affected his word retrieval, together with some damage to one of the inhibitory systems that meant it was hard for him to stop himself talking. Ralf's consciousness of other people's reactions to his babbling speech set up its own tensions and produced its own feedback loop. In some way Ralf sounds like a woman with Tourette syndrome that Oliver Sacks once saw on a New York street, where one tic set off another tic and people's reactions to her stimulated still more tics.

Ralf had not been able to make his way around his disability. He had reached the age of twenty-nine without ever being treated as normal in any way. His behavior, and the responses of those around him, had become entrenched, and people saw him as irritating and unacceptable. This has now changed somewhat. Ralf's control over his speech and behavior has improved, and some people around him are now aware that he doesn't mean what he says. Nonetheless, by the age of thirty his life seems to have been settled for him. Only limited change seems possible. He lives in a hostel for people labeled as intellectually impaired and attends a segregated day program. He had little academic education when he was a child, and it is now difficult for him to make up lost ground—the necessary support systems just aren't there.

Ralf needs people around him who understand his problems and react sympathetically and appropriately to his speech, and he also needs partners to practice his typing with. He doesn't have the skills that would allow him to use the telephone or write a letter, and without someone to help him he can't even get information on possible educational opportunities. He couldn't actually take a course without help with his transport, help with communication on campus, and help with producing his assignments. Like most people with severe difficulties, Ralf knows that ultimately his achievements will depend as much on others as on himself.

Wayne, a pleasant, well-mannered twenty-one-year-old living on a dairy farm, had problems similar to Ralf, but had the enormous advantage of dedicated family support. Wayne could cut his own sandwiches, which among our clients put him into the Olympic athlete class, but his speech was confined to wordless grunts, whispers and shouts, echolalia, and meaningless stereo-typed single words and short phrases like "Go away!" Like Ralf he laughed a lot for no apparent reason. There was some dispute about his capacity. His mother, Yvonne, said he under-stood everything that was said to him and could follow compli-cated instructions; his training-center instructor doubted whether he understood the meaning of "yes" and "no."

Yvonne wrote later that she'd nearly stopped Wayne from coming down to DEAL in the first place. She hadn't had any-thing against DEAL; it was just that she knew Wayne hated assessments, and she didn't expect him to receive any signifi-cant benefit from yet another one. In the end, though, his instructor got her permission and brought him to DEAL. We tried him out with a few straightforward yes/no questions. When he answered orally his answers seemed to be fairly random, which meant either that he didn't know the answers or that because of his speech problems he said "No" when he wanted "Yes" and vice versa. I wrote "Yes" and "No" down on a piece of paper and asked Wayne to point to the appropriate one to answer my questions. Not only did he always point at the right answer, he also said it, correctly, when he pointed at it. We moved to a Communicator and he typed, PLEASE TELL MUM I KNOW HOW TO SPELL. I told Wayne and his instructor about our experiences with other people who had unexpected spelling skills, which they had been able to use to compensate for their speech problems. Wayne asked, DOES ENYBODY NOT SPELL? Wayne had low muscle tone, an index finger with all the strength of cooked spaghetti, and trouble starting a movement, so we gave him finger exercises and supported his arm while he typed.

By the next visit Wayne's disconnected speech initially seemed to have lessened, possibly because this was his second visit and he was more relaxed, but when he became excited it came back. The tension level rose every time a new activity started. I ONLY LIKE DOING THINGS IF I'M GOING TO GET THEM RIGHT. I tried him on a multiple choice reading test designed for adults with aphasia; he was unwilling to try it, seeing it as a test, and looked away from the material, saying, "No, no." I encouraged him to go on, and he did well. He needed a lot of encouragement throughout, and it was clear that confidence was a major problem. DO YOU SEE MANY PEOPLE LIKE ME? EVERYONE THINKS IM STUPID.

Wayne came to DEAL once every two weeks, and showed reasonable progress while he was working with me. He wouldn't work with Yvonne, though. She made the fortnightly trip from the country for months without getting anything from him, and it's a credit to her that she didn't give up. Then she burst out, "He's working with you, and he's working with his new instructor—we're excited about that—but he won't work with me. And I'm getting jealous." Wayne reached out for her hand and typed, WELL, I SUPPOSE ILL HAVE TO BITE THE BULLET. It caught Yvonne completely off her guard, and she nearly fell off her chair.

Six months later Wayne was typing at home faster than he worked at DEAL. He produced pages on the family's old Commodore 64 computer. I WANT TO GO TO A PROPER SCHOOL, I WANT TO DO A PROPER COURSE IN ENGLISH SO I CAN WRITE BETTER AND I CAN HELP OTHER CHILDREN LIKE ME. I DONT WANT OTHER KIDS TO WAIT AS LONG AS I HAVE. He was enrolled in a bridging course in English at a tech college.

He worked with his father, with some difficulty. WOULD YOU LIKE TO WORK ON THE COMPUTER WITH ME THIS AFTERNOON? I LOVE YOU, BUT YOU DONT SEEM TO UNDERSTAND THAT I CANT HELP BEING SLOW. I DONT MEAN TO SOUND GRUMPY, BUT YOU GET SO IMPATIENT WITH ME. I DONT WANT YOU TO STOP LOVING ME, I NEED YOUR STRENGTH SO MUCH. I WOULD LOVE TO BE ABLE TO MOVE FAST.

Wayne wanted to be independent, but he didn't want to give up the closeness of the hand support.

One of the DEAL speech pathologists gave Wayne more speech therapy. I KNOW WHAT I WANT TO SAY BUT IT DOESNT COME OUT. He was dyspraxic and had poor lip control, which meant that his speech was short on consonants. She coached him in consonant sounds and mouth movements. He could copy some spoken words, but he couldn't copy the mouth movements if they were made silently, and he couldn't initiate them. I AM REALLY TIRED OF PEOPLE WANTING ME TO SUDDENLY BE NOISY. I WANT TO BE QUIET. Similarly, he could imitate hand signs but not initiate them.

His muscle tone and his speech varied from day to day. On days when his muscle tone was very low his irrelevant speech was much reduced but typing was a chore, and on days when he could type easily he also used more inappropriate speech, so that his overall communication didn't gain much either way. It reminded me of the early days with Penny, when her hand skills and her screaming had gone up and down together.

Wayne gave us new insight into the practical problems of people who had difficulty initiating movement. TO LEARN TO TYPE IS NOT EASY, BECAUSE MY MUSCLES KEEP TELLING ME TO STOP AND THEN I FIND IT HARD TO START UP AGAIN. JUST DOING THE SIMPLEST THINGS TAKES SUCH A LOT OF EFFORT ON MY PART, TO KEEP ON FLOWING ALONG IS A CONSTANT BATTLE. IT'S LIKE HAVING TO WALK UP HILL FOR KILOMETERS, ON AND ON.

On good days: I FEEL LIGHT AND FREE, EVERYTHING WORKS REALLY WELL, I LOVE DOING THINGS. I FEEL HAPPY. On less good days: I AM JUST ABLE TO GET MY MUSCLES TO WORK. I FEEL AS IF I AM PUSHING UP HILL ALL DAY, IT IS BEAUT TO GET TO BED. EMOTIONALLY I FEEL DRAINED ALL THE TIME. On bad days: ITS DREADFUL. I AM SO SLOW IT GETS ON MY NERVES. IM GRUMPY ALL DAY BECAUSE ITS SO HARD AND DRAINING TO GET GOING.

We may say that we all have days like that, but with Wayne it's not in the least metaphorical. He was sitting in the car one hot day while his mother went in shopping, and when she came out he was suffering from heat exhaustion. Wayne's mother knew he could wind the car window down, because she had seen him do it. She wouldn't have left him in the car if she'd thought he couldn't. When she asked him why he'd just sweltered without trying to do anything about it he replied, MY MUSCLES WOULDNT LET ME WIND DOWN THE WINDOW OR OPEN THE DOOR, THEY JAMMED UP ON ME.

He was serious in his wish to spare others going through the same trials. He told reporters from the local paper about it all. He said of me, I LOVE THE UNUSUAL WAY SHE MAKES FUNNY FACES AT HER CLIENTS, IT HELPS PUT YOU AT YOUR EASE.

Four years after starting at DEAL Wayne started to type without any physical support. In 1993 he passed Contemporary Society at senior level, and he is now taking a creative writing course. He has been working on his independent-living skills, but initiating movement is still a problem.

For Ralf and Wayne their personas are defined by the nonsense that comes from their mouths. Even when you know that there's someone inside, when you know that they can type sense, it's hard for your responses not to be governed by what's being said. The constant interference from their speech is worse for them than being mute, and their words make it harder for them to change the way the world sees them.

Ralf, Wayne, and many others like them are isolated by their speech. The very skill that most of our clients strive and pray for has turned and savaged them. They are the most unlikely sufferers of severe communication impairment.

12

Eventually We'll Know

Finding that Holmes was too absorbed for conversation I had tossed aside the paper and, leaning back in my chair, I fell into a brown study. Suddenly my companion's voice broke in upon my thoughts.

"You are right, Watson," said he. "It does seem a preposterous way of settling a dispute."

"Most preposterous!" I exclaimed, and then suddenly realizing how he had echoed the very thought of my soul, I sat up in my chair and stared at him in blank amazement.

"What is this, Holmes?" I cried. "This is beyond anything which I could have imagined."

He laughed heartily at my perplexity.

—Arthur Conan Doyle, "The Adventure
of the Cardboard Box," *The Memoirs of
Sherlock Holmes,* 1893

Jill was a plump fair-haired fourteen-year-old with blue-gray eyes and large blue-framed glasses. When her mother, Pam, first brought her to DEAL in 1987 Jill, diagnosed as autistic and intellectually impaired, attended the same special school as Marco, and lived at home with her parents.

Jill had various minor behavior problems (like pulling her

sweater up in public to scratch her naked stomach) and some major behavior problems (including screaming loudly when frustrated in any way). She was reported to have "largely irrelevant speech," and a reading age of six. Her score on a recent Peabody Picture Vocabulary Test was appropriate for a child of five and a half.

Jill's speech was loud and fluent, but mainly consisted of echolalia and confused repetitions unrelated to anything around her. When she was stressed in any way, her speech became louder and more compulsive. At these times she talked as much as Penny screamed, and with about the same amount of communicative success. We knew she wanted to tell us something, but it was hard to work out what. There was so much "rubbish" that if Jill did manage to get out what she meant, we were likely to miss it. It was as though she would try and say something, not get it out correctly, try again, fail, try again, fail, and repeat the sequence ad nauseam, becoming progressively louder and more frustrated. Jill could read single words aloud, but when asked to read a passage aloud only an occasional word bore any relation to the words on the page. She could write only a few words that she had practiced for years, and even then her handwriting was immature and ill-formed. As a substitute for her inadequate handwriting I offered her a keyboard.

Jill lacked index finger isolation, and in order to point with her index finger sticking out she needed her hand molded to hold her other fingers back. As well as helping Jill to hold her fingers back, the hand-holding also served to slow down her typing. Her partner needed to pull her hand back from the keyboard after each letter to prevent a recurrence of the perseverations, the unnecessary repetitions, and the inappropriate completions which plagued her speech.

With this restraint Jill's typing was fluent and she spelled, I NEED TO USE A CANON [Communicator]—I CAN'T TALK RIGHT. Given our experiences with Anne and Marco, this was not especially surprising. What was disconcerting was Jill's speech. If we asked her a question, she would say the wrong answer while typing the correct one. While she was typing she would even say a wrong letter aloud when hitting the right one.

Jill's mother, a secondary school teacher, was understandably confused. Here was Jill speaking rubbish but apparently typing sense; failing at reading aloud, but apparently typing correct answers to a reading comprehension test while at the same time saying incorrect answers.

We lent Pam a Talking Teacher, an educational toy with spelling activities and voice output, to use with Jill, and she replicated the DEAL assessment at home. Jill practiced spelling activities on the Talking Teacher every day, with her mother holding her hand to mold her fingers and to slow her down. At Jill's second appointment, one week after her first, I noted that "Jill didn't vocalize as much when using the Communicator this time, and the letters she did say matched the letters she was typing." Despite the rapidity of Jill's speech and the slowness of her typing she could communicate more effectively using the latter. Even though she might type only a few sentences at a session, at least they were sentences she wanted to say.

On Jill's third visit to DEAL her mother asked me to give her a second Peabody Picture Vocabulary Test, using a different set of words. In the Peabody the examinee has to indicate which out of four line drawings shows the word said by the examiner. Jill did the test with no hand support and obtained a score appropriate for an eleven-year-old. Words correctly answered included "precipitation" and "archaeologist."

As Jill's unfacilitated performance was still affected by perseveration, her score understated her actual word knowledge. Multiple choice tests are especially useful for assessing people who cannot speak or write, but they are unfortunately particularly vulnerable to the other problems that are often associated with hand function impairments—problems such as poor eye-hand coordination and perseveration. An examinee with perseveration may point repeatedly to the same location on the page. Each question in the test involved choosing from a different set of four pictures. If the correct answer to question one was the second picture in that set, and the correct answer to question two was the second picture in the next set, then Jill would point to the second picture in the third set whatever the correct answer was. It was impossible to prevent this unless I held her back physically. Whenever it became obvious that Jill was perseverating I would allow her a long pause between questions to break up the pattern, but it would only become obvious that she was perseverating after she'd already made several mistakes and thus lowered her score.

Our immediate aim was for Jill to use a keyboard to converse with her mother. Reducing the amount of physical support Jill was given was not a high priority at that stage. It was more important for her to start using a keyboard at her special school. Another goal—improving Jill's speech—was added unexpectedly when it became apparent that improvement was occurring spontaneously.

Initially Jill used the Talking Teacher with her mother only for structured activities, but within two months she was using it for general conversation. Her parents bought her a Communicator. Gradually support was faded from her hand to her elbow or sleeve. At first, when hand support was withdrawn, Jill needed to grasp a pencil in the palm of her hand to help her keep her unwanted fingers back.

It was easier to fade physical support than it was to achieve the goal of having Jill use a keyboard at her school. Her special school teacher came to DEAL for the first time some six months after Jill's first appointment. Jill behaved quite well. At the start of the session she typed sentences on her Communicator, saying the letters (correctly) *before* she hit them. She did some structured activities, in particular replacing missing letters in words, with her teacher facilitating. Despite this promising start, the Communicator was not a success at school. Apparently Jill became tense and aggressive under pressure, and there was a considerable amount of skepticism expressed about the possibility of her having the literacy skills that we were suggesting.

At the start of the next term Pam reported that the school did not want anything to do with the Communicator. By the end of the year, however, Jill was able to keep her fingers back without either being held or holding on to anything. By the start of 1988 she had become almost independent in her typing, only needing the person sitting beside her to put a hand on her leg for moral support.

It wasn't clear what the hand on the leg did, but it seemed like a security blanket. With it Jill was calm and focused, and her output made sense and was appropriate to the situation. Without it she became tense, her typing speeded up, and her output was like her speech—strings of recognizable words with no discernible meaning. At this stage her teachers became more accepting, and Jill did start using a keyboard at the school. As her academic skills became more evident, and as her speech and behaving improved, the school gave positive support to Pam's search for a secondary school prepared to accept Jill in 1989. Finding a secondary school for a fifteen-year-old who hasn't studied the regular curriculum is never easy. When that fifteen-year-old has a history of autism, negative intellectual assessments, and behavior problems, considerable diplomacy is required.

Jill's behavior had improved, but it still had some way to go. She had been known to walk into DEAL and punch me in the stomach before screaming (literally) down the corridor to raid the cookie jars in the kitchen. Cutting out the hitting and screaming was a substantial improvement, but it still left Jill raiding the cookies. The question was how much we should tell prospective schools and how much we should let them find out. If we could guarantee that Jill would behave perfectly in her interviews then the schools needn't be told anything, but unfortunately stress and unfamiliar situations frequently triggered explosions.

Later Jill wrote:

> I felt so angry that my life was about to turn around. I had a nice comfortable existence. Existence it was, rather than living; I never knew what living was, but existence I knew and I thought I had exactly what I wanted. My parents meant well and were doing the best they could for me. It really was a prisoner's existence.

Sometimes the prisoner doesn't want freedom. I felt the fortress walls I had built for my autistic survival were being besieged. The very idea that my mother should invade the world I had built for myself was too frightening. The enemy must be resisted. I hated the idea. Yet something within me wanted to be part of the human race.

However, having an alternative means of getting her message across had taken the pressure off Jill's speech. Once she could type she spoke far less, but what she said was generally appropriate (unless she was tired or stressed, when her old speech patterns reappeared). The reduction in Jill's echolalia and inappropriate speech after she began to use the Communicator was so heartening that she had regular sessions with Jane Remington-Gurney, a DEAL speech pathologist. Jane's efforts were largely directed to giving Jill a repertoire of routine responses and utterances that she could use spontaneously in predictable situations, such as when greeting someone. Jill's word-finding problem responded well to cueing, so her mother was shown how to cue her with the expected response by giving her the initial sound when necessary. If Jill was asked the capital of Australia, for example, and hesitated, her mother would say "cuh" and Jill would then say "Canberra."[1] Jill herself was encouraged to use her Communicator whenever she was nervous or her speech failed her, to reduce the risk of frustration.

These strategies worked well, and the amount of appropriate speech Jill used continued to increase while her inappropriate speech diminished. Toward the end of 1988 her special school principal recounted that at the conclusion of Jill's initial interview at what was to be her new school he had watched with some trepidation as she approached the high-school principal with her hand outstretched. To his relief Jill shook hands with aplomb and thanked him for having her.

Jill's communication at DEAL during her first year of typing

---

[1] The effectiveness of this cueing showed that Jill's problem in answering questions was not due to ignorance but was an information-retrieval problem. After all, if she hadn't known the capital of Australia all the cueing in the world wouldn't have enabled her to say it.

contained interesting insights on her disability and her view of herself.

She was making an effort to control her behavior. I'M DOING MY BEST TO MAKE MYSELF NORMAL. Her constant failure, though, contributed to her low self-esteem. I'M POTTY [slightly crazy] I HEAR VOICES I WANT TO BE NORMAL, BUT IF I CAN'T BE I WANT PEOPLE TO BE SCARED OF ME — NOBODY LIKES ME ANYWAY HOW CAN YOU HELP ME? I'M POTTY

She met Anne, and rather surprisingly, if you think of Anne's disabilities, wrote: I WISH I COULD BE LIKE ANN[e] I'M TOO RETARDED   I CAN'T HELP IT   I PUT MY FINGER UP MY NOSE BEFORE I CAN STOP MYSELF   I'M SORRY I'M SO STUPID I CAN'T HELP IT   I'M NOT CLEVER ENOUGH TO DO THINGS LIKE ANN[e] I did my best to explain that we thought her problems were neurological, not just stupidity or naughtiness. I STOPPED TALKING BEC[ause] I COULDN'T SAY WHAT I WANT TO   NOW I HAVE TO STOP MY HANDS DOING WHAT THEY SHOULDN'T.

She was occasionally aggressive. HATE THIS FIGHTING   WISH I DIDN'T HAVE TO DO IT I'M SADESTIC [*sic*] I LIKE HITTING PEOPLE Why? THEY CAN DO THINGS I DON'T. We tried to switch her over to other satisfactions. What did she like doing? I LIKE MATHS I CAN DO THEM ALL RIGHT. She was pulled in all directions. YOU MAKE IT SOUND SO WISE — HELP ME TO WORK WITH YOU PEACEFULLY. Then after another outburst, GO TO HELL — NO, HELP ME NOT TO SCREAM, I HATE SCREAMING. Even here she had mixed feelings. NOISE IS HARD TO DO WITHOUT, NOISE WAS FUN. LET ME LEAVE Why? TO GO HOME Why? TO FIGHT WITH MUM Whenever she made a mistake she tore the tape off the Communicator and ate it.

THE PRISONER IN ME WAS GOING TO BE DEFEATED, BUT NOT WITHOUT A FIGHT THAT WOULD BE BITTER AND CRUEL. I USED EVERY TRICK I KNEW TO RESIST HAVING TO COMMUNICATE. I DROVE MY FAMILY TO THE POINT OF DESPAIR AND MADE LIFE HELL FOR MY POOR TEACHER.

She could see that typing gave her a way around her speech problems, but that didn't mean she had to like it. I PUSH

WORDS OUT, BUT THEY AREN'T WHAT I WANT TO SAY. I LIKE
TYPING, BUT I WISH I COULD TALK. She knew she needed to
talk, not type. I HAVE TO TALK LIKE OTHER PEOPLE BECAUSE I
WON'T HAVE ANY FRIENDS IF I DON'T. . . . TO TALK IS MY
GREATEST WISH.

I TALK FUNNY SOMETIMES—YOU MUST HELP THE WRONG
WORD USUALLY COMES INTO MY MOUTH EVERY TIME. We tried
to work out strategies to deal with her speech problems. WHEN I
GET EXCITED I SOMETIMES SAY WORDS THAT DON'T MAKE SENSE.
HOW I DEAL WITH THIS IS TO MAKE MYSELF SAD. A WARY PERSON
HAS TO ASSIST ME WHEN THIS HAPPENS.

For a time she became more aggressive. I'M SICK OF BEING
TREATED LIKE A BABY. I CAN'T TALK, SO I GET ANGRY. BIND ME
UP—I CAN'T STOP HITTING PEOPLE. TILL NOW I THOUGHT IT
WAS BECAUSE I WAS EVIL. . . . VERY HARD TO STOP. Sometimes I
could hardly get a word in edgeways. SHUTUP—ARE YOU LIS-
TENING TO ME?

Her mother had a lot to put up with and a lot of changes to
go through. OF ALL THE MOTHERS I HAD TO HAVE I HAD TO
HAVE YOU I LOVE YOU MUM. I NEED TO TALK TO YOU ABOUT
MY COMMUNICATION PROBLEM LIKE MY SPEECH, MY LOUD VOICE
AND MY BODY.

On one visit she asked DOES ANNIE EVER BEHAVE BADLY? Perhaps a tiny tantrum now and again. TELL HER I FEEL SORRY FOR
HER HAVING SOMEONE LIKE YOU BOSSING HER ROUND.

When Jill was good, she was quite charming. I HAVE BEEN A
BIT OF A PILL I GET SAD I CAN'T TALK I CAN FORGET THAT
WHILE I'M WITH YOU BECAUSE YOU DON'T CARE

A lot of discussion centered on Jill's educational future. Over
the summer holidays Jill spent some time with another DEAL
client who had successfully moved to high school. She was keen
to follow her, but was understandably anxious about whether
she would be accepted.

DO YOU BELIEVE THAT I COULD FIT IN AT SCHOOL? I WORRY
THAT WHAT I WANT WON'T BE RIGHT. TEACHERS GET ANGRY
WHEN YOU GET THINGS WRONG Don't be silly, I said, of course
you can do it. YOU DON'T MEAN IT YOU'RE SAYING ALL THAT

JUST TO MAKE ME FEEL GOOD   RANTING AND RAVING ABOUT ME DOESNT BEEF ME UP—I KNOW YOU

If she didn't want me to praise her, and if she didn't want me to criticize her, what, then, pray, did she want me to do? TO INGEST MY EVERY WORD AND BELIEVE IT. Fifteen months after starting to type Jill wrote: TYPING MEANT I HAD THE MEANS OF MAKING MY OWN WISHES KNOWN. I FOUND THIS SCARY BE-CAUSE YOU CAN'T IMAGINE WHAT IT IS LIKE BEING LOCKED INSIDE YOURSELF ALL YOUR LIFE AND THEN HAVING THE KEY TO ESCAPE YOUR SELF IMPRISONMENT; SOMETIMES THE PRISONER LIKES SECURITY. Interestingly in the light of what was to hap-pen, she continued, SOME PEOPLE HOPE I AM MANIPULATED BY MY MOTHER WHEN I TYPE TO ORDINARY PEOPLE BUT THERE'S NO WAY I WOULD LET THIS HAPPEN.

Jill's typed language showed some signs of the word-finding problems that plagued her speech, but to a much reduced extent. There was no written "echolalia," and Jill's typed vo-cabulary was extensive and was used appropriately. The most significant problem she had was with perseveration or auto-matic completions. When perseverating Jill would get stuck and hit the same combination of letters repeatedly. Using a notepad computer with a liquid crystal display gave her the option of erasing her errors before printing, but sometimes she would type and retype the same error, erasing it each time.

Jill had a particular problem with some common words, a problem which had effects similar to Marco's obsession with "bread." Jill had no particular obsession with the words (most of which were structural, like "but"); rather, she appeared to have stored the motor patterns for typing certain common words so well that if she started typing any word starting with the same letters as these words she would automatically type her "standard" word unless she concentrated intently. For example, the most common word starting with an upper case "i" is the first-person singular pronoun. Correspondingly, every time Jill typed "I" she followed it with a space, and if she had in fact wanted to start a sentence with "It" or type "Ireland," or "I'm," she then had to erase the space. This difficulty had been lessened when Jill's hand was held by a facilitator because the facilitator slowed her down and broke the pattern by pulling her hand back from the keyboard. It continued to be a problem when Jill typed without facilitation, though she did monitor her output and erase mistakes.

At the start of 1989 after doing a lot of catch-up work with her mother over the summer vacation Jill moved to the local junior high school, the first time she had ever attended a regular school. She entered ninth grade. She had full-time integration aide support; that is, an aide was available to accompany Jill to all classes and monitor her behavior at breaks. The first essential was to inform her integration teacher and aides about Jill's communication impairment, and to teach them the skills necessary to act as her communication partners. Teacher and aides were very supportive and quickly acquired the skills necessary to facilitate Jill, who sought more support from unfamiliar communication partners and needed more support again to maintain the speed necessary to keep up with the class. Developing close relationships with a number of new people in an unfamiliar environment was of course not easy, and Jill's year was not without its problems. Nonetheless, by the end of the first semester she appeared to be achieving an acceptable academic standard in the subjects she was studying.

Some critics of facilitated communication training have suggested that the facilitator may in fact be the originator of the communication. One wrote,

> One explanation of this phenomenon is that with some clients any form of physical contact, such as a hand on the shoulder, can be used, even unconsciously, to provide cues to correct responding; a "Clever Hans Effect". . .

Clever Hans was a horse whose owner, Wilhelm von Osten, spent many years attempting to teach him arithmetic. Hans appeared to be an excellent pupil, and correctly answered his teacher's questions by tapping his hoof the requisite number of times. It eventually transpired that Hans's responses were being cued, unintentionally, by tiny postural cues given by his teacher:

Even a slight elevation of von Osten's eyebrows, a subtle flaring of his nostrils, were sufficient to halt the counting.

Unfortunately, the investigation into Clever Hans was concerned only with whether he could or could not do sums. Equally important questions about the cooperative nature of the communication involved and the broader implications for interspecies communication were not even asked. Ever since Clever Hans's "unmasking" in 1904, his name has been synonymous with the production of desired behavior by unintentional cueing.

Clever Hans responded to his teacher's cueing to get the piece of carrot he was given for each correct answer. The standard scenario for the Clever Hans Effect involves an alert interested subject (A), a task (B), a reward (C) desired by A, a trainer (D) who wants A to achieve B, and a cueing system (E) recognized and understood by A, and used but unrecognized by D, who is nonetheless the controlling figure in the interaction. That is, D manipulates A through C and E to achieve B. The situation in which A manipulates D through E to obtain C—that is, a situation in which the "horse" manipulates its trainer, using information unwittingly provided by the trainer—has not previously been described. (It has been pictured, however, in a cartoon beloved of psychology lecturers—one rat saying to another, "Gee, we've got that psychologist well trained. Every time we push the lever he gives us some food.")

The possibility of a facilitator exerting undue influence certainly cannot be discounted. Deliberate, conscious assistance is probably rare, if only because it is likely to be obvious. The degree of movement and control needed to direct another person's finger to a given typewriter key, without any participation by that person, is considerable. For complete accuracy it would be necessary to grasp the person's finger. Subconscious cueing, however, would in its nature be more subtle, and hence more difficult to detect. It could also only work with a cooperative subject—a person who was interested, for whatever reason, in taking cues, and who voluntarily moved a finger toward the communication display or keyboard. My experience with Jill sheds light both on the facilitation process and on the risk of applying to people analogies derived from animals.

Near the end of Jill's first year at her new school her integration teacher, Alice, who had always provided excellent support for Jill, her mother, her teachers, and her aides, called me about an unusual problem the aides were having.

Jill was generally typing with physical contact from her aides, the level of physical contact varying from a touch on the knee to actual hand support. She had just completed the final ninth-grade examination, and Alice had two problems. The first problem was that none of Jill's integration aides wanted to work with her next year—not because she was behaving badly, but because they believed that Jill was telepathic and that she was intruding into their private lives. Earlier in the year one aide with whom Jill had developed a very close relationship had felt that Jill was telepathic. The aide had been worried about the effect this was having on her, and she had left half-way through the year. Alice had discouraged discussion of the incident, but most of the other aides had since had similar experiences.

The second problem was that there was now considerable skepticism about Jill's exam results, because the aides were saying that the results were not hers—she had picked up the answers from their thoughts. They said that if they deliberately tried to turn themselves off, Jill gave no answers, and they had therefore decided that they were transmitting the answers to Jill.

An appointment was made for Jill to come to DEAL with her mother one Friday afternoon after school. I started the session by making it clear that I had heard from Alice about the problems Jill had been having at school. I suggested a few possible explanations and asked Jill if she had anything to say. She picked up my hand, showing that she wanted full hand support. We had previously worked through hand support to light shoulder contact or independent typing, but I had not partnered her for six months, and the last time she had come to DEAL with her aides she had not been at all cooperative.

Pam interrupted. She said that she had experienced

telepathy herself. She knew she could make Jill type things. She would be helping Jill type (Pam did not hold Jill's hand; she just put a hand on Jill's knee, a touch on her shoulder, or a hand on her waist) and then what would come out would be something Pam was thinking of and that Jill did not know about. Pam could not think of any explanation for this that did not include telepathy.

First, I asked Pam to make me type something in the same way that she thought she made Jill type. Pam wrote down a message without showing me and put her hand on my leg. I tried the mind-reader trick of circling the keyboard limply with my hand and dropping it whenever I felt an increase in pressure, but it did not work. I did not get Pam's message; when I dropped my hand on a letter Pam was surprised, not approving, and if she was giving signals I did not register them.

Second, I asked Pam to show me how it worked with Jill. Pam thought of a message, one that she said Jill would not know, put her hand on Jill's leg, and looked over at Jill's typing as it appeared on the display of the laptop computer Jill was using. Yes, Pam said, looking distinctly worried, Jill was typing what Pam was suggesting to her.

There was no reason to doubt it, because what I could see when I was watching the pair of them work was a lot of hand movement on Pam's part, far more than when her hand had been on my leg. There was a clearly visible change of pressure across the fingers, and a visible change of pressure from back to front of the hand. I pointed this out to Pam, saying, "There's your explanation. You mightn't be aware that you're doing it, but you're cueing her." Pam was theoretically aware that she might be cueing Jill; she just could not see how she was, and she really did not believe my explanation. She said, "Well, yes, you say I move my fingers and my hand, but how on earth do I do it when I'm just touching her ponytail?" I imagined Pam did it the same way as when she had her hand on Jill's knee, so I asked her to let me run a third trial, in which Pam was to transmit a message I had chosen to Jill by holding on to her ponytail. Jill was quite cooperative through all this. The message, chosen with some care, was "Eventually I'll know."

There is a magician's trick that works the same way. The quirky physicist Richard Feynman describes it in his wonderful book *Surely You're Joking, Mr. Feynman*. A carnival comes to town, and a respected citizen is asked to hide a five-dollar bill anywhere in the town he wants to. And then the mind reader gets to work.

> He takes the hand of the banker and the judge, who had hidden the five-dollar bill, and starts to walk down the street. He gets to an intersection, turns the corner, walks down another street, then another, to the correct house. He goes with them, always holding their hands, into the house, up to the second floor, into the right room, walks up to a bureau, lets go of their hands, opens the correct drawer, and there's the five-dollar bill. Very dramatic!

This isn't Ouija board influence, and the banker wasn't pushing an inert mass. The mind reader was reading bodies. As he explained,

> . . . you hold on to their hands, loosely, and as you move, you jiggle a little bit. You come to an intersection, where you can go forward, to the left, or to the right. You jiggle a bit to the left, and if it's incorrect, you feel a certain amount of resistance, because they don't expect you to move that way. But when you move in the right direction, because they think you might be able to do it, they give way more easily, and there's no resistance. So you seem always to be jiggling a little bit, testing out which seems to be the easiest way.

It was unlikely that the kind of pressure Pam had been using was accurate enough to direct Jill to a specific letter on the keyboard, particularly as all her cueing appeared to be subconscious, ruling out the use of a formal code such as Morse. Pam could cue Jill to a general area of the keyboard by giving rough signals—an up or a down or a left or a right—and she must have had some sort of acceptance signal: perhaps she relaxed when the letter typed was what she expected and tensed up when it was not.

For such a crude cueing system to work at all Jill had to be a very active participant, with a good knowledge of spelling.

My hypothesis was that Jill was doing two things: she was picking up Pam's unconscious signals, and she was checking on her guesses and extending them through the use of word-prediction and message-prediction strategies. One useful thing about the English language is that it is highly redundant. That means, among other things, that it is often easy to look at a few letters and guess what the rest of the word is, and to look at a few words and guess what the rest of the sentence is going to be. The partial sentence "Ca__y___gue___wha__I_hav__wr_____" is easy to read even though it employs only fifteen of the thirty-four symbols (including spaces) in the full sentence. That is what I thought Jill had been doing. Again, it must be stressed that to use such word-prediction strategies as a component of a system for interpreting nonverbal signals requires a highly sophisticated knowledge of vocabulary and language structures on the part of the student.

The message "Eventually I'll know" started with the letter most frequently used in English, but as the message had very low redundancy, it was not easy to predict, and it should show something about the strategies Jill and/or Pam used.

Jill started off extremely well. She got the first letter, which must always be the most difficult one, E, and continued V E N, without an error or a backspace. And then she guessed it was a whole word, and of course typed a space. Pam obviously gave some kind of a "no" signal, and Jill erased the space. Then she actually got the T, which, again, was very impressive. But then she did another space, making EVENT; got Pam's subconscious "no" signal, erased the space, and then went further back and erased the T. Still no "yes." After erasing the T she erased the N, so that she was back to EVE, and then she put an R and space to make EVER. She presumably got the "no" signal again, so she erased the space and put Y and space to make EVERY. Her mother's response was still negative, and Jill got up and threw a tantrum. It was a very minor tantrum, for Jill, but if the session had been in the classroom, it would have stopped at that point.

What was really interesting in the exercise was how Jill had got the first E and the V. What Pam was doing—and again, I could tell by looking very closely—was putting pressure on Jill's ponytail, tensing up when Jill moved. By this time Jill was obviously very good indeed at picking out signals. I had noticed that when she had picked up my hand earlier she had used a very light grasp. A firm grasp would have meant that the pressure would blank out any subtle unconscious signals. She had moved her hand around with very low muscle tone, and if I had any messages to give her, either consciously or unconsciously, she would have received them. All this was very interesting, even in the unlikely event that Jill had no spelling skills at all. Remember, Jill has autism. What are people with autism singularly bad at, and apparently very uninterested in doing? Picking up cues. Whether Jill was typing sentences, or whether everything she typed was cued, she was doing things that were thought to be impossible for people with autism including sitting still, in close contact with another person, for hours. Of course, finding out how Jill had worked her "telepathy" did not solve all our problems; in some ways it made them worse. At the beginning Pam had been very worried about the possibility of ESP. Once she was shown that she had in fact been cueing Jill, she accepted it, and that brought her to the next worry: if she had been cueing, what did that say about Jill's output in general? She was very anxious to know how much of it was Jill's and how much was her facilitators'.

We did a bit of good old-fashioned message-passing to reassure her. Pam picked up a list from the table—a sheet of work, consisting of thirty or forty different questions, which had been made up for another client—and said, "Let me ask her something from that and you won't know what I've asked her; I'll just show her the written question and you won't know what it is." "No," I said, "let's do it a bit better than that; we'll do it double-blind and you won't know what it is either, because if you're cueing her . . ." At this time Pam was sitting on the other side of Jill, but she tended to get anxious and move in closer and closer until she put her hand on Jill's legs without realizing she was doing it. I shut my eyes, folded and refolded the paper, held it out to Jill, and said, "Okay, now type the answer to the question that's at the head of the page." Which she did, correctly. When we tried it again with another question, a sentence completion, "Bunch of_____" however, she typed PEOPLE—a possible answer, but only just; "a bunch of people" is colloquial and unlikely. Still, Pam was starting to cheer up a bit.

Next I quizzed Jill about what she had been doing at school, what they had actually studied in history, what they had actually studied in geography, et cetera, questions to which Jill and Pam knew the answers and I did not. What we got was more evidence of her communication problem and another demonstration of the difficulties of getting something unknown out of a person subject to automatic completions. Jill would type the first letter or couple of letters of an answer, Pam would say yes, that's correct, and then Jill would switch into her stereotypes—that is, common words starting with a particular letter or letters—that Jill seemed unable to prevent herself from typing once she had typed the first letter(s). Jill's stereotype words—"very," "feel," et cetera—are well known to her aides. One of her major problems in school was that if she started typing any word beginning with *V* she would type VERY. The word she wanted to spell now turned out to be "vegetation," which had not only the *V* but the *E*. This was fatal. Jill spent a long time typing VERYs and erasing them. A facilitator who does not know the answer cannot stop the rubbish. Jill did eventually answer the questions, about what they were studying in history and in geography, in detail. (I wouldn't accept generalities; she had to give the details right down to the ecology of the seashore.)

All this took about two hours. One interesting thing was that apart from a few excursions to the kitchen to get cookies (quite understandable, since it was now after six o'clock and she hadn't had anything to eat since lunch), Jill was staying in the room. On previous sessions at DEAL she had left the room every five minutes. She had been at secondary school all year, of course, obliged to stay in the classroom, and her behavior had changed very markedly for the better.

Nonetheless, her persistence on this occasion was exceptional and was possibly due to a desire to get to the bottom of the problem. Jill certainly realized that she was in trouble; there were no aides prepared to work with her next year, and even her exam results were in doubt.

When Jill was questioned about why she had been playing games with her aides and mother she was not very forthcoming on the subject. However, she was at least now prepared to admit that it was not ESP, that she was picking up physical cues. I outlined a few scenarios that I thought were about right, and Jill sat there smiling at me. The explanation that she was happiest with (partly because it reflected the most credit on her) was the Sherlock Holmes model, where Holmes tells Watson what Watson's been thinking about, by putting together what Watson has looked at, where he has been, and what he has done previously; magician's cold readings are done along the same kind of lines. On some occasions, too, I suggested, it might not be Jill picking up cues from the person concerned, it would be Jill flying a kite. She knew a fair bit about her aides, and their families, and their social situation, through ordinary conversation, and it would be very easy to start typing out something speculatively. If she got a response—increased interest from the aide, say—she would keep on going on the same topic, and if she got no reaction the interpolation would be assumed to be one of her stereotyped phrases. At this point Jill actually managed to wink, which for her was really quite a feat.

If the exercise with Pam was a sample of how Jill had used "telepathy" at school with her aides, she could not lose. If she was guessing well, she went on; if she seemed to be losing her facilitator she could return to regular work as though she had just lost track for a minute, or throw a tantrum and stop. Because Jill had such a problem with automatic completions, her aides were used to her typing something and then immediately erasing it. She often had several goes before she completed a perfectly ordinary sentence, so a false start wouldn't attract any attention. She didn't have to score every time—just one hit a week would be enough to get her the reputation of being telepathic.

The next step was to prevent a recurrence and to reestablish Jill's credibility by getting her typing without any physical contact. I had moved Pam well away from Jill in order to be sure that I was the only person she could see or touch when she answered questions about her school subjects. However, Pam was always edging back—it was not that she wanted to fake things, but she was really interested in what was coming up on the display—and when she moved nearer, Jill would of course reach out for her. I asked Pam to go outside while I battled on with Jill.

I told Jill, "The way out of this is to type by yourself. You don't need support. You've got to type by yourself. And you are going to do it by yourself before you leave here today. I do not care how long it takes. I am going to sit here and you are going to type me a sentence about what you did in geography in first semester, without me touching you." She had told me the topic, seashore ecology, earlier. I said, "Type me something—anything—that shows me you learned something in geography in first semester." I sat back so Jill could not see my face. She began by mucking around, typing garbage words and stereotypes. Each time I had to let her type a couple of words before I could see that they were not going to make a sentence, when I would erase them, and Jill would start over. This went on for half an hour or so. It was really difficult, and I did not have any obvious sanctions if Jill chose to give up. She seemed tired and depressed. At one stage she did get up and try and go to the room where her mother was, but only once. Given her readiness to leave the scene when placed under pressure on other occasions, this was quite remarkable. On the other hand, she sat there screaming *Eeeeeeeeeeeeeeeeeeeeee* in my ear for quite some time.

After half an hour we finally got to the point where if I counted "one—two—three" Jill would hit a letter on the "three," which would make sense. This would go on for five or six words, and then the rubbish would come out again and Jill would muck up. The rule I established was that if Jill did not hit a letter by the time I counted to three I would erase the last letter, regardless of whether it looked right or wrong. I did that a few times, and she did not come back on task, so I erased the whole lot and told her to start over, which she did. We got almost complete sentences typed without any physical contact five times. It was a very slow process and clearly not functional. Jill looked like death. She seemed to be trying, but she certainly was not getting anywhere very much, and the stereotyped words kept coming. And then at last I remembered a technique I'd used with Marco. When people perseverate on one letter, and keep hitting it again and again rather than moving on to the next one, occupational therapists teach them that after they hit the letter they have to pull their hand back and tap the table in front of them. Sometimes at DEAL we put a red dot there, for a target. It is a standard occupational-therapy technique, and it has been used for over fifty years. "Okay, this is what you do," I told Jill, holding her hand to start her off, to show her the movement pattern, while we typed THE QUICK BROWN FOX JUMPS OVER THE LAZY DOG a few times. "Now you try. Tell us what the problem is—tell us why you're mucking up like this— tell me why I'm getting all this crap."

We had fought our way through what must have been no more than a dozen sensible words in the past hour. Suddenly, with the new technique Jill's typing came together. And it was fast! I started off saying, "Letter, table, letter, table," to give her the pattern. She very quickly got so fast that I could not fit the two words in before she hit the letter, so I would just say "table" after she hit the letter, and I would still keep getting out of the rhythm because she was too fast for me. And it was all there! And it was all making sense! We had broken out of the stereo-types. And Jill was beaming from ear to ear obviously thinking "I can do it! I really can do it!" By this stage she may have been doubting herself. She typed that she couldn't stop herself typing stereotyped words; she would hit a letter, and then the other letters would come so quickly, automatically, they wouldn't stop. Even now, every now and again, if she lost her concentration, the obsession words would come in, but she would erase them by herself. It was wonderful. After she had typed a couple of paragraphs I said, "Yaaay, you've got it, you've got it, it's wonderful!" and her mother could hear that we were both suddenly very cheerful and came in. I explained what had happened, and she could read the sentences that were on the display.

Of course Pam wanted to see Jill typing with no contact, so I said, "Okay Jill, type me a sensible sentence about a specific assignment you did in geography in first semester," and she did. It was about the roots of plants on sand dunes. It was not quite as fluent as her earlier sentences, and I had to halt her twice when she went off into stereotyped words, but, as Pam said, "Now that I've come in the stress level has gone up." I pointed out that we were now three and three-quarter hours into the session, Jill had not had any dinner, it was a quarter to eight on Friday evening, and I thought that had something to do with it too. But Jill's typing was still functional. It was still independent. If the aides limited themselves to restraining her every fourth word or so to stop an obsession word coming through, that would be enough, and they would not be making her type the right answer. Jill was still beaming.

If Pam and Jill practiced a lot over the summer vacation—no hands-on, or hands-on only when it was necessary for speed or in a difficult public situation—my hope was that Jill would get better at overcoming the stereotyped words herself. She probably would not have to go on tapping the table; after people have been doing that for a while they just pull their hand(s) back a little way before they go to the next letter, and that is usually enough. It is programming this microsecond break into the routine that is helped by the table tapping.

Why had Jill pretended to be telepathic? I think that once she realized that she could play people for suckers she quite enjoyed it; many children would, and a person who had had no power over others for most of her life might obtain additional satisfaction from successful manipulation. She had been devalued all her life because of her disabilities, and was now being given special status as someone who had uncanny powers. What student, furthermore, would pass up the opportunity to have someone telling them the right answers? This meant, of course, that her exam results *were* suspect. How long Jill had been picking up cues from her communication partners, and how much of her communication had been cued, was a question it was impossible to answer.[2]

The content of her early typing appears unlikely to have come from her partners—her style was consistent, regardless of whether she was partnered by her mother or me, she made spelling mistakes, and her sentences were shorter and simpler than ours. Certainly Jill had never typed my thoughts, if only because I had mainly partnered her in the early days, when she needed to be slowed down, and hence had been pulling her back quite firmly, making it much harder to pick up any cues. Also, I suspect, Jill probably didn't initially have good enough spelling skills to use the sophisticated prediction techniques that she'd shown when trying to get "eventually." Her typing without any physical contact confirmed that she did have good literacy skills and that she had absorbed something from her high school lessons, so it was also possible that a lot of Jill's work was in fact her own. The problem was, which bits?

Why did Jill's mother move her hand on Jill's leg or when holding her ponytail? The answer to that probably relates as much to the slowness of nonspeech communication as to the nature of the relationship between Jill and Pam. Communication through spelling and typing is slow. People generally speak at a rate of 150 to 200 words a minute. A one-finger typist may not produce more than twenty words a minute, significantly slower than handwriting, much less speech.

Jill was using typing to replace both speech and handwriting. Once she went to secondary school she had a significant amount of homework to do. Both this and her everyday conversation required Pam's involvement. Many individuals find it stressful to sit back and watch a person do something slowly that they could do much more quickly themselves. Pam had this experience every day with Jill's homework. At the same time, she was having to devote a significant part of her evenings and weekends to facilitating Jill's typing.

---

[2] This episode left many questions unanswered. Unfortunately, DEAL, a tiny organization with a long waiting list, did not have the resources to pursue them.

One integration teacher described her own experience of facilitation as being similar to being a passenger in a car with a novice driver. The passenger moves her body as if she is driving, pressing the floor at the lights and moving into the turns. If Pam experienced facilitation in this way, when Jill was answering questions to which she knew the answer—for example, "What is the capital of Japan?"—her own subconscious movement may well have provided cues, as she both expected Jill to get the answer right and wanted to speed up her typing. Once Jill registered how her mother moved she may then have had a choice of starting any answer herself or waiting for her mother to cue it for her. After Jill had developed this technique with her mother it must have been very tempting to use it at school.

Because everyone was conscious of the difficulties in integrating someone with autism into the regular classroom, all energies had been focused on enabling Jill to control her behavior so she wouldn't cause a disturbance. Her aides were instructed to make any minor accommodations necessary for Jill to remain calm. If holding her hand was what it took, well, that was what they did. And this may have been how it started. At first Jill may have genuinely wanted her hand held for emotional support, even though she was well past the stage of needing that kind of physical support when she was typing. Once she started to relax she obviously realized that handholding had other possibilities.

It's important to reiterate that not everyone who has her hand held is seeking or receiving cues. To do what Jill was doing actually requires more skills than most beginning typists have. By no means all facilitators give cues, and not all students have any interest in seeking them. Marco attended the same secondary school as Jill, and for a while they shared aides, including a couple who said Jill was "telepathic." At no stage did any of the aides feel that Marco was "telepathic," or that he was picking up cues. His movements were always so forceful and his determination to do his own thing so great that I doubt if even deliberate cueing would work. Certainly I had precious little success in trying to prevent him typing anything he had set his mind on. Jill's search for cues had two rewards for her. Firstly, she liked being a drama queen and center of attention—she enjoyed the notoriety of being "telepathic." Secondly, she wanted to get things right, and she didn't mind sacrificing her individuality to do so.

Following on this incident, and aware that there had been some discussion of telepathy and cueing by other academics and facilitators, I asked Anne if she was telepathic. She said no, and went on to illustrate how such mistakes may arise.

> I'm not telepathic but I can pick up vibes. I notice where people look and how they respond when I start to spell something. I can spell what they want me to, if I want to and they are not good facilitators.
> I can pick up how people feel by their hand contact and hand movements, but I can't pick up what they are thinking about without other cues. If I know what has formed their opinions I can sometimes get the subject. Only some people give cues, not every facilitator does. I have met two that I could fool into thinking I was mind reading.

The existence of unconscious cues may also cast some light on one form of experiment devised to test communication occurring through facilitation. Several studies have recorded that when different questions are set to facilitators and students, the students occasionally respond with answers appropriate to the facilitator's question (Hudson et al 1993). While it is clear that any such answer comes from the facilitator, Jill's story shows that simply to state that baldly does not necessarily end the story. To date, the presumption of the test givers has been that any evidence of cueing indicates that the test takers are empty vessels merely being "filled" by their partners, in the way that Clever Hans presumably was. This explanation always was questionable; after all, taking cues (or stealing the exam paper) doesn't necessarily mean you don't have any skills, just that you feel you can do better if you don't have to risk having them break down.

Jill's story and Anne's comment indicate that experienced communication-aid users can sometimes tell what answers their partners expect them to give. During a test which deliberately sets out to make communication difficult and sets up maximum interference, it is possible that a student, able to tell that his facilitator expects an answer different from the one he thinks is right, might lack sufficient confidence to choose his own answer. There are a number of common undergraduate psychology experiments which demonstrate this phenomenon with subjects who are college students with a dozen years of schooling and test-taking experience behind them, not people with severe disabilities just learning to communicate. In both the psychology experiments and the facilitation tests a minority of responses involve a straight swap in which the student gives the other party's answer. In the case of facilitated communication the student has to either accept the facilitator's influence or have the skills necessary to pick up the cues given by the facilitator for the swap to be possible.

When issues of telepathy or cueing come up it is important not to throw out the baby with the bathwater. Pam's first reaction when Jill's "telepathy" was shown to be the outcome of her ability to pick up cues was to assume that everything Jill had ever typed resulted from cueing. This was not so. In order to use the minimal cues she was getting, Jill needed excellent literacy skills and considerable experience with facilitation. Showing that a person has picked up cues does not mean that she has no communication skills or that all her communication is tainted.

Jill practiced the table-tapping technique with her mother over the summer vacation. She gradually became more confident in typing without physical contact. Halfway through the next year Alice reported that she was typing with no physical contact or table tapping unless she was stressed, and was able to use ten fingers when she was copy-typing. No further stories of telepathy emerged, and her next set of exam results, which were still satisfactory, were accepted as her own. After another year, she chose to leave school and concentrate on acquiring the skills necessary to live independently in the community.

Jill's speech continued to improve and when I last heard of her she was working in a regular part-time job, traveling by public transport, and using a mobile phone. She now uses typing like the rest of us, for correspondence and other writing tasks.

13

No Way In

The people I've written about so far have been people who have had problems getting words out. They may have had problems understanding language, but they've been ordinary problems; like the rest of us, they have difficulties understanding some things, and how much they understand in a given situation varies depending on the familiarity of the situation, their age, their experience, and their vocabulary.

There is another, much smaller, group of people who can hear but who cannot process speech—the word-blind.

The study of the neurology of language began in the 1860s when Paul Broca, a nineteenth-century French surgeon and anthropologist, described the damage which he found on post-mortem in the left brains of people who had expressive aphasia—problems with speaking—after strokes. Thirteen years later a German neurologist, Carl Wernicke, identified another area behind Broca's area that was associated with the reception of speech. People with damage to what has come to be known as Wernicke's area have difficulty decoding speech; they have what is called "receptive aphasia." As with other impairments, there is a continuum of difficulty, from people who can decode short routine utterances but not complex sentences to people who don't even recognize that other people are talking at all. Some adults who have had damage to

Wernicke's area can still read, and in those cases written language provides an alternative way in, but some people also lose the ability to decode print.

Broca's and Wernicke's areas are not like the nose and chin, found in invariant locations. In some people the corresponding functions are carried out by the right-hand side of the brain. Furthermore, the difference between the two forms of damage is not as clear-cut as I have just made it sound. People with Wernicke's (receptive) aphasia may have fluent but disordered speech, and people with Broca's (expressive) aphasia may have problems with both the expression and the reception of speech. And finally, Broca's and Wernicke's areas are certainly not the only brain areas associated with the expression and decoding of speech, and the expression and decoding of speech may not be the only functions in which they participate. As is often the case, the initial explorers produced a simple map of the main features, leaving it to later travelers to add the details.

Receptive aphasia most commonly occurs as a result of damage to a mature brain, typically as a result of a stroke. It is distressing and frustrating, but at least the person with the problem knows the function of speech, even if he can no longer decode it. He understands social situations and is generally still able to decode gestures and facial expressions. Some people with acquired receptive problems can still read and write; their communication can take place purely in the visual mode; their overall understanding of language has not been affected, just their ability to decode speech.

Most people with severe receptive aphasia as the result of a stroke also have expressive aphasia, meaning that they cannot talk or cannot talk very much. Sometimes, however, speech comes back to a greater or lesser degree without any improvement in the receptive problem. This is no problem if everyone around the person with the receptive problem *realizes* that she has a receptive problem. My aunt Judy was a case in point. She was living in a hostel when she had a stroke and lost speech. It took some time for everyone to realize that she had also lost the ability to decode speech, but had retained the ability to read.

She had severe arthritis and could not write, and her ability to read was discovered by giving her written instructions and observing her response. After some months her speech slowly started to return, and this confused the issue more than somewhat. The staff who had been with her since the stroke knew that Judy still did not understand when they spoke to her and that you had to write things down, but when Judy moved to a new unit most of the staff just thought she was going deaf.

The main problem arose with Judy's family, who did not see her as often. They had no trouble accepting that she couldn't understand them while she couldn't speak. However, when her speech returned they assumed her understanding had come back also, and all the explaining in the world would not convince them otherwise. "But she can hear," her sister would say; "she turned around when the door banged." And of course Judy *could* hear—she just could not decode speech. So her sister would ask Judy questions and be frustrated when she got no answer, and would tell her to do things and be angry when she didn't, ending up shouting at her like the archetypal cartoon Englishman shouting at the foreigner who willfully refuses to understand perfectly good English.

Judy had disabilities other than her aphasia and was not out and about in the community. Bridget was, and her receptive aphasia caused major problems for her and her family.

Bridget spoke beautifully and could talk intelligently about art and literature. Her hair was stylish, her clothes elegant and expensive. She could still process written language to some extent, at least sufficiently to get some information from newspapers. She had perfect manners and was very aware of facial expressions and the nuances of body language and behavior, but as far as our speech pathologist could determine she had no understanding of speech at all.

A pharmacist before her stroke, Bridget, a widow, insisted that she was perfectly competent to live alone and manage her own affairs. Most people meeting her casually would have agreed, but currently she was staying with her married daughter. It was the daughter who brought her to DEAL, and she was having real problems. Bridget's lack of speech comprehension would have been problem enough, but it was exacerbated by the fact that Bridget covered it up.

Bridget did not tell people she could not understand them. She pretended she did understand, and gave all the right body language responses, smiling and nodding to show she was following. If the person she was talking to stopped talking and waited for a response Bridget responded to what she thought had been said. If it was just a brief predictable interaction she would often be quite successful. I used to meet her when she came to monthly meetings of the stroke group we ran. She would come in smiling, look at my badge, and say, "Hello, Rosie, how are you?" I'd say, "Fine, thanks, how are you?" and she'd say she was fine and make some comment on the weather. I would respond predictably. We would agree that it was cold and she'd say, "See you later," and go into the meeting. No one listening would have thought there was any problem, and indeed other people in the waiting room often assumed Bridget was on the staff, because clearly there was nothing wrong with her speech. The difficulty came when new topics were introduced. Bridget would comment on the weather, I would respond by saying that I hoped it would be better before my holidays started next week, and her receptive problems would show up—she would nod and smile and say, "Yes, it is cold for this time of year, isn't it?" I've often wondered since whether Bridget consciously covered up her receptive problems (in the same way that some people try and hide deafness) or whether the concealment was unconscious. Could she have been confabulating the other channel of conversation, "hearing" what she expected to hear?

This would all have been trivial if Bridget had only been engaging in routine social interactions, but she wasn't—she was trying to run her affairs exactly as she had before her stroke. Like some people with acquired deafness, she was becoming mildly paranoid as things kept going wrong, and she accused her daughter of messing up her arrangements. For example, Bridget still insisted on using the telephone. This would have been fine if she had just used it to pass on news to people who knew of her disability, but she didn't. Bridget had been a professional woman. She was used to giving orders and expected her orders to be obeyed without questions. She would ring up a plumber and ask him to come and fix the blocked sink on Thursday afternoon. The plumber would say he couldn't make it in the afternoon, what about the morning, and Bridget would assume he was saying the afternoon was fine and say okay. He'd arrive in the morning and find she'd gone shopping; she would stay in for the afternoon wondering why he didn't come, and eventually her daughter would have to sort it out. Often the daughter was blamed by both parties, by the plumber for not keeping the appointment he thought she'd made and her mother for interfering with her arrangements. This was trying enough, but worse was to come.

One day the daughter called in some distress to say that Bridget had told her that she'd been to the family lawyer to seek his advice about cashing in some investments to buy an apartment so she could live by herself, away from her interfering daughter. Could we possibly call the lawyer and warn him about Bridget's receptive problems, and at least suggest he write everything down for her? Unfortunately, the speech pathologist felt there was also some doubt about Bridget's ability to comprehend complex written language, so that wasn't going to resolve all of Bridget's problems—and anyway, we had no right to intervene. The daughter called the lawyer herself and described her mother's difficulties. He refused to believe her. Understandably, given the everyday experiences of lawyers, he accused her of having ulterior motives. "Your mother is an exceptionally intelligent and articulate woman," he said. "She listened carefully to all my advice and agreed with it." Reluctantly he agreed to call us, but was totally unreceptive to our therapist's explanation of receptive aphasia. Bridget spoke beautifully, she responded appropriately to his greetings, and she outlined her financial situation clearly—how could there be anything wrong? He had prepared various documents for her to sign and she had looked at them carefully before signing. There was no question of her capacity. In one sense he was right—Bridget *was* perfectly capable of making intelligent decisions given good information. It was getting that information in to her that was the problem. There was no question of duplicity on the lawyer's part. He was genuinely convinced of Bridget's understanding, and we could not convince him to ask her the questions that would have shown him otherwise—just asking Bridget her name, out of context, would have been enough. Where there was a context, such as a form to be filled in, Bridget could usually either read or predict the questions and answer appropriately. How the lawyer felt later when Bridget complained to the Law Institute that he had not followed her instructions I don't know.

Bridget was somewhat unusual in that it is relatively uncommon for someone to retain perfect speech and have such severe processing difficulties, but the cause and timing of her problems were typical: a stroke in late middle age. It is possible to have similar problems from birth or early infancy, a prelingual receptive aphasia,[1] which, like prelingual deafness, has more wide-ranging effects than the acquired disability. Severe developmental receptive problems in isolation are rare. A standard textbook, *The Development and Disorders of Speech in Childhood* (Morley and Court 1963), said: "In over 20 years we have seen only two children who could be described as having a true receptive disability for speech." Morley and Court were talking about children without any other disabilities. Unfortunately, severe developmental receptive problems are more likely to accompany other disabilities, in which case their true nature may be overlooked, and the lack of understanding equated with overall learning difficulties.

Terry was one child whose receptive problems had been overlooked. I first met him in St. Nicholas Hospital. The hospital was a miserable place, and Terry had been just about the most miserable child in it. He had an unusually long face and unusually short hair. His hands were unusually thin, with long palms and thin blush fingers. He had cerebral palsy. In St. Nicholas terms Terry was physically able—at the age of ten he

---

[1]Here, as in many areas, U.S. usage is different from Australian and British usage. In the United States the term "aphasia" is applied only to adults with acquired speech problems. Elsewhere it is used to refer to children who have similar problems from birth.

could sit up and shuffle around, though not walk. For years he was the only mobile child in his ward, and in the hospital environment this mobility, ironically, was an additional handicap. When Terry was crawling or bunny-hopping around he tended to fall over the quadriplegic children lying on the floor, and to prevent this he was restrained all day in a small playpen. Terry could also use his hands more than most other residents. In St. Nicholas this wasn't an advantage either. What Terry did with his hands was put them into his mouth, often making himself sick, and then wipe the saliva or the vomit off on his hair, which is why the staff kept it so short. He was totally without aggression, he wasn't destructive, and he had absolutely no activity other than putting his hands in his mouth. He had no speech.

None of the other children in his ward had anything like normal speech, and all of them had severe movement impairments. Most of the staff were not native English speakers. Possibilities for personal interaction were very limited indeed. Despite this, nearly every child had relationships with some other children or some staff. Terry didn't. His unattractive personal habits accounted for his lack of relationships with the staff, but they didn't account for his lack of interaction with the other children or their lack of interaction with him. Even in St. Nicholas, there was communication. We on the staff couldn't understand what the children said, but some of them could understand each other. They all had similar severe articulation problems, the environment was so restricted that there was a predictable range of issues of interest, and they'd been together for long enough to decipher the "noises" or gestures they made to each other. Those children who could not make any attempts at speech themselves still had the possibility of responding to others' interactions, or laughing at staff jokes. Terry only vocalized when he was very distressed, which was generally when he had a temperature, and showed no interest in the speech or vocalization of others.

It was very, very hard to like Terry—not because he was deliberately nasty, but because he looked funny and smelled funny and felt funny. Even when Terry had just been bathed, force of association made me flinch if he touched me. His long weak fingers felt somehow creepy. He was rarely dressed in day clothes—there just weren't enough clothes around to keep up with Terry, so he was usually dressed in hospital nightdresses. He always had a diaper tied around his neck. The staff could spend almost the whole day bathing him and changing him. His situation was profoundly depressing.

When St. Nicholas finally closed down in 1985 Terry was among the residents moved out to group homes. The rehousing provided a hundred young people with severe disabilities with a chance at a decent life. The changes were in many cases spectacular, and Terry was among the program's biggest successes. In 1986 I was thrilled to see him at a party— smartly dressed, sitting in a wheelchair, joining in wheelchair dancing, and wheeling himself out into the kitchen to help himself to chips and a drink. He was clearly much happier than he'd been in St. Nicholas, and he was clearly much better liked. The behaviors that made him so unpopular had died away as he got more control over his life, in particular as he had achieved mobility through his wheelchair. Pushing the chair gave him something purposeful to do with his hands too.

Terry's improvement showed that communication isn't everything, because it had happened without any change taking place in his communication. He still didn't speak, and more significantly, he didn't respond to speech. He showed pleasure when people talked to him, but he didn't ever do anything that showed any comprehension of what they had said, unless they also gave a gestural cue. The staff would tell Terry that dinner was ready and he would wheel himself to the dining room, if they pointed toward the dining room when they spoke. They had noticed that while Terry liked radio and TV, what he liked to do was put his ear right on the speakers and feel the vibrations. He never showed any response to what was said—he didn't laugh at the jokes, for instance—but he loved music. Hearing tests had found no auditory acuity problem. His only reported communication strategies were vocalizing when upset and using his wheelchair to take staff members to things he wanted.

Staff from his group home brought Terry to DEAL in 1990,

when he was in his twenties. Thinking back on the Terry I used to know, and questioning the house staff about his present preferences, it seemed to me likely that from birth or infancy he had been one of those rare children with an almost total auditory word blindness.

Congenital receptive aphasia is an extraordinarily distressing handicap; people talk to you, and not only do you not understand them, you may not even register that communication is taking place. You have absolutely no concept of what's going on. Terry smiled at me, and he may have recognized me from St. Nicholas. He sat quietly while the staff and I talked, and didn't attempt to explore the room or take anything from the shelves—polite of him, but unusual for one of our clients. I began the session by asking Terry to wheel his chair over to me. He was looking at me, he could see my lips move, and he could presumably hear me, but he made no response. That could have been, of course, because he didn't want to wheel his chair over. I asked him again, again with no response. I made a come-hither gesture, and he reached for his wheels.

I had absolutely no idea what skills, if any, Terry had, but that experience made it seem that Terry was going to require different approaches from other clients with cerebral palsy. I brought out a child's toy called a Touch and Tell. It has five pictures on the front: a cat, a ball, a tree, a dog, and a toy red wagon. If you turn it on and hit the ball, say, it goes, "This is the ball"—it has quite good speech, for a toy—and if you hit the cat it goes, "This is the cat, meow." To start Terry off I took him around the five pictures several times, helping him to hit the pictures and saying what he'd hit as well as waiting for the machine's response.

After a couple of repetitions of each picture I put the machine into the mode where it asked Terry to find the pictures. In case the Touch and Tell, which had an electronic voice with an American accent, wasn't totally clear, I repeated the questions after it. The Touch and Tell rewards correct responses with snatches of music and after each correct response I signed and smiled approval. For incorrect responses, when the machine spoke, I made a Kabuki grimace, shook my head, asked the question again, and helped Terry to answer it correctly. Initially the only requests Terry was able to carry out correctly were finding the cat and the dog, when he was asked to "Find the picture of the cat—meow" or "Find the dog—woof." He was, that is, able to answer the questions which included a sound cue that did not require interpretation of speech.

When it became clear after many repetitions that Terry wasn't going to get the other pictures right I paired the picture of the ball with a circle I drew in the air; every time the Touch and Tell asked Terry to find the ball I'd draw a circle in the air. With this cue, Terry cottoned on to the round ball straightaway. I paired the picture of the wagon with a hand movement to and fro as if I were pushing and pulling the wagon. He didn't get the connection automatically, as he had with the ball, and I had to demonstrate it to him. When he was asked for the wagon I did the movement, he didn't do anything, and I helped him hit the wagon on the display and did the movement again while the Touch and Tell said, "That's right. That's the red wagon." From then on Terry consistently got four out of the five pictures right.

I didn't pair the tree with anything, firstly because it was hard to think of a movement or a noise that would adequately represent it and secondly because I wanted a check on the other items. Would Terry go on finding only those items that had a sound or movement cue? He did. Whenever he was asked to point to the tree he just didn't move. He wasn't being given a nonspeech instruction to point to the dog, the cat, the ball, or the wagon, and he didn't register that if he was being asked for something that wasn't any of those then it must be the tree. He may not have realized that it wasn't one of the others. The machine wasn't meowing or barking, so he'd know it couldn't be the cat or the dog, but if his word blindness was really severe he may have thought the machine was asking for the ball or the wagon and I just wasn't doing my cue. After showing Terry the tree repeatedly after each spoken question without any indication that he was getting the connection, I changed strategies and turned his head toward me every time the tree was requested. When he made eye contact I'd nod and help him to hit the tree. By the fourth time the tree was called for Terry looked at me spontaneously before I touched him. After that he looked at me each time the tree was requested and after my confirmatory nod he would select it. That indicated that he was differentiating between "Find the tree" and the other instructions, but I didn't know whether he was cottoning on to the word "tree," the lack of any of the other cues, or my lip movements as I repeated the machine's instructions.

I picked up a visual yes/no box, two switches labeled with "yes" or "no" in words and symbols. When the "yes" switch was pressed, a green light came on, and when the "no" switch was pressed, a red light. I tried to give Terry an extra cue by saying a bright high artificial "yes" and a very deep growly "no." Terry was very fond of coffee, and his responses were predictable, so I used the switches coactively with him to enable him to get coffee. I showed him the coffee, made "Do you want?" gestures, and assisted him to respond. With some prompting Terry reached for the "Yes."

At the end of the session receptive aphasia was an obvious possibility. In some ways developmental receptive aphasia is a more severe impairment than deafness, even prelingual deafness. The child who's born deaf is enormously disadvantaged, but in our society the defect is likely to be picked up early in life and remedial steps taken. Receptive aphasia is harder to pick up because the child can still hear. It is the decoding of speech, not the hearing of it, which is impaired, so an infant will still do perfectly well on infant hearing tests which don't rely on speech comprehension.

Lack of comprehension may be seen as behavioral, in that the child appears to be deliberately ignoring instructions that we know he can hear, or as evidence of global deficit, overall intellectual impairment. Consequently, the true nature of the inevitable lack of speech is likely to be elucidated later than deafness even in children with no other impairments. Where there are other impairments and intellectual disability is expected, the existence of a specific language problem may never be picked up. There were so many other oddities about

Terry that his failure to respond to spoken language had just been put down to intellectual impairment.

Some of Terry's behavior at St. Nicholas became clearer. I said Terry was put in a playpen, but in fact there wasn't much play to the pen; he wasn't given any toys, just left to sit. In such a barren environment the radio or television were the only sources of stimulation. Apart from music, which Terry was known to enjoy, there was nothing for someone for whom language was a blank.[2] Even the limited speech that the staff addressed to the children was a closed book to Terry. Unlike the other children, he could glean no information about what was going on from staff conversations. Some prelingually deaf people who have come to sign late in life, or have regained some hearing through surgery and developed speech, have said that prior to having access to language they thought in pictures and had memories that were basically pictorial. If Terry had global receptive aphasia he had no internal language. He may have stored the past in pictures but how could he picture the future?

On his second visit four weeks later Terry was a lot cheerier than he had been in the first session. He clearly remembered me and showed excellent recall of the activities we had done together. We started straight in with the Touch and Tell with no rehearsals or reminders and he picked all the pictures correctly on the first request with the same nonspeech cues as before, the "cues" here being my substitutes for the spoken question; I wasn't cueing Terry with the answer, I was using nonspeech signals to give him the question. He didn't make any mistakes, but if I didn't give him his nonspeech signals he wouldn't move at all. I checked Terry's ability to generalize these cues to other representations of similar items by using pictures we had around the center of other wagons, trees, and balls. He did perfectly well with this, and he enjoyed it. When I asked him a question and he knew what I wanted—not when

---

[2] There may have been other residents like Terry who nonetheless didn't respond to the deprivation as Terry did. There were certainly children who were deaf and blind, and they led miserable and distressing lives. Apart from them most of the children at least understood what speech was, though their levels of comprehension and ability to respond were very variable.

he knew the answer to the question, that is, but when he understood what the question was—his face showed real pleasure. When he wasn't sure he frowned anxiously. If he wasn't sure what was being asked he withdrew rather than give the wrong answer. He was a delight to work with.

Terry clearly had a visual memory good enough to be usable, and his motivation was good. How were we to capitalize on this? He wasn't a child anymore, he was in his twenties. The main problem was that we didn't just have to develop a communication strategy for Terry, we had to develop a communication strategy for people who talked to him. Everybody around Terry had to develop new ways of interacting with him. Sign language wasn't the answer; Terry could probably have remembered signs—he had a good memory for my gestural cues—but his cerebral palsy would prevent him duplicating them accurately. Signing could only provide a means of input, not output. Even then there would be problems. At present Terry had very little idea of what language did, of how people used it. He would need to learn not just representations and structures, but the whys and wherefores. At the moment he was in a similar position to Anne going into the supermarket for the first time, but with the difference that he not only didn't know what all those packets and cans contained; he didn't even recognize them as food.

We would need to have a sign that would indicate to Terry that someone was asking a question—a sign that meant "I am asking you . . ." that could be used to cue him to respond appropriately to ". . . do you want a cup of coffee?" Pictures are powerful, and if we taught Terry that a question mark meant "Do you want?" then he could use a picture communication book of the kind initially devised for adults who had been left with receptive aphasias after strokes. If we wanted to ask Terry what he wanted to drink we'd open the book to the drinks page and point to "?". Terry would then point to the picture of, say, the cup of coffee. Communication using this type of strategy is obviously limited, but as Terry had at the moment no formal communication at all it would still be an improvement.

On Terry's third visit three weeks later I brought out the

Touch and Tell again. He had no difficulties and remembered all the cues perfectly. The next thing we needed to find out was which of the possible stimuli Terry was responding to. When the Touch and Tell said, "Point to the tree," I woofed. Terry pointed to the dog. Next time the Touch and Tell asked him to point to the tree I repeated the question, as I always did, but drew a circle in the air. Terry pointed to the ball. So Terry wasn't responding either to the spoken words or to my lips— indeed, he didn't appear to register that he was getting conflicting information. If Terry didn't know what I wanted he would frown and do nothing. Here he seemed quite confident and responded to the nonspeech message without hesitation, interpreting my imitation of the machine's "woof" without difficulty. In retrospect, though, I'm not sure that he really registered that he was being asked to do anything before he looked at me and pointed at the tree. It may well have been that he had learned that if there was a gap when nothing (as he perceived it) happened he should look at me, and if I nodded he should press the tree.

I wanted to see what kind of concept of time and relationship Terry had, and so I asked him to rearrange a sequence of black-and-white photos in the correct order to show a simple series of actions which I knew he would have seen at his group home: boy getting milk out of refrigerator, for example, boy pouring milk into glass, boy drinking milk, empty glass, boy at sink washing glass. It was hard to get any idea of whether Terry could perform the sequencing tasks, however, because I found it virtually impossible to make him understand what the task was. If I put down a sequence of pictures in the correct order and then shuffled them up he could certainly replace the pictures in the correct order. If I didn't lay them out first, though, he wouldn't move.

There was no a priori reason why a person with an auditory word blindness shouldn't switch on to written language. Had Terry already done so? I showed Terry the words that went with pictures he was already familiar with, such as "ball" and "cat," and paired them with the appropriate pictures. (Given Terry's limited access to print I might have been better off using brand names like Nescafé, which he would have seen more often.) He quickly understood that if I showed him two words and just one picture he should point to the word for that picture, and vice versa if I showed him two pictures and one word, and he did that successfully. However, if I included in the choice a word that I hadn't shown him previously in connection with its picture and asked Terry to choose that picture he withdrew his hand and looked upset. If I showed him the words "dog" and "cat," for instance, where I'd taught him "dog" but not "cat," and a picture of a cat, he wouldn't make a selection. In theory he could have gone for the word "cat" on the ground that the picture wasn't the one that went with the word "dog," which he knew, but that wasn't the way he played it.

It appeared that Terry hadn't already developed any word-recognition skills, at least not including these words. When he refused to make a selection I'd show him which word went with the picture, that c-a-t went with the picture of a cat, whereupon he'd smile and perform selections involving the new word without hesitation, which would tend to indicate that given the good visual memory Terry had shown earlier he could learn to recognize words.

Unfortunately there is no one available to give Terry the one-to-one instruction such a program would require, so he is unlikely to have a chance to try. Like many people with developmental disabilities, Terry had missed out on therapy and education as a child—he probably did not have any language assessment until St. Nicholas was due to close, when therapists were brought in for the first time to assess the residents. Unfortunately, whatever the outcome, the community resources were not there to carry out intensive programs for adults—after all, the assumption in the community is that everyone has received all the education and therapy they need in childhood. Consequently, those who miss out in childhood are unlikely to get this omission redressed as adults. Nonetheless, Terry was at least out in the community. The last time I saw him was at a big concert of African music in the new concert hall. Seated up in the back, he was wheeling himself back and forth in time to the music with great enjoyment. There were, however, gaps between items when techniques were explained and artists introduced, and these were of course meaningless to Terry. He would shake his wheelchair with impatience, waiting for them to get on with it.

Unachieved potential is also unknown potential. What Terry could have achieved in different circumstances is impossible to say. He was clearly interested in learning, and when tasks were presented in a form that he could understand, and involved responses that he was physically able to give, he had the ability to learn.

Developmental aphasia is not insuperable. Adam, a young man in England who has cerebral palsy and no understanding of spoken language, was lucky enough to have his receptive problem correctly diagnosed in childhood and appropriately treated. Despite not being introduced to sign language (his first language) until age seven Adam is now fully literate, and types and signs fluently.[3] His hand skills were certainly better than Terry's (as a young child he depicted the world around him through drawings) and he had the benefit of a devoted family and creative teachers and therapists, but I don't think we can say with certainty that he was intrinsically more able. We just don't know.

[3] In a joint paper, Adam and Prue Fuller, his one-time teacher, said, "There is need for in-depth assessment which will capture the potential of young children with multiple disabilities. Too may professionals . . . still see what they expect to see when confronted with a young non-speaking child and so fail to identify all the skills and talents which may be masked by disability." (Fuller and Wright, 1994)

14

On the Front Line

Few people living in North America and reading newspapers and watching television current affairs programs in the early nineties could have missed seeing something about facilitated communication training. Some reports hailed it as a miracle, others derided it as a cruel fraud. Unsurprisingly, reality is more complex.

Let's begin with the basics:

1. Most people with severe communication impairments know more words than they are able to say.
2. People who know more words than they are able to say may be able to expand their expressive communication by using alternative communication strategies.
3. Many people with communication impairments have hand-function impairments which affect their ability to write or use manual sign or make selections from communication displays.
4. Some people with impaired speech and hand function can use equipment which does not require hand skills[1] to expand their expressive communication. Other people cannot use such equipment, either for practical reasons[2]

---

[1] For example, headpointers or scanners controlled with foot switches.

[2] You cannot walk and wear a headpointer or use a foot switch.

or because of the nature of their neuromotor impairments.

5. People who cannot use other communication strategies
   may be able to use their hands to access communication
   aids if their hand-function impairments are remedied
   either temporarily or permanently.

6. For some people facilitation can provide a temporary
   remedy for hand-function impairments affecting communication-aid use, and when used as part of a structured
   teaching program may result in a permanent improvement in hand function.

Facilitated communication training certainly isn't a miracle.
At best, it can give nonspeakers a means of communication. It
doesn't give them speech (or only rarely) and it doesn't cure
their underlying disability. It's a treatment, not a cure.

In itself, facilitated communication training can no more be
a fraud than golf lessons. The technique the professional (the
facilitator) uses either works for you or it doesn't. Your swing
(your pointing) either improves or it doesn't, and your game
(your overall communication) either improves or it doesn't,
depending on the skills of the professional (the facilitator),
your rapport, your natural aptitude, the level of skill you had
before lessons started, how much you practice, and the number
of lessons you receive.

Facilitation only came into wide use in America after the
Harvard Educational Review published an article by Dr. Douglas
Biklen entitled "Communication Unbound: Autism and
Praxis." in 1990. This article came about because when
DEAL began getting unexpectedly good results with people
diagnosed as autistic my partner, Chris, wrote to all our
contacts telling them about it. One of these contacts was
Doug Biklen, a professor at Syracuse University in New York
State and an authority on deinstitutionalization and integra-
tion for people with disabilities. We had met a few years before when he was out advising the Victorian government on
its disability services. He'd read and liked *Annie's Coming*

Out,[3] and we'd had a pleasant evening together. We knew he'd be interested in what we were saying, if he accepted it, and because he had met us we hoped he wouldn't just think we were crazy.

> I didn't know what to think about this claim. It seemed conceivable to me that Crossley and her colleagues had happened on a *few* people with autism for whom communication was possible. But it made no sense that people with severe autism would have normal or even near normal literacy skills. By definition, people with severe autism were thought to have a severe intellectual disability as well. . . . Whether consciously or unconsciously, I set the matter aside in my mind. (Biklen, 1993)

Almost uniquely, though, Biklen didn't leave it at that. The next time he was in Australia he dropped by DEAL and saw us at work with clients. He was impressed enough to come back to DEAL for a whole month in 1989. He then went back, wrote us up for the *Harvard Educational Review*, and started his own facilitated communication training program at Syracuse. Biklen's article spurred the establishment of facilitated communication programs across the United States and Canada. While Biklen covered the downside of facilitation and said it was a technique to be used with care, these caveats were generally overlooked in the enthusiasm to release those imprisoned in silence. Thousands of individuals labeled autistic or intellectually impaired were soon using communication aids with facilitation. Many of these people were being given their first chance to communicate verbally through typing. FC, as facilitated communication training became known, became synonymous with the production of unexpected spelled communication. Children diagnosed as autistic were said to be typing that they were lonely. Nonspeakers who had been diagnosed as severely retarded and shut away in institutions for

---

[3] Crossley and McDonald (1980). Biklen should have been warned—as well as describing the use of facilitated communication by people with cerebral palsy, *Annie's Coming Out* describes the controversy which ensued.

twenty years were said to be spelling out complaints about the treatment they had received.

In the fall of 1992 I taught a course in augmentative communication at Syracuse University. It gave me the chance to observe the American FC phenomenon firsthand. The media had run a stream of "miracle" stories: "Shattering the Silence," "The Magic Touch," "The Miracle of Arthur." Parents whose children couldn't speak, and who had been told nothing could be done, were desperate for help. Teachers and therapists working with people who couldn't speak wanted to help. They flocked to lectures and workshops, and they went home and tried facilitation with their children or students. Those who couldn't get to workshops picked up what they could from the newspapers or the television coverage and improvised. It is to their credit that they tried; it is scarcely surprising that their lack of detailed information on what, why, how, and with whom led to mistakes and misapprehensions. Some people did surprisingly well. Others, unsurprisingly, did badly.

Getting facilitation wrong had two main effects. Some people who could have benefited from facilitated communication training were incorrectly assessed as unsuitable, and some people were at risk of having words put into their mouths (or at least their hands) by unskilled facilitators.

As portrayed in the media, FC appeared deceptively simple. Write out the alphabet on a sheet of paper, put it in front of a nonspeaker, hold his or her hand, and wait for words and sentences to be spelled out. This was a description, of sorts, but it wasn't an explanation, and there is only a short step from the unexplained to the inexplicable. What surprised me, in fact, was not the skepticism which such media reports often aroused but rather that so many people were prepared to embrace reports of spelled communication without having any explanation for them. If you didn't have any information about the reasons for using facilitation, and if you didn't know the ways in which literacy skills could be acquired, you just had to accept FC on faith; and many people did.

This faith was buttressed by a mythology which quickly sprang up among parents and professionals, most of whom had little or no previous experience of nonspeech communication. This mythology was founded on the erroneous belief that facilitated communication was the only communication strategy available for people without speech. Therapists who worked with people with cerebral palsy or acquired brain damage knew better; however, services in the disability field are typically provided for a diagnosis and not a need—nonspeakers with cerebral palsy received communication aids, nonspeakers with Down syndrome didn't—and these therapists were not in contact with the people who had taken up FC with such enthusiasm. Few caregivers or teachers had any familiarity with other nonspeech communication techniques, and so they saw facilitated communication training as *the* alternative to speech. Consequently, they gave it all they had.

They were encouraged by a second myth which spread along with FC, which was that most nonspeaking individuals have a mysteriously acquired ability to spell. Expecting literacy skills in nonspeakers was certainly a positive change from the earlier negative mythology that people who could not talk could not learn to read, but it was still absurd to suggest that these literacy skills were innate. The ability to acquire language—written or spoken—is innate but exposure to text or speech is necessary for learning to occur. If not specifically taught, literacy must be picked up from exposure to written language in newspapers, magazines, junk mail, product labels, TV commercials, and so on.

It isn't dangerous to believe that everyone has the potential to acquire literacy, but it may be dangerous to believe that literacy is innate. A belief in universal potential should lead to the supply of print-rich environments for all children, regardless of disability. A belief in universal literacy could and did lead to people who were blind and had not been taught to read "spelling" sentences by pointing to letters with their hands held.[4]

---

[4] People who have always been blind cannot have learned to read from incidental exposure to print and can only acquire reading or spelling skills through formal instruction. This does not mean blind nonspeakers who are illiterate can't express themselves. They can either use sign language or select from options presented in auditory or tactile form. In the early nineties many families were unaware of these strategies, presumably because the professionals with whom they were in contact were also unaware of them.

In 1990 "training" people with disabilities was no longer politically correct in North America. Training was seen as something that you did to animals, and hence the local acronym was FC—facilitated communication—and not FCT—facilitated communication training. Getting facilitators to implement movement training, whatever you called it, was complicated by a widespread belief that the "natural" behaviors of people with disabilities should not be challenged—that if you attempted to correct or change unusual behavior you were not accepting the person or showing respect.

The most common example of unwillingness to interfere with "natural" behaviors occurred with people who pointed or typed without looking at the display, typically because they could not coordinate their eye and hand movements or because they found it hard to keep their eyes on task. Ten-finger touch typists can type without looking at the keyboard by using the home keys for reference, but people pointing or typing with one finger need to look at what they are doing. FC mythology said that these people were using peripheral vision or had an image of the keyboard in their heads. This may have been true in some cases, but whether it was true or not it was certainly true that someone who doesn't look at the board can only generate utterances reliably if he gets feedback after each selection and if he has a reliable way of deleting errors. Because people had learned their techniques from TV reports, many facilitators didn't realize the importance of feedback and correction.

At one conference a woman brought up her son to talk to me. She held his hand over a card containing the letters of the alphabet but no "Delete" or "No" or "That's not what I meant." The boy's eyes were on the ceiling while his hand moved around the board. After a few minutes of silence his mother said, "He spelled 'I want to thank you for discovering FC. I use it all the time.' " Judging by appearances I wasn't sure he'd ever used it—used it, that is, to communicate his own thoughts. This kind of facilitation created understandable skepticism.

People who accepted inexplicable literacy and typing

without looking were well equipped to accept even more implausible things. Many people seemed to believe that everything typed with facilitation was true, however far-fetched, up to and including claims of guidance by the divinity in person. This willingness to believe may have been bound up with a stereotype of people with disabilities—innocents, "holy fools," people who did not participate in the wickedness of the world and who therefore could not be telling lies. Inexperienced communication-aid users with a history of dependency have emotional (and practical) difficulties in correcting misunderstandings, and misinterpretation is always a more likely explanation for inherently implausible communication than either miracles or mendacity, but that was too prosaic for many people.

Such credulity would probably have produced problems whenever it arose, but the United States in the early nineties was the worst possible place and time for it. Sexual assault, and especially sexual assault by caregivers, was a hot topic. Any communication from a nonspeaker that could possibly have a sexual connection produced an immediate reaction. The reaction was intensified when the communication was typed: written language is generally taken as more serious, more considered, than speech, and it certainly stays around in a way that speech doesn't. Some allegations of abuse were based on a few gnomic typed words, which were passed around, mulled over, and analyzed in the search for meaning as if they were utterances from the Delphic oracle. As with the oracle, reality often didn't match the interpretation.

The obverse of the belief that everything typed with facilitation was gospel truth was that if something was proved to be untrue then that was taken to mean that the person couldn't communicate at all. It was politically incorrect to suggest that a nonspeaker might tell lies, exaggerate, or make mistakes just like other people, so if the communication was wrong then the blame must rest with the facilitator. This was then usually taken to involve complete self-delusion involving the manufacture of all communication from scratch.[5] A more careful explanation would have considered the difficulties inherent in nonspeech communication and allowed for the possibility of error on both sides. The typical FC user was a novice communicator; even experienced, competent communicators and partners get it wrong sometimes; by no means were all facilitators either experienced or competent.

Some apparently unjustified allegations of abuse were made using facilitation, and lawyers in these cases attacked Doug Biklen for the uncontrolled spread of FC. To an outsider this seemed absurd. Biklen had published his article in the *Harvard Educational Review*, after all, not the *National Enquirer*. The spread of FC reflected aspects of American society that were not controllable by any individual: a more positive attitude to people with disabilities than generally prevailed in Australia, a readiness to accept that people with severe disabilities might also have significant skills, and a voracious appetite for human interest stories in the U.S. media fed by many people's willingness to call their local television station whenever anything out of the ordinary happened.

Most Australians place a high value on privacy, which meant that if a young Australian man spelled "I love you Mum" most families didn't think of going to the media; but if a twenty-five-year-old American communicated "I love you Mom" for the first time, that was news. Australians and Americans also respond differently to these stories. If Australian parents were interested in a media report on a new therapy they would contact professionals about it but would not try it themselves without professional input. Anne McDonald's use of facilitation

---

[5] A highly publicized Australian case that never came to court involved a young woman known as "Carla" who typed similar allegations of abuse with nine facilitators. After she failed a message-passing test while partnered by a novice facilitator it was said that all nine facilitators, some of whom had no prior knowledge of Carla or her circumstances, had manufactured her allegations. On the sole occasion when I was brought in to partner Carla after she had alleged abuse she typed quite unbelievable stories with no facilitation other than my hand on her shoulder (and I certainly wasn't cueing her). My obvious skepticism angered Carla and was dismissed by social workers who had been taught that children (Carla was in her twenties) don't manufacture allegations of abuse.

got widespread media coverage here, but I have only heard of one example of an Australian caregiver trying facilitation with a child with CP as a result. The American response, on the other hand, was "Let's give it a go."

After the miracle stories came the hoax stories. These originated with professionals, usually psychologists, who had tested people using facilitation and found them wanting. The presumption behind the testing was that if these people could spell at all they would be able to do the same kinds of tasks that nondisabled spellers are able to do. If they couldn't, that was taken as proof that they couldn't spell. This sounds reasonable until you consider the differences between the groups.

The FC users tested, whatever their ages, had just started to communicate. Any ordinary testee—any nondisabled child or adult who could spell well enough to do the psychologists' tests—would have been talking for five or six years at least, and would have had many thousands of conversations to practice the necessary language skills. All of the FC users have speech/language impairments. The typical child speaks fluently. All FC users have difficulties in generating text which necessitate the involvement of a facilitator. The typical child writes with relative ease.

A reasonable analogy for facilitated communication may be a transistor radio with low batteries, which works okay as long as you get it tuned and positioned exactly right and there's no interference. There's a signal there and the radio is trying to receive the signal, but it comes through more clearly in some situations than in others. If there's interference you can't hear the signal and if you turn up the volume to try and beat the interference the signal disappears in woofs and whistles. Some messages get through the interference better than others; we can make out well-known songs because we use our previous knowledge to fill in the gaps in the transmission, but someone talking on an unknown topic isn't comprehensible because we can't anticipate what's going to be said and we have no contextual knowledge to fill in the gaps.

Typical tests given to FC users removed all the predictability and redundancy usual in human communication. Users were asked to give one single word detached from its surrounding context, and the facilitators had to receive the word in a situation of maximum interference—interference from the test setup, with screens, earphones, and white noise, and from the stress that is part of any test. Feedback, which is integral to communication board use, was sometimes deliberately excluded; facilitators were told not to repeat the letters or words aloud as they were selected, and the aid user thus had no chance of finding out about or correcting any misunderstandings. Under these circumstances it would have been difficult for the people tested to get a message through even if they hadn't had the literacy or language problems they did have. If their communication partner/facilitator had been set up to expect a completely different message communication was likely to be impossible.

These problems aren't only found with people who use FC. People with severe dysarthria—people whose speech is so distorted that they are intelligible only to family members, say—find tasks like this difficult for exactly the same reasons. Just as with FC, some speakers can get their messages across only when the partners are familiar and the context known.

The procedures used to test FC rested on a binary model of communication. The test designers appeared to believe that communication ability, the capacity to send a message, was either present or absent—you either had it consistently or you didn't have it. This model certainly did make testing easier. If you believed that communication is either always present or always absent, then if people could communicate at all they could be expected to communicate under test conditions. If they could not communicate under test conditions, then this indicated that they could not communicate at all.

It was all rather like IQ testing. Both IQ testing and FC testing record a person's performance on given questions on a given day and use that to draw conclusions about their basic capacity. Both kinds of test regard the testee's previous educational and environmental experience as irrelevant to the interpretation of the results. Results obtained on either test are said to be reliable predictors of future performance. It is not surprising that many of the people who were administering one-off communication tests to FC users were psychologists working in the mental retardation industry, an industry built on the classification and segregation of people with severe communication impairments on the basis of IQ scores obtained from one-off tests. Both IQ testing and communication testing assumed that the test results predicted future performance so reliably that it was unnecessary to provide for the possibility of error. People who were unsuccessful in IQ tests—people whose test scores indicated to the psychologist that they could not benefit from an academic education—were not provided with an academic education, and their later lack of academic skills confirmed the validity of the original prediction. People who were unsuccessful in one-off communication tests usually had their facilitated communication training programs terminated immediately, and their later lack of success in using communication aids or keyboards confirmed the validity of the test result.

There is an alternative model of communication. A message is originated by a sender. The message is dispatched through a communication channel. In the process of transmission a variable amount of noise is overlaid on the signal. The task of the person receiving the communication is first to separate the signal from the noise and then to decode the message, providing sufficient feedback to the sender to permit the message to be repaired if it has been distorted. This model allows for the possibility that communication between a particular sender and a particular receiver will succeed on one occasion and fail on another, and for the possibility that a particular sender will communicate successfully with one receiver and not another. It is a more difficult model to test because it allows for the possibility of there being more than one significant variable. If communication breaks down you can't simply write off the user as congenitally incapable; you have to analyze the capacity of the user, the nature of the message, the particular circumstances of the interaction, and the skills of the receiver or facilitator before you can determine anything about the cause of the problem.

Even a radio transmitter and a radio receiver have more variables than a binary on/off. The strength of the signal and the power of the receiver can both be adjusted, which means that a given amount of interference will have a different effect under different circumstances. In human communication there are an enormous number of variables that can alter the effectiveness of sender and receiver—the amount of experience and the level of training of either party, for example. Experience and training inevitably change over time, which means that any given test result will have only limited predictive value.[6] Under this model, just establishing whether a single aid user can communicate given information in a given situation to a single facilitator may require a significant investment of time and effort in tweaking all possible variables.[7]

There is no theoretical basis for saying that if communication competence cannot be achieved in a set time then a communication therapy cannot be considered valid, although practical resources-allocation issues may mean setting an arbitrary time limit in particular cases. A child whose speech shows no improvement after a year of speech therapy, for example, may discontinue therapy even though it can't be proved that no improvement will ever occur. When there is some improvement, but nothing spectacular, a judgment call has to be made. Decisions to continue or discontinue therapy should be based on the person's progress, on the availability of resources, and on how important that skill is to that person.

The ability to communicate is probably the most important skill a child can acquire. Children who don't have disabilities take years to acquire fluent spoken and written communication, and it is reasonable to expect that you would have to devote years to teaching children with disabilities nonspeech communication before they reached competency. The long time lines involved had been thoroughly documented in previous nonspeech communication work, but, as I said, few of

[6] See Cardinal et al. (1996) in which all 43 participants failed a validation test one week which 32 out of the 43 passed five weeks later (with different questions).

[7] See Marcus and Shevin in Biklen and Cardinal (1997).

FC's critics and few of its supporters had had much contact with this work.

Expectations of instant competence may have been encouraged by the unexpected literacy skills reported in many FC users. The naive view held by both critics and supporters was that if these people really were spelling then they should have all the other skills of people who can spell. In effect, this view saw starting to communicate as equivalent to getting the telephone connected, as if all that had been missing from the nonspeaker's life was a technology. This view ignored both the primary effects of the disability that had left the nonspeakers mute and the secondary effects of having been treated differently all their lives.

One of the more extraordinary research projects took twenty-one students aged between eleven and twenty-one who had been diagnosed as autistic and mentally retarded, only two of whom were believed able to spell words, and sat them at keyboards with "facilitators" whose only training came from the researchers. The students were allowed twenty hours—twenty hours!—to acquire literacy and keyboard skills. They were then given a test which required them to type the answers to questions asked while the facilitators heard white noise played through headphones. Somewhat surprisingly, six students did answer at least one question correctly, including the two students known prior to the study to have some spelling skills. After twenty hours' training both these students answered more questions correctly by typing with facilitation with their facilitators screened from the question than they had previously answered correctly by typing independently. One increased his total correct typed responses from fifteen to twenty-four, and the other from eight to fifteen. Nonetheless, the researchers still stated that "no student demonstrated emerging literacy skills . . . that exceeded their already established communicative abilities" and said that these students "could type as well without physical assistance as they could with FC" (Eberlin et al., 1993). The experimenters' biases blinded them even to their own data. Today this article is still cited as evidence that facilitation has nothing to offer children with autism.

Biklen's 1990 article in the *Harvard Educational Review* drew immediate criticism, but the lag time for academic journals meant that it was 1992 before many papers on facilitated communication training appeared. The flood of publications that followed could be divided into three groups: instructional and theoretical articles, qualitative research and case studies, and quantitative research and test results. The qualitative articles were generally positive. In the nature of things, however, a study which gives students a once-and-for-all test after twenty hours of training is quicker to carry out than a study which evaluates students' competence in different areas over a period of years, and the first batch of quantitative studies to appear was consequently skewed toward the binary model of communication and assessed the validity of FC through one-off tests.[8] Virtually all the students failed their tests, and some facilitators were shown to have cued some responses.

These negative studies stimulated further research into the factors that can affect test success for people using facilitation, and researchers examined the effect the nature of the tasks set, the training of the facilitators and the aid users, and what effect their experience in undertaking tests had on test outcomes. The first results of this research are appearing as I write, and show that test outcomes are in fact predictable. Studies in which students are allowed to develop competency in taking tests and to practice the skills required produce a high proportion of successes; studies which don't allow any practice produce almost one hundred percent failures (Biklen and Cardinal, 1997).

Longitudinal research looking at the ability of students to communicate about a variety of topics in various situations with multiple partners takes longer than one-off tests. In an ideal world, people would have withheld judgment about the general usefulness of facilitation in nonspeech communication until this research had been completed and there had been time enough to see if facilitation produced any improvements in speech or independent typing. Allegations of physical or

---

[8] Not that the articles acknowledged this; they contained no discussion of the nature of communication, or the difficulties inherent in its assessment.

sexual abuse made with facilitation made this impossible. The legal system doesn't wait for academics to complete research, and the criminal court is not an ideal situation to develop and test theories of communication.

Sexual abuse is a hot topic, and the media didn't need much urging to take an interest in allegations of abuse made through FC. Several major U.S. television current affairs programs ran stories in 1993 suggesting that all the allegations of abuse made with facilitation must be unfounded because there was no evidence that any of the complainants (or anyone else, for that matter) could communicate with facilitation. One such story was *Frontline*'s "Prisoners of Silence," which went to air on PBS on October 19, 1993. It contained a savage attack on facilitated communication training and those who espouse it. I was accused of manufacturing communication by moving a person's communication board in front of his head pointer while he was in a coma. They even showed a video.

> "Rosemary Crossley, the founder of FC, is facilitating with a head injury victim in a coma to make a very important decision on where he will live. Because the man is in a coma, his head pointer barely moves through the taping. By drawing a line on the screen it is easy to see that Rosemary Crossley is ever so slowly moving the board."

After thirty seconds of watching the top of the board move away from the line Howard Shane, a Boston speech pathologist, comes on screen to say, "I don't think they're doing it consciously, but they're absolutely manipulating these individuals and they're communicating for them."

There you are, then; I've been caught out manipulating communication. The camera does not lie. Depending, of course, on where you draw the line. Draw it as *Frontline* did, along the top of the board at the top of the screen, and the top of the board moves away from the line. Draw a line around my thumb supporting the bottom of the board and it is obvious that my hand moves fractionally, if at all.

So how come the top of the board moved down and the

bottom didn't budge? Because the camera, like all cameras, "lied." Movement of the top of the board away from the camera was transformed into movement down the screen. Why did the board move away from the camera? Because the man, who was not in a coma, was pressing on the board as he pushed his head pointer up toward his target.

Now you know something the *Frontline* producer and the "scientists" apparently didn't know: the difference between three dimensions and two, and the difficulty of converting one into the other.

The main message of the *Frontline* program was that communication through facilitation had been disproved by scientific testing—that dozens of scientific studies had now been carried out, that none of them have shown valid communication, and that all had shown facilitator influence. This just wasn't true. There were studies that showed facilitator influence in some cases, there were studies in which none of the subjects succeeded in communicating, and there were studies that showed valid communication. More were coming through all the time, together with reports of students typing independently and students whose speech had improved significantly.[9]

Since 1993 a number of convictions for abuse have been recorded because the plaintiff passed communication tests, the perpetrator confessed, or there was medical and other evidence (Dwyer, 1996). Proceedings in one case dragged on so long that the victim learned to type without facilitation, whereupon the perpetrator confessed (Kochmeister, 1994). In one case which did not go to court it appeared that the false "allegations" typed by an autistic child using facilitation may have been word-for-word accounts of adult conversations, a sort of written echolalia (Heckler, 1994). Anne Botash, a pediatrician at the Child Abuse Referral and Evaluation Program at the State University of New York Health Science Center in Syracuse and her colleagues have published a study of one group of

[9] For a detailed examination of the research, both negative and positive, see Biklen and Cardinal, 1997. Ironically I have just heard, in late 1996, that *Frontline* proposes to rescreen "Prisoners of Silence" without any correction or reference to the positive test results obtained since 1993.

cases (Botash et al., 1994). Over a three-year period 1,096 children with suspected abuse were referred to the program. In 13 of these cases the children were said to have used facilitated communication to disclose the abuse. There was corroborative or supportive evidence in 9 of the 13 cases—at least as many as would be expected in a similar number of cases involving speaking children. The authors suggested that in the absence of other investigations "it does not seem prudent for clinicians to attempt to prove or disprove sexual abuse allegations by testing facilitated communication validity."

Botash's research hasn't attracted anything like the amount of media coverage given to the initial abuse allegations. These almost gave the impression that more complaints of abuse were made with FC than with speech, and that every person using FC was complaining of abuse. The 13 allegations of abuse cited by Botash came from a pool of hundreds of FC users. This may still seem a high rate of abuse allegations, but it should be viewed in the light of research suggesting that upwards of twenty-five percent of nonspeakers have been subject to abuse over their lifetimes (Sobsey, 1994).

Only a small percentage of professionals in the field of developmental disability have come any closer to FC than their TV sets. Most people who have been involved in facilitated communication training programs have never been involved in either court cases or communication testing. Some professional organizations—the American Psychological Association, for example—have nonetheless been influenced by the negative media coverage of such court cases, and have passed resolutions critical of facilitated communication training. Other organizations, such as The Association for People with Severe Handicaps (TASH), have passed supportive resolutions. As a result of the negative publicity and resolutions, many agencies have terminated facilitated communication training programs. Their clients have had their communication aids removed. The great majority of these people have never had their communication skills tested and had not used their communication aids for anything more controversial than asking for a cup of coffee. Returned to silence, they cannot complain.

15

This Is Where We Came In

In 1979, when the Victoria Health Commission was opposing Anne McDonald's application for habeas corpus, one of the measurements they relied on in court was Anne's size. If she was the size of a five-year-old, how could she have the intelligence of an adult? This was always an extraordinary contention; our intelligence is not determined by the distance of our heads from the ground, whatever else may affect it. In Anne's case the Health Commission adduced her size as evidence that she had a form of cerebral palsy described as being "inevitably" associated with severe mental retardation. This notion was to be disproved in a most unexpected manner.

When Anne was admitted to St. Nicholas a month before her fourth birthday she was two feet ten inches tall and weighed twenty-seven pounds, approximately the height and weight of a two-year-old. Twelve years later she was three feet four inches tall, the height of an average four-year-old, and weighed twenty-eight pounds, still the weight of a two-year-old. Between the ages of four and sixteen Anne had grown six inches (18 percent) and her weight had increased by one pound (4 percent) as opposed to height and weight gains in the average child over those years of one foot ten inches (51 percent) and seventy-eight pounds (203 percent). When Anne left St. Nicholas Hospital at the age of eighteen she was the size of a five-year-old. She had been putting on weight since I had started feeding her in 1977, and for the first time since her admission to St. Nicholas her weight, now thirty-five pounds, was appropriate for her height, now three foot six.

Nonetheless, even if you didn't believe the Health Commission, Anne's size was a problem. Shortness isn't a criminal offense, but it certainly affects the way people treat you. People with severe disabilities always run the risk of being patronized, and so do people who are significantly shorter than average. The combination of severe disability and childlike stature and appearance made it almost impossible for casual acquaintances to treat Anne like an adult.

> I didn't like littleness. Everybody treated me like a baby. My tiny little body appealed to sentimentalists and drunks. They would sit next to my baby buggy and stare lovingly into my eyes. The worst ones would pat me on the head. Their breath smelt of stale beer and their hands were wet and sticky. I asked Chris to have a T-shirt painted with PAT ME AND I'LL BITE YOUR HAND OFF. I was sitting in the park wearing it when an old lady came up. She read it, said, "Oh, how *cute*," and patted me on the head. There were also practical disadvantages; I couldn't see over the top of a table in a restaurant, for example, let alone a bar. One of the first things I did after leaving the hospital was to ask my doctors if there was any way to increase my height.

Growth is a complex phenomenon, with our eventual stature the result of a complicated interaction between nutrition and metabolism, environment and hormones, combined with the growth potential we inherit from our parents. Anne's parents were of average height, so her short stature wasn't likely to be the result of inheritance. Unstimulating environments can contribute to failure to thrive, and part of Anne's growth lag might be due to that. She hadn't had a pubertal growth spurt;

menstruation doesn't start in girls who are severely malnourished. The simplest explanation seemed the best: she was small because she hadn't had enough to eat.

Anne had an X ray to see what her bone age was. The bones of children have uncalcified areas at the ends, called epiphyses, which is where growth takes place. The extent of these areas can be observed on an X ray, and matched with the average areas left uncalcified at a given age. Typically the result is close to a child's chronological age, and is in fact often used to estimate the ages of nondisabled children whose birth dates aren't available. At the end of puberty the epiphyses close and then no further growth is possible, but Anne hadn't reached puberty. In fact, at the age of eighteen Anne's bone age was that of a six-year-old.

We were initially appalled—an eighteen-year-old with a six-year-old bone age didn't sound like good news—but in fact this was the best news Anne could have had. Hypothetically, she had the growth potential of a six-year-old. No one could predict what would happen in such an unusual situation, but as Anne's height age and bone age were quite close no special treatment seemed called for. Theoretically, she should now start growing. And grow Anne did. Between sixteen and twenty-six the average woman grows by less than half an inch (0.2 percent) and her weight increases by three pounds (2 percent). Anne grew by one foot six inches (46 percent) and her weight increased by seventy-eight pounds (277 percent). She will always be slightly shorter than average because the long bones of the legs do not grow as much in people who do not stand or walk, but she may have grown more after the age of eighteen than any other human being now alive.

When she entered St. Nicholas Anne's height was 80 percent of the average four-year-old's and her weight 70 percent.

For the next twelve years her weight and height increased only slightly, and at the age of sixteen her height was 63 percent of the average sixteen-year-old's and her weight 24 percent. After that delay she entered onto a growth curve similar to that of normal growth but displaced sideways by fourteen years, and by twenty-six her height was 91 percent of the average and her weight 88 percent.

The Bible (King James version) says at one point, "Which of you by taking thought can add one cubit unto his stature?" A cubit was the length from elbow to fingertip, often taken as eighteen inches, the amount Anne grew. In many ways it was as if Anne's biological clock had shut down in the years immediately after her admission to St. Nicholas, and started again after she came out. Initially her growth was so accelerated that she needed several complete new wardrobes each year—a great thrill for a young woman who hadn't previously had any clothes of her own, much less the opportunity to shop for them.

Anne's teeth started to wobble and one fell out. Horrified, and presuming that this was the result of the gum disease endemic in the institution, we rushed her to a dentist. There was nothing to worry about, he explained; it was just a deciduous tooth, pushed out in the normal way by the second tooth coming through. He looked at us very strangely—after all, why were we so concerned about an apparent six-year-old losing teeth? Anne's dental age was similar to her bone age, and as she grew she lost more deciduous molars. Most of these were replaced, though her dental development was not as regular as her growth curve.

Now in 1995 I'm still living with Chris and Rose, still don't back institutions, and still play at being a student. St. Nicholas has been closed and my friends have moved out into homes in the suburbs where I can visit them. I let Rose fight new battles while I just tried sitting back and enjoying freedom and friendship. Taking attendants for friends, I made many friends, but my reputation always took lots of work to overthrow. I seemed like a modern icon. The new attendants would wet themselves with reverent adoration, and I had to drink a rum for breakfast to show them I wasn't a saint. I'm really not a martyr either— I didn't choose my part. In living the role of heroine I wished I could change it for that of romantic lead.

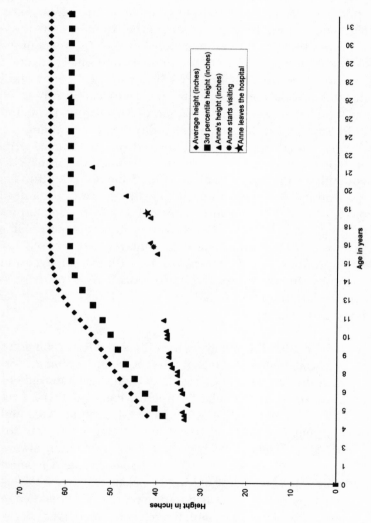

Anne McDonald - Height

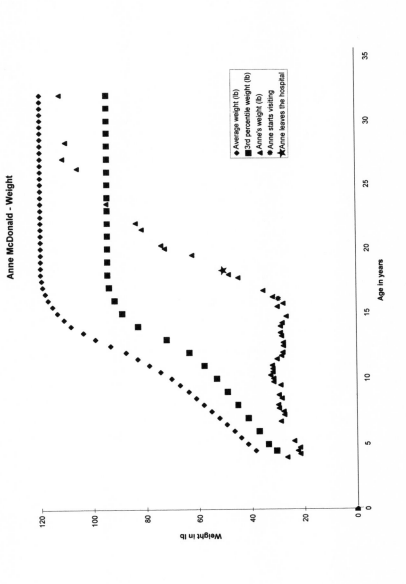

Anne McDonald - Weight

Weight in lb

Age in years

- ◆ Average weight (lb)
- ■ 3rd percentile weight (lb)
- ▲ Anne's weight (lb)
- ✶ Anne starts visiting
- ★ Anne leaves the hospital

Anne's story is not just that of a single misdiagnosed child placed in a bad institution. It exemplifies a tendency among professionals to band together when their expertise is challenged and to deny resolutely the existence of evidence which, if admitted, would force a reevaluation of established practice. My failure to appreciate and extend Anne's communication in 1974 provides a demonstration of just how difficult it is for anyone with severe disabilities to change other people's preconceptions, and the limitations these preconceptions impose on their development.

The most important thing Anne has tried to teach me is not to set limits—not to judge people by appearance, or by label.

Intelligence is a concept which is due for revision. As more is discovered about the neurological impairments which affect performance both in everyday life and on IQ tests it is clear that each individual has so many different strengths and weaknesses that it is impossible to even design a test which will fit every body, much less make reliable predictions from people's scores on the current tests. The important concern is not to improve the tests but to stop people being graded on any measures which can be used to restrict the rights and opportunities of those who rank lowest. Making low IQ a crime warranting imprisonment is as humane as making shortness a criminal offence. Both measurements indicate difference. The judgment that one difference warrants imprisonment and the other does not is based on prejudice about the relative desirability of particular human characteristics.

St. Nicholas, sadly, was not unique. There were and are other St. Nicholases around the world. Their similarity is worrying. One such institution could be explained as an aberration, but the existence of many suggests that there is an endemic human tendency to treat as less than human children with disabilities who cannot speak. Our humanity to others appears to be dependent on the feedback they give us, and in the absence of that feedback we may overlook their essential humanity.

Anne got out. She got a wheelchair and grew and went to university and traveled overseas. Obviously this didn't make her normal—she still couldn't talk, walk, or feed herself—but did it make her normal for someone with that degree of physical disability? Unfortunately, the answer is no. You don't just spend fourteen years of your life in a place like St. Nicholas and leave unscathed. Recovery from physical and academic deprivation is easy compared to the ongoing pain caused by the social and emotional deprivation of life in the hospital.

I rotted in St. Nicholas for 14 years, and you expect me to be a woman like any other? Do remember that I saw my friends die—over and over, time after time. In the hospital you couldn't afford friends. Kids who tired of fighting rusted away; and if you rust young you don't live to be old. I fought, and I survived—survived to wonder which of my enemies I had beaten and which I had just put away inside myself. I suffer jealously whenever Rose works with another person with a disability. What if they take her fancy and she swaps me for them? I want to be normal, to love and be loved, crisp new love, but I still prefer not to make close bonds with mortals.

Mine is the troll's motto, "To thyself be enough."

16

Thoughts of Voices
Never Heard

In the eighteenth century society discovered it had been making a mistake about one group of people who behaved like idiots. These people weren't intellectually impaired at all, they had a sensory problem; they were deaf. The true nature of their impairment was discovered and an educational system developed to capitalize on the language of sign.

However, these advances still left a group of people who made funny noises and who waved their arms around in the asylums or poorhouses. This group often walked unsteadily. They dropped or spilled things. They were not able to do the manual work which was available for deaf people. The worst could not walk at all and could not feed themselves. It was possible to show that most of them could hear, and it was clear, therefore, that they had no excuse for not talking. Their lack of speech or their distressingly garbled attempts had to be due to imbecility.

Many of these people had cerebral palsy. In the middle of the twentieth century society made another reevaluation. It was realized that some people who did not move or speak properly did not have anything wrong with their thinking either—they had a physical problem, not an intellectual one. Cerebral palsy—neurological impairment resulting in problems with controlled movement—became recognized as an entity separate from "mental deficiency."

This still left other people in the asylums—people who didn't speak normally, some of whom waved their arms around and made funny noises. Most of them were classified as mentally retarded or autistic. What we should have learned from our experiences with people who are deaf or have cerebral palsy is that you shouldn't assume that every aspect of a nonspeaking person's thinking is defective until you have looked for other explanations—that you shouldn't assume that if people are not talking it's because they haven't got the capacity to use language. Once you start looking you find that there are other possible explanations, explanations that do not involve global cognitive defects but instead have to do with specific neurological dysfunctions.

It's time for another revision.

The pervasive stereotype applied to people with communication impairments has been that mute = dumb, as in stupid. Indeed the word "dumb" originally meant stupid, and was applied to people who couldn't talk as a matter of course. Only later was it "upgraded" and used as a synonym of mute.

While the general view has always been that you could rank people on the basis of their speech and actions, it is only in the last century that a "scientific" basis for doing so has been devised: the intelligence test.

The people I write of in this book all have severe disabilities. Some can walk, some use wheelchairs. Some can talk, some are mute. What they share is the difficulty they have all experienced in getting out what they wanted to say, in letting us know what they were thinking. Once they had access to nonspeech communication they all showed more skills than they had been expected to have, more skills than they had been able to show without communication. In most cases their emerging skills were initially greeted with skepticism by some of the people around them because of something else that they all shared: preexisting negative assessments of their intellectual functioning.

To be officially mentally retarded you must have an IQ score of 70 or below. In 1994, the widely used manual of the American Psychiatric Association *DSM-iv* made a clear connection between speech impairment and mental retardation. Mildly retarded people ". . . can learn academic skills up to approximately sixth-grade level" including, presumably, literacy. Moderately retarded people ". . . can acquire communication skills . . . (but) are unlikely to progress beyond the second-grade level in academic subjects. . . ." Severely retarded people "During the early childhood years . . . acquire little or no communicative speech. . . . During the school-age period, they may learn to talk. . . ." With profoundly retarded people ". . . communication skills may improve [from an unspecified base] if appropriate training is provided." It is assumed that someone who cannot speak will not be able to spell; speech is referred to as if it were cognitively identical with language. While this does not say that every child who doesn't talk is profoundly retarded, that was (and is) a common presumption.

Devaluation dignified by the trappings of science or medicine cannot be easily dismissed. As many experiments have shown, we believe men in white coats and tend to obey their instructions and trust the information they give us. There is a general assumption that the labels which are used in medical and paramedical fields have a factual basis. A coronary occlusion is a real event, phenylketonuria is a real condition. So what is mental retardation?

Actual damage to the substance of the brain, from a head injury, say, will show up on a CAT scan. Mental retardation doesn't. None of the brain-imaging techniques we currently have available, none of the biochemical tests we can do, can see it. We can easily show that someone has an extra chromosome or has PKU, but we cannot do any physiological test that will pick up mental retardation. Mental retardation is a social construct. Like Kannerian autism, it is a construct developed to answer a question. In this case, the question is "Why are these people different?"

A diagnosis of "mental retardation" provides a simple explanation—they're different because their brains are no good. However, mental retardation is diagnosed not by a test of brain matter but on the basis of performance, which is where it falls

down as a construct.[1] Diagnosing mental retardation is not
unlike a dog chasing its tail. We find retardation because we
already know it's there. Very, very few people have mental
retardation diagnosed for the first time after an intelligence
test administered blind. Rather, the tests are given to people
who are already believed to be "retarded" with a view to ascer-
taining just how retarded they are. We see someone whose performance isn't up to par, then we give them tests which require
them to use the functions that aren't up to par, and then we
add up the results and use them as an explanation for why the
person's performance isn't up to par.

The basic flaw in the diagnosis of mental retardation is that
the retardation industry in all its facets depends on the premise
that your behavior is an accurate reflection of all your internal
mental processes. In the most obvious sense, what you do *does*
reflect what your central nervous system does—Anne's inability
to reach for the pediatrician's plastic ring reflects her brain
damage; Marco's limited speech reflects some kind of brain
dysfunction—but our ability to go beyond this kind of crude
equivalence is very limited.

The most widely read book of the last few years to focus on
IQ testing is *The Bell Curve*. Its main concern is social engi-
neering rather than the assessment of intelligence and it virtually omits any mention of the people (around a million in the
United Sates, the vast majority of whom are white) who are currently viewed as having significant intellectual impairments.
This disregard is one of the few things *The Bell Curve* shares with
Stephen Jay Gould's *The Mismeasure of Man*. While the books are
written from very different perspectives, they are both concerned with the accuracy and applicability of intellectual assessment, and it is perhaps surprising that they do not investigate
the situation of those people whose lives are most affected by IQ
tests, people who have obvious impairments. While Gould does
review some examples of misdiagnosis and mistreatment from

[1] In *The Mismeasure of Man* Stephen Jay Gould discusses some of the more
absurd efforts to find a physiological basis for presumed differences in intellectual ability.

early in this century, he does not discuss the current situation of this group, and *The Bell Curve* omits them totally.

As many people including Gould have pointed out, *The Bell Curve*, along with all other books which rest their arguments on IQ scores, has to prove two points. First, that it is valid and meaningful to reduce all the mental abilities of an individual to a single figure, an IQ score. Second, that this IQ score is validly derived from tests which accurately measure individual mental abilities without bias.

If it were possible to encapsulate all of a person's mental abilities in one meaningful figure, presumably that figure would have significant import for that person's life. If individual IQ scores have no predictive value, either the assumptions on which the test scores are based are questionable or mental ability is not as important as the testers would like us to think. Consequently, it came as something of a surprise to read in *The Bell Curve* that "you cannot predict what a given person will do from his IQ score." It's not the statement which surprises but its source. Obviously Hernstein and Murray didn't think that was the end of the story, or they wouldn't have written the book. They went on to say that "large differences in social behavior separate groups of people when the groups differ intellectually." Apart from adducing evidence in support of this assertion, Hernstein and Murray also attempt to answer the chicken-and-egg question, arguing that differences in group social behavior including unemployment and teenage pregnancy spring from differences in intelligence rather than that differing social circumstances will affect academic performance and IQ test results. All of this would be no more than an academic entertainment if we didn't place so much store on intelligence. Telling a group that their average life expectancy is five years less than that of their neighbors is less likely to provoke outrage than telling them that their average IQ is five points lower.

Bias in IQ testing has typically been envisaged as relating to class, race, or education. More easily demonstrable bias is usually disregarded. It is as though prejudice on the basis of preexisting disability is unimportant.

The central question of intellectual assessment is how do you measure something you can't get at? The general assumption used to be that mental retardation was like the mark of Cain. You could see it, or its accurate reflection, in the awkward movements of cerebral palsy and the epicanthic folds of Down syndrome. Until very recently most people admitted to institutional care because they were mentally retarded had been diagnosed using the eyeball test. They were looked over, and if the stigmata associated with mental retardation were evident then that was sufficient. Anne wasn't given an intelligence test before she was admitted to St. Nicholas; she was given one before she was allowed to leave.

But that was then, this is now, and today a child with a disability would be given an intelligence test before admission to residential care. True—but would that change anything? Anne Two turns up for assessment at age three—no speech, no fine motor skills, no gross motor skills, no head control, no eye movement control, and therefore no ability to perform any existing intelligence test. She flunks her Denver, at best achieving a three-month level. The only certain thing that anyone can say is that her knowledge (if any) is inaccessible and she is therefore untestable. How you react to that finding depends on your prejudices about severe disability.

Anne Two is only an extreme example of the general problem. Tests of intelligence purport to assess how well you take information in, and what you are able to do with it, on the basis of what comes out. If nothing quantifiable comes out you are untestable. If anything quantifiable comes out you may be tested as though you have no disability, so that a six-year-old child with ten words of speech may be given a test requiring spoken answers and a teenager with no speech who perseverates and repeatedly points at the same spot may be given a test to be answered by pointing. Obviously the child and teenager won't do well on their tests. That isn't surprising. What is surprising is that the results are assumed to reflect what the child and teenager are thinking and what they are able to learn, and are used as a basis of making decisions about their futures.

The fatal flaw in intelligence testing is that we don't know what intelligence is or where it resides. Sure, we've got a general concept, as we've got general concepts of beauty and pain, but having a concept of intelligence doesn't mean that it is a tangible, measurable entity. At best, intellectual impairment is no more than the shadow cast by real neurological and physical and sensory and social abnormalities, as we might make a wobbly rabbit in a shadow play; if we want to know what is not illusion, we must look not at the rabbit but at the fingers.

I am not just saying that we should redraw the boundaries of mental retardation and exempt from the label or move up a grading or two those who can, with the communication techniques we have now, demonstrate their capacity. I am saying that the notion that we can meaningfully compact the strengths and weaknesses of an individual into two or three digits, or even into two categories like "retarded" and "normal," is intellectually bankrupt and must go.

"But the Emperor has nothing on at all!" said a little child.

And under the clothes there is no Emperor.

When I started work at St. Nicholas Hospital I really hadn't thought much about intellectual assessment. Finding deaf-blind infants in the wards made me concerned about a system that labeled as severely retarded children whose intellectual abilities were completely inaccessible. Finding that Anne and other residents were far more able than their labels of profound retardation would imply made me conscious of the difficulties of assessing people with severe physical impairments. Working with people with acquired brain damage was salutary. Derek, Penny, and Carolyn were all as severely disabled when I first saw them as the most disabled child in St. Nicholas. Okay, they'd been normal, and okay, when they started to communicate they were using or recovering old skills, but they showed that lack of any obvious response didn't mean there wasn't someone home.

That still left people who could walk but not talk. When I was removed from St. Nicholas in 1980 I still thought that those children who were more physically able could demonstrate any abilities they had. Correspondingly, any abilities they didn't show were abilities they didn't have. I still saw this group as having relatively limited potential, until I met Amy.

Amy was sixteen years old and had been diagnosed as autistic and severely/profoundly intellectually impaired in infancy. I first saw her at a residential center early in 1986. She was being led around like a virtual zombie. Her face was expressionless. She had no speech and no method of communication other than leading people by the hand to things she wanted and pushing away things she didn't want. Unless she was prompted she did absolutely nothing. Her muscle tone was usually very low and her hands were weak.

Nonetheless, Amy wasn't what I would then have described as physically disabled. She could walk and pick up food, and I'd assumed that if you had these skills you had to have enough physical ability to be able to communicate, by pointing or signing if not by speech. I assumed that if you had enough physical ability to be able to communicate and didn't communicate you were severely emotionally or intellectually disabled. I said in chapter 1 that Anne taught me not to set upper limits. What I should have said was that I had learned not to set upper limits for people with severe physical impairments. It took Amy to teach me that not setting upper limits is a rule that has no exceptions.

At the center that first day Amy surprised me and the residential staff by pressing the "yes" and "no" buttons on a speech synthesizer to answer some simple questions. According to the staff this was just about the first clear indication they'd ever had that Amy understood any speech at all. Next time they came to DEAL to look at equipment for some of their other clients, they brought Amy along for the ride. She sat next to me while I went through the equipment and talked to the staff.

I had a Vocaid on my lap, an early speech synthesizer designed for use by adults who could read. One overlay displayed a set of thirty-six written utterances, each of which could be spoken by pressing the appropriate words. At the residential center Amy never did anything, apart from occasional raids on the sugar bowl, without a physical cue. Now she suddenly reached across and pressed the UPSET key repeatedly.

I thought it was a random selection. I asked her, "What do you want?"

UPSET.

"You're upset?"

WRITE/RIGHT. (The Vocaid used homonyms to expand the limited vocabulary.)

"Right, you're upset. Why?"

READ.

"Do you want to read?"

I WOULD LIKE TO READ. (two keys)

"Can you read?"

WRITE/RIGHT.

"Do you want to try spelling on the alphabet overlay?"

WRITE/RIGHT.

At my request Amy spelled her name using the alphabetic overlay. Amy's previous utterances had only taken two presses at most. When she started to spell her name her hand dropped after the first few letters and I supported her under her forearm so she could continue. She also needed reminders to keep her eyes on what she was doing.

She then went on to I CAN TYPE and I POOSH NO ONE TO TALK Y DO U ("I push no one to talk. Why do you?").

When I asked the staff where Amy had learned to read and spell the answer was straightforward—school. Unlike many residential centers, Amy's had an intensive academic program. She had never contributed anything to it, and it was assumed she was getting nothing out of it, but as there wasn't a better alternative she had sat at the back of the class for years.

Amy had a major neurological problem, which should have been obvious to me when I first met her, regardless of whether she could walk, regardless, in fact, of whether she could do ballet. She couldn't talk. After infancy, not being able to talk indicates a neurological problem, whether or not we can specify the nature of that problem. Saying the problem is due to "mental retardation" is the same as saying there's something wrong in the black box but we don't know what. Personally I prefer Donald Duck's "blinkus in the thinkus"—it's more user-friendly.

Apart from her lack of speech Amy had difficulty in initiating movement, in starting to move. Obviously her low muscle tone had something to do with this, but it also seemed that she had a problem recalling and executing patterns of movement when she wanted to, an apraxia. Apraxia leaves spontaneous movements (like raiding the sugar bowl) relatively unimpaired but affects the carrying out of more deliberate movements. There are several types of apraxia, and in them, or something like them, may be found part of the explanation for why many people diagnosed as autistic or intellectually impaired look fine but have problems doing some of the things the rest of us take for granted.

After two more visits care staff reported that Amy's confidence, hand control, and communication skills had all improved greatly. She required less support, and her attention and eye-hand coordination was generally good. She spelled on the Vocaid, "I'M A SLOW SPELLER. . . . I'M TRYING TURNING MY THOUGHTS INTO WORDS   I'M PLEASED TO BE TALKING. . . . IS TEACHING ME STILL POSSIBLE   I HOPE TO LEARN TESTING SO I CAN TEST DUMB KIDS [spelling corrected].

By this time I wasn't sure exactly who was dumb.

By the middle of the next year Amy was able to type on a small keyboard with no support, though muscle tone was still a problem if she wanted to type more than one or two short sentences. Questioned about this she spelled, somewhat surprisingly, MORNINGS ARE WORST   MY MUSCLES [are] WEAKER. By September 1987, her independent typing had become established. In some respects she had changed little—she still tended to rock, cover her ears, or shut her eyes at inappropriate moments—but the videotapes from this time show a smiling responsive teenager very different from the "zombie." She was now an active participant in more advanced educational programs her center had set up to help her and others similarly misassessed catch up on literacy, general knowledge, and current affairs. On this visit she spelled, I STILL HAVE TROUBLE IN STARTING   IS ENYONE DOING ENY WORK ON HELPING PEOPLE LIKE ME START MOVING. The occupational therapist spoke to Amy about initiation problems. At a later session I asked Amy what she saw her major problems being. NOT BEING ABLE TO TALK OR INITIATE MOVEMENT. I'M NOT MENTALLY RETARDED OR MAD. I'M A BIT ODD BUT NOT CRAZY.

Having finally shown me that light could be found under even the least likely bushel, Amy went on to demonstrate vividly a range of the problems that could occur if you acquired a voice for the first time at the age of sixteen. She used her new communication skills to ask staff at the residential center about all kinds of things, her past, her future, where babies come from, whether she could have babies, and so on. It was the last question which started the problems. No, Amy could not have babies. She had been sterilized at the age of twelve, when her parents still thought she was profoundly intellectually impaired. And not just sterilized; Amy had been given a complete hysterectomy. She was a Peter Pan who could never grow up. Without the hormones produced by her ovaries she was doomed to remain an eternal child in body, though not in mind. Her anger was palpable and she let fly in all directions, accusing people of abusing and maltreating her. Reports of these incidents created great anxiety in the parents of other adults living in the same hostel, adults who themselves were starting to use nonspeech communication for the first time, and the facilitated communication training program was first placed under tight control and then terminated. The residents weren't asked whether they wanted this; once their communication aids were taken away they certainly couldn't complain.

I don't know what has happened to Amy.

One thing we have learned from people who can't talk is that while speech is relatively fragile, language isn't. It appears to be extraordinarily difficult to erase language. It may not have a way out, it may not be easy to find it or use it, it may be disturbed or distorted, but language does stick around. It is one of the fundamental organizing structures of the human brain. Where there's human life, there's language.

We should also have learned that it is impossible to judge from appearances whether anyone is home. Decades after encephalitis lethargica had left a ward of people frozen in a kind of neurological Alaska, Oliver Sacks gave them L-dopa and they came to. As he records in *Awakenings*, language (and, in most cases, even speech) was there. If he stopped providing the L-dopa that thawed them, they froze up again and their speech stopped.

Hilary Pole, totally immobile, with no facial response, was never thought to have lost language, but for years her communication still hung by a thread—a real thread, connecting her big toe to a bell.

I am *not* saying that no one has learning problems and that everyone can learn to read. I *am* saying that virtually everyone can use some form of communication, and that most people, whatever their diagnosis, can use complex language. I am saying that we need to look very carefully for the specific reasons that prevent people communicating and try and address those, rather than neatly shoveling them all to one side in black boxes labeled "mental retardation" or "persistent vegetative state." If we don't know exactly what is going on, we should presume normal language reception and processing. We should then try to find a communication strategy that allows the person to use whatever language he has.

But, as someone said to me at a presentation on Down syndrome, what does it matter whether they're retarded or not—they're still disabled, aren't they? True. And people with disabilities are devalued not just because of their IQ scores. They're devalued because they cannot do some of the things we value. But nonetheless it does matter whether we address the problems they actually have rather than the label that covers and obscures those problems. Over the last two hundred years we have advanced to the point where some diagnoses—deafness, and to a lesser extent cerebral palsy—have been moved out from under the retardation umbrella, and some individuals like Anne have escaped. A lot of other people haven't. The answer to their problem isn't to move yet another group out from under, but to close the umbrella and, once everyone is out of its shadow, look at them and what they can do and the lives they can live.

This is not a small thing, or an easy thing. It will involve changing virtually all elements of the systems we have set up to care for and educate people who have been labeled retarded. They will have to be taught, not minded. They will have to be given genuine occupations. They will have the same right as other people to determine the direction of their lives.

On my last brief meeting with Jan, the teenage poet with Down syndrome, she typed (at full speed, fighting the clock as well as disability and disbelief):

Can anyone hear the voice inside?
Give me some light and I can see.
Give me some pain and I can feel.

Give me a call and I will hear;
But give me credit—
That's for some too hard.

Remember:
My words, like pearls,
Are found in an oyster.

It isn't her best poem, but I am sure it's her most heartfelt. Unless things change, it will also be her last.

Communication doesn't cure anything. The people in this book all still have severe disabilities. Some of these people have learning difficulties and some don't. Some of these people have the potential to be academic achievers and some don't. All are able to do more than their initial diagnoses and prognoses suggested. All are participants—they are part of their communities, however small their communities may be. They are contributors—they add to the richness and diversity of life in their communities. They are creators—and some can do some things better than we can. Their participation, their lives depend on communication, on their ability to interact with other people and the willingness of other people to interact with them.

The last word is Anne McDonald's:

People who can talk have built-in voices. People who can't have add-ons. Nonetheless the add-on voice is part of the person. After the ball I put my voice in a corner, but it is mine far more than the clothes I wear or the chair I sit in. It contains my identity. Without it I am a tin man—I am heartless, a body with no way of sharing thoughts or emotions. My voice is me. Take it from me and you leave a handful of dust.

I have a voice.

Hear me!

Glossary of Terms

Communication

Communication: Sharing of ideas and information using a mutually known system. For example, you can communicate with a deaf person who uses sign language *if* you also know sign language.

Aided communication: Any communication strategy requiring the use of a communication aid, that is, any tangible object used to assist a nonspeaker to communicate. Communication aids range from cards showing symbols for "yes" and "no" to laptop computers that translate typed utterances into speech. Speech, gesture, and manual sign are all *unaided* communication strategies.

Alternative communication: Forms of communication, such as signing, using communication boards or communication aids, used instead of speech when speech is nonexistent or unintelligible.

Assisted communication: Communication by a person in which the response of that person is expressed through the use of equipment and is dependent upon the assistance of another person, e.g., a person using an eye-pointing board needs the assistance of a partner, who has to observe and translate the user's eye movements.

Augmentative communication: Forms of communication that augment, or add to speech (e.g., Jane's speech is understood by her family but not by strangers, so when she is out and about she *augments* her speech by using a communication book containing useful words and phrases). The same strategies which are used as alternatives to speech can be used to augment speech.

Facilitated communication: An assistive communication technique in which the primary message receiver makes physical contact with the sender to help them overcome motor or emotional problems, e.g., poor muscle tone, lack of confidence. It differs from coactive movement in that the initiation of movement and intention to complete an action are solely the responsibility of the message sender. Facilitation is mainly used when training people to use communication aids.

Nonverbal communication: Nonverbal means not involving words, e.g., gesture. It is often incorrectly used as meaning without speech, for which the appropriate terms are nonspeech or nonoral. People who type but do not talk are *not* nonverbal.

Communication Aid Use

A communication aid is any tangible object used to assist a nonspeaker in communication. Communication aids are varied to suit the different ages, needs, and abilities of their users.

Access: Ways of using or accessing a communication aid. Access is split into two types:

Direct access includes any communication aid usage in which the aid user has enough controlled movement to select wanted items directly by touching them with a finger or fist, or by eye pointing, head pointing, etc.

Indirect access involves scanning. The items on a communication display are indicated in turn, either manually by a partner or electronically by a light or a pointer. The communication aid user stops the scanner when the item they want is reached, either by signalling or by hitting a switch.

Dedicated device: A piece of communication equipment

specially designed for use by people with severe communication impairments, and not used by people without disabilities, e.g., Canon Communicator, Wolf, Macaw. Typewriters, electronic organizers, and regular computers are not dedicated devices; though they may be used as communication aids by people with disabilities they are also used by the community at large.

Display: A set of visible items from which a communication aid user can make selections to compose a message, e.g., a board with six pictures on it, an alphabet board, a computer screen showing words and letters.

Fading: Gradually reducing the amount of facilitation provided to a communication aid user, e.g., support may be faded from wrist to elbow to shoulder before being withdrawn.

Phonetic spelling: Spelling words as they sound, e.g.,

ornj = orange

jon u shood cum to skool = John you should come to school.

Sometimes aid users use letters to represent similar sounding words, e.g.,

ruok = are you okay

Word prediction: "On_Tuesd___I_wa__ver__sa__becau___my_pet_do__die_."

Often when a communication aid user is spelling you can fill in the whole word. Many computerized communication aids use similar-word prediction strategies to speed up message production.

Neuro-Motor Impairments

Problems with producing desired movement patterns, e.g., speech, due to neurological dysfunction, such as brain damage.

Eye/hand coordination: The ability to coordinate eye and hand movements. In the simplest sense, the ability to keep your eyes on what you're doing. More complex aspects include the ability to correlate perception of depth and strength of movement.

Inhibition: The ability to stop unnecessary or inappropriate movements, e.g., we inhibit ourselves from scratching our noses when being photographed. To make controlled voluntary movements it is necessary to inhibit involuntary movement, and to point correctly to the answer to a question it is necessary to inhibit movement until the question is finished.

Disinhibition is the opposite of inhibition. Many people with poor eye/hand coordination are visually disinhibited—that is, they are unable to inhibit the automatic movement of their eyes to anything in their environment that moves or makes a noise.

Initiation problem: Difficulty in starting a movement, even though the person knows a movement is required and wants to move. People with initiation problems may need a spoken or physical prompt to start moving, e.g., a tap on the elbow to start typing.

Muscle tone: Tone refers to the readiness of a muscle for movement. Normal muscle tone is the state of the muscle that allows natural movement. Some people's muscle tone is too low **(hypotonia)**; their limbs feel floppy and heavy. They have difficulty moving against gravity, and they are likely to tire quickly. Some people's muscle tone is too high **(hypertonia)**; their muscles feel tight, and their limbs feel stiff. Their range of movement may be restricted, and their movements may be jerky.

Perseveration: Repetition of a movement sequence more often than is necessary or appropriate. There can be perseveration in speech: "I went to the shops, shops, went to the shops to shops to buy shops." There can be perseveration in written words: "I am in in inside in my class." Sometimes perseveration of a sequence will cue another unwanted word, as in the above example of *in* and *inside*. Sometimes a typist cannot get as far as a word—they get stuck on the first letter and hit it again and again, or (in a variant form) they hit a wanted leter then every other letter along the row.

Speech Impairments

Aphasia: Loss or impairment of the ability to use words or sounds. **Receptive** (Wernicke's) **aphasia** affects the ability to decode spoken and/or written language. It is less common than expressive aphasia (which it may accompany).

Expressive (Broca's) **aphasia** affects the ability to speak and/or write. There may be problems with recall of words, confusion between words with similar sounds (e.g., saying "knife" for "life"), or difficulty in repeating something just heard.

Apraxia (also referred to as **Dyspraxia**): A neurological impairment which prevents a person from reproducing sequences of voluntary movements. A person who has this condition may be able to reproduce the same movements spontaneously or involuntarily, e.g., a woman who could not touch her nose on command despite indicating understanding of the request was observed doing so when brushing away an insect. A person with severe oral apraxia is often said, quite incorrectly, to be able to "speak when he wants to" because he has been heard to speak. In fact, what he said may have been **involuntary** (e.g., swear words) **automatic** (e.g., completions—"Shut the _____") or **spontaneous** (e.g., greetings), and it's precisely considered **voluntary speech** that he is unable to produce, for example, he *cannot* talk when he wants to. (This distinguishes oral dyspraxia from dysarthria (below) as in the latter there is a motor deficit in *both* voluntary and involuntary speech.)

Dysarthria: An impairment in the functioning of the muscles involved in respiration, phonation and articulation due to a lesion in the peripheral nervous system, central nervous system, or both. Involvement of muscle groups controlling the tongue, the palate, the vocal cords, and breathing can seriously affect the intelligibility of speech. Total lack of speech, for this reason, is called anarthria.

Echolalia: The involuntary repetition of the last word of another person's sentence or a previously heard utterance. Echolalic speech is often associated with word-finding problems. Individuals with echolalia are often diagnosed as autistic.

Word finding problem: Frequent inability to find the correct word. We all experience occasional word finding difficulties: "Can you bring me the whatsit from the whosits?" For some individuals the problem is very severe and causes communication difficulties similar to expressive aphasia.

Resources

Periodicals

Augmentative and Alternative Communication (AAC)
   (International)
Communicating Together (Canada)
Communication Matters (United Kingdom)
Communication Outlook (United States)
Facilitated Communication Digest (United States)

Information Sources

These agencies can supply subscription details for the periodicals and the addresses of regional nonspeech communication centers or practitioners.

International Society for Augmentative & Alternative
   Communication
ISAAC Secretariat,
P.O. Box 1762,
Station R,
Toronto, Ontario,
Canada M4G 4A3

Facilitated Communication Institute
Syracuse University,
370 Huntington Hall,
Syracuse, NY 13244-2340,
U.S.A.

Fax: 1-315-443-2274

Homepage: http://web.syr.edu/~thefci/

DEAL Communication Centre Inc.,
538 Dandenong Road,
Caulfield 3162
Victoria, Australia

Fax: 61-3-9386 0761

Homepage: http://www.vicnet.net.au/~dealccinc

A Selection of Further Reading

Personal Accounts

Brown, C. *My left foot*. London: Secker and Warburg, 1954 (autobiography of a man with cerebral palsy).

Crossley, R., & McDonald, A. *Annie's coming out*. Melbourne: Penguin Books, 1980 (autobiography of a young woman with cerebral palsy).

Deacon, J. *Tongue-tied*. London: Spastics Society, 1968 (autobiography of a man with cerebral palsy).

Eastham, M. *Silent words: A biography*. Ottawa: Oliver-Pate, 1992 (biography of a young man with autism).

Horwood, W. *Skallagrigg*. Harmondsworth, U.K.: Penguin, 1988 (novel about people with cerebral palsy).

Itard, J. *The wild boy of Aveyron*. New York: Appelton-Century-Crofts, 1992 (biography of a young man without speech).

Martin, R. *Out of silence*. New York: Henry Holt, 1994 (biography of a boy with autism).

Nolan, C. *Under the eye of the clock*. London: Weidenfeld &

Nicolson, 1987 (autobiography of a young man with cerebral palsy).

Perske, R. *Don't stop the music*, Nashville: Abingdon, 1982 (novel about teenagers with cerebral palsy).

Sienkiewicz-Mercer, R. *I raise my eyes to say yes.* New York: Whole Health, 1990 (autobiography of a woman with cerebral palsy).

Sellin, B. *I don't want to be inside me anymore*, New York: Basic Books, 1995 (autobiography of a young man with autism).

Wilson, D. C. *Hilary: The brave world of Hilary Pole.* London: Hodder & Stoughton, 1972 (biography of a woman with acquired severe communication impairment).

Textbooks and Historical Accounts

Sign Language

Groce, N. *Everybody here spoke sign language.* Cambridge, MA: Harvard University Press, 1985.

Lane, H. *When the mind hears: A history of the deaf.* New York: Random House, 1984.

Sacks, O. *Seeing voices.* London: Picador, 1990.

Augmentative and Alternative Communication

Beukelman, D., & Mirenda, P. *Augmentative and alternative communication: Management of severe communication disorders in children and adults.* Baltimore: Paul H. Brookes, 1992.

Beukelman, D. R., Yorkston, K., & Dowden, P. *Communication augmentation: A casebook of clinical management.* San Diego: College-Hill, 1985.

Bloomberg, K., & Johnson, H. (Eds.). *Communication without speech: A guide for parents and teachers.* Melbourne: ACER, 1991.

Burkardt, L. *Total augmentative communication in the early childhood classroom.* Eldersburg, MD: n.p., 1993.

Munson, J. H., Nordquist, C. L. & Thuma-Rew, S. L. *Communication systems for persons with severe neuromotor impairment.* Iowa City: University of Iowa, 1987.

Facilitated Communication Training

Biklen, D. *Communication unbound.* New York: Teachers College Press, 1993.

Biklen, D., & Cardinal, D. (Eds.). *Presuming competence: Empirical investigations of facilitated communication.* New York: Teachers College Press, 1997.

Crossley, R. *Facilitated communication training.* New York: Teachers College Press, 1994.

Oppenheim, R. F. *Effective teaching methods for autistic children.* Springfield, IL: Thomas, 1977.

Seminal Publications

Biklen, D. Communication unbound: Autism and praxis, *Harvard Educational Review, 60, 3* (1990), 291–322 (facilitated communication).

Cornforth, A. R. T., Johnson, K., & Walker, M. Makaton vocabulary: Teaching sign language to the deaf mentally handicapped, *Apex, 1* (1974), 23–24.

McDonald, E. T., & Schultz, A. R. Communication boards for cerebral palsied children, *Journal of Speech and Hearing Disorders, 38* (1973), 73–88.

Silverman, F. H., McNaughton, S., & Kates, B. *Handbook of blissymbolics.* Toronto: Blissymbolics Communication Institute, 1978.

Vanderheiden G. *Synthesized speech as a communication mode for non-vocal severely handicapped individuals.* Madison: University of Wisconsin, 1975.

Bibliography

Alpern, G. (1967). Measurement of "untestable" autistic children, *Journal of Abnormal Psychology*, 72, 478.

American Psychiatric Association (1994). *Diagnostic and statistical manual of mental disorders*, Fourth Edition (DSM-IV), New York, American Psychiatric Association.

Andrew, K., Murphy, L., Munday, R., & Littlewood, C. (1996). Misdiagnosis of the vegetative state: Retrospective study in a rehabilitation unit, *British Medical Journal*, 313, 13–16.

Bannister, R. (1985). *Brain's clinical neurology*. Oxford: Oxford University Press.

Biklen, D. (1990). Communication unbound: Autism and praxis, *Harvard Educational Review*, 60, 3, 291–322.

———. (1993). *Communication unbound*. New York: Teachers College Press.

Biklen, D., and Cardinal, D. (Eds.) (1997). *Contested words, contested science*. New York: Teachers College Press.

Botash, A., Babuts, D., Mitchell, N., O'Hara, M., Manuel, J., & Lynch, L. (1994). Evaluations of children who have disclosed sexual abuse via facilitated communication, *Archives of Pediatrics and Adolescent Medicine*, 148, 1282–1287.

Brown, C. (1954). *My left foot*. London: Secker and Warburg.

Buck, J. N. (1955). The Sage: An unusual mongoloid. In *Clinical Studies of Personality, 3*, A. Burton and R. Harris (Eds.). New York: Harper and Row.

Campbell, J. (1992). *Grammatical man.* New York: Simon and Schuster.

Cardinal D. N., Hanson, D., & Wakeham, J. (1996). An investigation of authorship in facilitated communication, *Mental Retardation*, 34, 4, 231–242.

Clunies-Ross, G. (1986). The development of children with Down syndrome, *Australian Pediatric Journal*, 22, 167.

Crossley, R., and McDonald, A. (1980). *Annie's coming out.* Melbourne: Penguin.

Crossley, R. (1994). *Facilitated communication training.* New York: Teachers College Press.

Deacon, J. (1968). *Tongue-tied.* London: Spastics Society.

De Myer, M., Barton, S., Alpern, G., Kimberlin, C., Allen, J., Yang, E., & Stelle, R. (1974). The measured intelligence of autistic children, *Journal of Autism and Childhood Schizophrenia*, 4, 42–9.

Donellan, A. (Ed.) (1985). *Classic readings in autism.* New York: Teachers College Press.

Doyle, A. (1893). The adventure of the cardboard box. In *The memoirs of Sherlock Holmes.* London: Pan.

Dumas, A. (1845). *The Count of Monte Cristo,* trans. Blair (1956). New York: Bantam.

Dwyer, J. (1996). Access to justice for people with severe communication impairment, *Australian Journal of Administrative Law*, 3, 2, 175–199.

Eastham, D. (1992). *Silent words: A biography.* Ottawa: Oliver-Pate.

Eberlin, M., McConnachie, G., Ibel, S., & Volpe, L. (1993). "Facilitated communication": A failure to replicate the phenomenon, *Journal of Autism and Developmental Disorders, 23, 3,* 507–529.

Ellis, D. (1982). Joey Deacon: A suitable case for labelling? *Developmental Medicine and Child Neurology, 24,* 485–488.

Feynman, R. (1985). *Surely you're joking, Mr. Feynman.* New York: Norton.

Fuller, P., & Wright, A. (1994). The beauty of the unspoken: The development of language without either recognition or production of speech. In *Internal Society for Augmentative and Alternative Communication Conference Proceedings.* Maastricht: ISAAC, 89–91.

Gould, S. J. (1981). *The mismeasure of man.* New York: Norton.

Gregory, R. (Ed.) (1987). *Oxford companion to the mind.* Oxford: Oxford University Press.

Groce, N. (1985). *Everybody here spoke sign language.* Cambridge, MA: Harvard University Press.

Hagberg, B. (1993). *Rett syndrome—clinical and biological aspects.* Cambridge: Cambridge University Press.

Heckler, S. (1994). Facilitated communication—a response by Child Protection, *Child Abuse and Neglect, 18, 6,* 529–530.

Herrnstein, R., and Murray, C. (1994). *The bell curve.* New York: Free Press.

Horwood, W. (1987). *Skallagrig.* London: Penguin.

Hudson, A., Melita, B., & Arnold N. (1993). Brief report: A case study assessing the validity of facilitated communication, *Journal of Autism and Developmental Disorders, 23, 1,* 165.

Intellectual Disability Review Panel (IDRP) (1989). *Report to the Director-General on the reliability and validity of assisted communication.* Melbourne: Office of Intellectual Disability Services.

In the matter of Karen Quinlan: The complete briefs, court proceedings and decision in the Superior Court of New Jersey. (1976). New York: University Publications of America.

In the matter of Anne Therese McDonald and In the matter of the Public Trustee Act. Supreme Court of Victoria, 1979, unreported case.

Itard, J. (1801). *The wild boy of Aveyron,* trans. Humphrey, G., and Humphrey, N. (1992). New York: Appleton-Century-Crofts.

Kanner, L. (1943). Autistic disturbances of affective contact, *Nervous Child,* 2, 217–250 (reprinted in Donellan, 1985).

Kochmeister, S. J. (1994). Reflections on a year of turmoil and growth, *Facilitated Communication Digest,* 2, 4, 6–8.

Lane, H. (1984). *When the mind hears: A history of the deaf.* New York: Random House.

Levin, H., Saydjari, C., Eisenberg, H., Foulkes, M., Marshall, L., & Ruff, M. (1991). Vegetative state after closed head injury: A traumatic coma data bank report, *Archives of Neurology, 48,* 580–585.

Luria, A. R. (1976). *The working brain,* trans. Haigh. New York: Basic Books.

Luria, S. (1975). *The man with the shattered world.* London: Penguin.

Martin, R. (1994). *Out of silence.* New York: Henry Holt.

McNaughton, S. (1990). Gaining the most from AAC's growing years, *AAC Augmentative and Alternative Communication, 2,* 2–14.

Mitchell, K., Kerridge, I., & Lovat, T. (1993). Medical futility, treatment withdrawal, and the persistent vegetative state, *Journal of Medical Ethics, 19,* 71–76.

Morley, R, & Court, C. (1968). *The Development and disorders of speech in childhood,* London, Routledge.

Nolan, C. (1987). *Under the eye of the clock.* London: Weidenfeld and Nicolson.

Oppenheim, R. F. (1974). *Effective teaching methods for autistic children.* Springfield, IL: Thomas.

Queensland Department of Family Services and Aboriginal and Islander Affairs (QDFSAIA). (1993). *The Queensland report on facilitated communication.* Brisbane: Author.

R v. Health Commission of Victoria, ex parte Anne McDonald. Supreme Court of Victoria, 1979, unreported case.

Rose, S. (1994). *The meaning of memory.* London: Penguin.

Sacks, O. (1986). *The man who mistook his wife for a hat.* London: Picador.

———. (1990). *Awakenings.* London: Picador.

———. (1990). *Seeing voices.* London: Picador.

Schawlow, A., & Schawlow, A. (1985). The endless search for help. In *Integrating moderately and severely handicapped learners— strategies that work,* M. Brady and P. Gunther (Eds.). Springfield, IL: Thomas.

Sellin, B. (1995). *I don't want to be inside me anymore.* New York: Basic Books.

Sienkiewicz-Mercer, R. (1990). *I raise my eyes to say yes.* New York: Whole Health.

Snow, P. (1991). Fringe therapies in the management of brain damage. In *Ockham's Razor 3,* J. Caluiy (Ed.). Melbourne: ABC.

Sobsey, D. (1994). *Violence and abuse in the lives of people with disabilities.* Baltimore: Paul H. Brookes.

Wheeler, D. D., Jacobson, J., Paglieri, R., & Schwartz, A. (1992). *An Experimental assessment of facilitated communication.* New York: New York State Office of Mental Retardation and Developmental Disabilities.

Wilson, D. (1972). *Hilary.* London: Hodder and Staughton.

Index

· A NOTE ON THE TYPE ·

The typeface used in this book is a version of Baskerville, originally designed by John Baskerville (1706–1775) and considered to be one of the first "transitional" typefaces between the "old style" of the continental humanist printers and the "modern" style of the nineteenth century. With a determination bordering on the eccentric to produce the finest possible printing, Baskerville set out at age forty-five and with no previous experience to become a typefounder and printer (his first fourteen letters took him two years). Besides the letter forms, his innovations included an improved printing press, smoother paper, and better inks, all of which made Baskerville decidedly uncompetitive as a businessman. Franklin, Beaumarchais, and Bodoni were among his admirers, but his typeface had to wait for the twentieth century to achieve its due.